D0661668

BLESSED BY THUNDER

MEMOIR OF A
CUBAN GIRLHOOD

FLOR FERNANDEZ BARRIOS

SEAL PRESS

Copyright © 1999 by Flor Fernandez Barrios

All rights reserved. No portion of this book may be reproduced in any form, with the exception of brief passages in reviews, without prior written permission from Seal Press.

Seal Press
3131 Western Avenue, Suite 410
Seattle, WA 98121
sealprss@scn.org

Cover design by Trina Stahl
Text design by Clare Conrad
Frontispiece photo: The author as a small child in front of her grandparents' home, Villa Petra.

Library of Congress Cataloging-in-Publication Data
Fernandez Barrios, Flor.
    Blessed by thunder : memoir of a Cuban girlhood /
Flor Fernandez Barrios.
1. Fernandez Barrios, Flor—Childhood and youth.
2. Cuban Americans Biography. 3. Refugees—United States Biography.
4. Cuba—History—1959– 5. Cuba—Rural conditions.
6. Cabaigüán (Cuba) Biography. I. Title.
E184.C97F47   1999   972.9106'4'092—dc21   99-20902
ISBN: 1-58005-042-5 (paper)

Printed in Canada
First paperback edition, September 2000.

10   9   8   7   6   5   4   3   2   1

Distributed to the trade by Publishers Group West
In Canada: Publishers Group West Canada, Toronto, Ontario
In the U.K. and Europe: Airlift Book Company, Middlesex, England
In Australia: Banyan Tree Book Distributors, Kent Town, South Australia

To all the Doñas past, present and future . . .

ACKNOWLEDGMENTS

The vision to write this book was inspired by the spirits of all those allies whose love held me in the light during the dark moments of my childhood in Cuba. The stories in this book are a tribute to the wisdom, courage and compassion they shared with me. From them I learned about the power of the human spirit to endure trauma and heal.

I treasure the many gifts I have received from my grandmothers Patricia Hernandez and Petra Alvarez. My grandfathers José Maria Barrios and Victor Fernandez. The comforting and healing presence of Carmen. The wise elders Graciela and Salvador. The nurturing care of my childhood neighbors Nena and Veita. The loving support of my childhood friends Maria Victoria Rodriguez, Enrrique Evelio and Mariluz Nieda.

My deep gratitude to my father, Antonio Fernandez, whose vision of freedom carried me to a new land of choices and opportunities. Thank you, Father, for your courage and for always encouraging me to follow my own dreams. To my mother, Felicia Barrios, whose strength and warmth kept our family anchored amidst the shifting sands of exile. Thank you, Mother, for your support and your faith in me. And to my brother, Jose Antonio Fernandez, who held hands with me during the turmoil and uncertainty of the Revolution. To my niece Danielle Fernandez, young curandera, and to my nephew Esteban Fernandez, gentle spirit. They have been a delightful source of inspiration and love in my life.

I feel very blessed by the consistent reminders of feminine strength I found in all my aunts: Ana, Caridad, Herlinda, Juana, Mensa and Nelda. Each one of them gave me invaluable gifts throughout different phases of my life.

My uncle, Dr. Tomás Barrios, whose letters from Cuba helped me keep faith while in exile with his thoughts and words of wisdom. Special thanks to my uncle, José Manuel Barrios, who sponsored my family into this country and to my aunt Herlinda Scorza, whose sensitive listening and support has been a soothing balm.

I have been very fortunate to find in my path the friendship of many great allies who came my way as if guided by the magic of our spiritual and loving connections. They all appeared in my life at the right moment, to hold my hand just when I needed a helping hand. In one way or another they have all shared this journey with me and contributed their own individual gifts to the process of writing *Blessed by Thunder*. Thanks to my dear soul sister Maureen Murdock, whose insightful council and empathetic listening was always there during the difficult times of many storms. To my great ally and wise yerbera, Keri Shaw, whose knowledge of herbs, health advice and nurturance made it possible for me to stay healthy throughout the rough spots of this journey.

Thanks to my sister-friend Helga Kahr for watching over me in the legal domain and for keeping an eye on my writing. To my compassionate and wise guide Anne DeVore, who helped me walk through the underworld of my emotions. To Emily Batlan, whose computer skills rescued me more than once. To Brenda Peterson, who encouraged me to write this book. To Kate Thompson, Penny Rosewasser, Kathleen Kinney, Jessica Young, Heather McIsaac, Mooh Hood, Carmen Carrion and Los Norteños. Thank you all for your time, insights, humor and play, wonderful meals and encouragement.

My deepest appreciation to my mentor and compassionate friend Carole Glickfield. Your wisdom, patience and generous teachings made it possible for this book to come alive. To my editor Faith Conlon, whose guidance and sensitive editing helped me get through the completion of this book. To Cathy Johnson for her thoughtful copyediting. To the staff at Seal Press: Lee Damsky, Ingrid Emerick, Jennie Goode, Laura Gronewold, Kate Loeb, Lisa Okey and Lynn Siniscalchi. Thanks for your support, dedication and enthusiasm.

Finally, I want to thank my faithful dogs and companions, Cinque and Clue. They have walked with me and kept me in physical shape throughout the many months of hard work.

CONTENTS

1. *Two Births*   3

2. *La Revolución*   13

3. *La Finca*   22

4. *Petra and Alazana*   34

5. *Carmen*   49

6. *Patricia*   65

7. *Stories from My Hometown*   77

8. *La Libreta*   87

9. *School Goes to the Countryside*   98

10. *Life in the Camps*   111

11. *Las Capitanas*   124

12. *Ten Million Tons of Sugar*   141

13. *Canta Rana—Where the Frogs Sing*   150

14. *The Telegram*   160

15. *Good-bye, Cabaigüán*   170

16. *Night from Hell*   182

17. *Flight to Freedom*   193

18. *City of Angels*   203

19. *Grandmother's Visit*   215

20. *The Crow*   229

Glossary   239

1

TWO BIRTHS

I WAS BORN in the town of Cabaigüán,
Cuba, in the middle of a hurricane. Just as I was entering the world, a
few minutes past midnight, a thunderbolt struck nearby with such
force that all the lights went out in the hospital. At least that's how
Grandmother Patricia told the story. "Negrita," she would say to me,
"you have a don, a gift. Never forget that thunder greeted you into this
life." Then she would explain that thunder and lightning were the
powers of the Yoruba deity Changó, also known as Saint Barbara in the
Catholic religion.

My name is Flor Teresa, but my Grandmother Patricia always
called me Negrita, which means "little black one." It was her way of
expressing affection and love for me, her favorite grandchild, the one
she believed would carry on the tradition of healing and become a
curandera, like her. Therefore, it was her responsibility to prepare me
to use this don.

Because of these circumstances, Grandmother Patricia was more
than just a grandmother to me. She was a protector and a teacher who
spent endless hours instructing me in the mysteries of life, from its
most mundane aspects, such as how to mop the ceramic floors of her
kitchen, to the serious subjects of spirituality and healing. A gifted storyteller by nature, Grandmother was able to weave into her stories a

kind of wisdom that was both magical and practical.

Doña Patricia, as everyone in town called her with respect, was convinced that it was during the stormy night of my birth that she received the signs confirming my destiny as her apprentice in the arts of curanderismo. For me, this story is an important link to my roots— not only to the place of my origin, but to the line of women whose identities were created in a healing practice, in a place where women were considered wise.

The last time I heard Grandmother's tales of my birth was right before my family and I left Cuba forever. I was fourteen and had gone to visit her on a Sunday afternoon. Grandmother greeted me with the usual kiss on my forehead and the blessing "Dios te bendiga." Then she stood there looking at me. She didn't say a word but signaled me to follow her to the kitchen. Grandmother walked slowly in front of me, as if suddenly all the years of her life were beginning to weigh on her. She pulled a couple of chairs away from the table.

"Negrita, come and sit." Then she placed her hand over my knee. "I'm sixty-five years old now, and the images of your birth are as if time had never passed. In the hurricane season, the winds blow so hard that the slender palm trees sway like pendulums. The rain pours down with fury and the rivers swell and swell till the valleys finally flood with a brown mix of soil and water.

"The night when you were born, the cyclone was at its peak. It entered through the eastern part of the island in the province of Oriente. Even though we were in the central area, in Cabaigüán, we had winds of at least forty to sixty miles per hour. In the dark, rain poured down without mercy. A big thunderstorm was on its way, lighting the sky with the fierce passion of Changó.

"I knew then that you, my long-awaited granddaughter, must be someone special to come into this world on such a night. I said to your mother, 'Your child has a strong soul, Felicia.'"

Grandmother paused, and her eyes looked into mine, making sure I was listening to her.

"You know, Negrita, I must say this, your mother Felicia was not my choice of a wife for my son. I didn't think it was going to work. She was a niña adinerada from the Barrios family. They were wealthy all the way to the bone, and we were poor. When I met your mother for the first time, she had the well-manicured hands of a princess—with long red fingernails! Felicia spent most of her afternoons glancing through the fashion magazines—*Vanidades*, *La Familia* and *Ella* . . . But in all fairness, after the marriage, she kept the house clean and fed my Pepe like a king."

Grandmother looked down as if she felt ashamed of the words she had just said. She patted me on the knee gently.

"That night of your birth," she continued, "I chose to be there by her side, in the delivery room of our small town's hospital, holding her hand. Her face was pale and thick drops of sweat fell on the white sheets of the bed.

"As I ran my fingers through Felicia's damp hair, I prayed to the Virgen del Cobre to give Felicia strength. In moments like that, when you're watching someone in pain, time moves so slow. I swear, the black hands of the old silver clock on the wall stopped at midnight."

I asked Grandmother to tell me more about the hospital room. I was curious about the place where I was born.

"Oh, Negrita, I remember a small window, maybe three by four feet, on the west wall, overlooking one of the neighborhood streets— that was the only opening to the world. Outside, the street lights were flickering from the force of the wind. Near the bed was a metal table, its top covered by sharp gleaming tools—scissors, knives, needles—that sent waves of chills down my spine.

"To me, hospitals smell of death, of sick bodies rotting on sterile beds. Ghost houses, mi niña. People die with no one to assist them in shedding the shell. Then their souls wander forever in confusion around the halls and rooms, searching for a way out. To me, hospitals are not the place to give birth, but your mother, like any woman of her time, wanted to do it 'the modern way.' She also wanted me to be there, as in the old way, when women knew women. It was unheard of before, going to a hospital to have a child. Women took care of childbirth in the privacy of their homes, and the men waited outside till they were told to come in."

I interrupted to ask how many women Grandmother had seen give birth.

"Oh . . . so many I've forgotten the number. But you I'll never forget—it was past midnight when Dr. Gamboa said, 'The baby is coming, the baby is coming!' and right at that moment, a lightning bolt hit a pole outside, and the electrical power in the hospital went out.

"Oh, my dear child! I couldn't believe it. You were making your entrance into this world accompanied by nature's powerful roar. I took it as a message from the skies. One cannot disregard such a good omen as thunder and lightning.

"The room was pitch dark. At first, I could see only shadows. Gradually my eyes began to adjust, and I saw Dr. Gamboa, his long, thin fingers running over the top of the table, searching for the instruments but knocking them instead to the floor. The nurse tried to help him, but Dr. Gamboa was young and inexperienced and that only angered him. 'Stay away till I ask for your help!' he yelled. I knew he was afraid of losing you.

"Then, I heard your mother screaming. 'Doña Patricia, ahhhhh Patricia, no puedo más. This pain, no aguanto! I feel like I'm going to die. Please do something . . . Help me! Why is it so dark in here?' Felicia was writhing and grabbing my arm so hard I thought she was going to pull it from its socket. 'Calmate, everything is going to be okay,' I told her. 'Take a deep breath.'

"'Where is Pepe, where is he?' I assured her your father was in the waiting room, like the other men, pacing up and down and smoking their cigars.

"'I'm afraid we're going to lose this baby!' I heard Dr. Gamboa say. Softly, I began to pray. 'Stop praying, señora!' the young doctor shouted at me. 'Patricia . . . uhm, uhm, ay, don't let my baby die!' your mother cried."

Grandmother's voice was louder now. I felt myself caught up in the storm, the wind blowing, the darkness, and my struggle through the birth canal, trying to find an opening into the world. I even saw my mother's face contorted with pain, and Dr. Gamboa nervously trying to see under the white sheets that formed a tent around my mother's legs.

"It was at that moment." Grandmother stood up from her chair and looked out to the mango tree just beyond her kitchen window. "It was at that moment I felt a strong presence in the room. My eyes turned to the the window. At first, only a glow of light was visible, and then it began to take the form of a young woman. The image was somewhat transparent but very vivid. She was dressed in the usual habit of nuns—a long black dress, a white wimple around her neck and chin, a black cloth over her head. I was so captivated by her radiance that I forgot where I was. 'Oh, mi Dios! What's going on? Did I fall asleep while waiting?' I said to myself."

Grandmother paused. Her body was shaking. She always got caught up in the drama of her own stories. Like a fine actress, she allowed the voices of the characters to flow through her, spilling out their emotions.

"Then, Negrita, you wouldn't believe it. The young woman spoke to me: 'Don't you recognize me, Patricia? I am Santa Teresa de Avila.'"

I couldn't help but express my disbelief in Grandmother's words. It was difficult for me to picture Saint Teresa in the hospital room.

"Well, believe what you want, Negrita, but that is what happened. I asked what she was doing there. And you know what she said? 'How could I possibly miss the birth of your first grandchild?' She was even upset with me that I wasn't taking over to help deliver you. She told me Dr. Gamboa had lost his confidence and that it was my job as a midwife to be in charge."

Grandmother came back to her chair and took my hand into hers.

"It's nothing I can explain to you in any other way, but you must know she was there protecting you. She was there! I could see her as clearly as I see you right now.

"And a few minutes later you were out of your mother's womb, in my arms, screaming with healthy lungs."

She looked at me now with the same expression of adoration I imagined she'd had when she first held me.

"Joy filled my heart when I saw you, Teresa," Grandmother continued, her voice trembling ever so slightly. "Not quite five pounds, but well formed with a moon face and dark eyes wide open to the world. Even with your skin bluish and wrinkled, you were like a doll, with thick black hair and a small round nose just like your mother's.

"I checked your fingers and toes, ears and mouth, legs and arms, back and buttocks. You were whole and healthy. Then, I turned to the window where I had seen Santa Teresa. She was still there. I raised your little body in my arms, facing the Virgin. I asked her blessings. She smiled and simply lifted her right hand. She sent a beam of light that touched your forehead, and then she disappeared before I could even thank her."

I was moved by my grandmother's tale, but I wondered whether, being the charming storyteller she was, she had added a bit of her imagination to what had really occurred.

"You could say I'm just a crazy old woman," she continued as if she had read my mind, "but I know Santa Teresa was there that night, and that's why I named you Teresa, in her honor."

"Why her?" I wanted to know.

"Santa Teresa is the one saint we curanderas call to for help during difficult situations, but in your case, I must be honest with you, la Virgencita came without my calling her, which means she is your protector and guide. She blessed you.

"I remember bathing your little body in the lukewarm water. Under the candlelight, I gently sponged your soft skin. What a magical moment in my life!"

No one, not even my mother, had talked about my birth with such passion and excitement. At fourteen, I felt uncomfortable with the attention the old woman gave me and the weight of unknown responsibilities I was not mature enough to comprehend.

"I was so happy you were born a girl. And as I was washing your tiny fingers," Grandmother turned my hand so the palm faced up, "I couldn't contain my excitement. Yes . . . yes . . . it is all in here. I saw it then, and I see now. Your destiny is to become a curandera. Your path is that of the healer. Curanderismo, Negrita, runs in families and you're my blood. My mother was a yerbera. She was the kind of curandera who worked with herbs and plants to help people heal. My mother taught me what she knew and the night you were born, I knew you had been chosen by the spirit to be my apprentice. I knew it the second that lightning illuminated the sky. The healing power God has given me is like the energy of thunder. That's my don, my gift. You have it, too, Teresa! Someday you will be called to learn about this don, and it will be important for you to hear the call."

"What if I don't hear it?"

Grandmother frowned. She got up from her chair and stood in the middle of the kitchen with her hands pushed down inside the pockets of her skirt. Then, in a dramatic gesture she moved towards me and lifted my chin with her hand.

"Negrita." She stared into my eyes. "Don't you ever forget, you have been blessed by thunder. No matter where you go, you must remember my words! Look at this wrinkled skin. This old woman you see knows how dangerous this don of thunder can be. I almost lost my own life."

For a few seconds, I failed to recognize my own grandmother. This woman in front of me was as fierce as a thunderbolt. My head was spinning with images of fire and of lightning flashing across the sky. Grandmother went back to her chair. We sat in silence for what seemed to me like a long time. Then she placed her hand over my knee again.

"Don't be afraid, Negrita, thunder doesn't just kill. It also heals." Grandmother leaned back in her chair and began to tell me the story of her own birth to the thunder don. At the age of twenty-two, Grandmother had developed a series of illnesses that plagued her with debilitating fatigue, high fevers and loss of weight. The doctors couldn't find the cause, no matter how hard they tried.

Doña Antonia, her mother, having exhausted her repertoire of herbal remedies, decided to call a friend, Doña Mariana, an old curandera with great wisdom.

The healer arrived at the house early in the morning, carrying an old leather bag. She was no taller than five feet and as skinny as a bamboo cane.

"I remember her blouse was so white it seemed to glow. And she wore a straw hat with a red cloth flower on the side," Grandmother reminisced. "Doña Mariana looked more like a rancher's wife than a curandera. She took her hat off, sat right next to my bed and examinined me carefully with her deep, black eyes."

Grandmother tilted her head back and, with her eyes half closed, described how Doña Mariana's gaze felt like the warm, soothing waters of the ocean washing the sickness from her feverish body.

"Doña Mariana looked so ancient!" Grandmother said in a low voice. "Deep wrinkles ran across her forehead like dry riverbeds across the land. Spider webs of lines around her eyes gently pulled her eyelids down, and time had carved long canyons in her cheeks and around her mouth."

The wise woman talked to Grandmother about the healing energy of thunder and lightning, and from her leather bag she pulled a bundle of fresh herbs tied with a piece of white cloth and proceeded to brush Grandmother's body with long, rhythmic strokes.

"This don is so powerful that if you don't learn how to use it, it will kill you," Doña Mariana said to young Patricia.

The old curandera asked Grandmother to close her eyes and began to chant some prayers. Soon Grandmother Patricia found herself feeling lighter and lighter, as if she were a feather floating in the air.

"Suddenly, a beam of light struck me right on the chest. At first I was very afraid. I could feel a current of energy moving through my body. Even with my eyes closed, I could see zigzags of lightning in the skies."

After this visit from Doña Mariana, Grandmother recovered quickly. In a few days, she was back helping her mother in the kitchen, peeling potatoes, cutting vegetables and cleaning the house. One afternoon, not long after Grandmother's recovery, the sky turned dark and the clouds became swollen with rain. Anticipating the storm, the workers left the fields and took refuge in the house.

Everyone found something to do—some were carefully rolling a fresh supply of cigars, others were mending the fishing nets used to catch river trout, and old Armando found pleasure in weaving a new hat out of palm leaves. Arturo was playing his guitar softly when lightning suddenly bolted across the sky. A few seconds later, the roar of thunder shook the house, shattering a couple of empty glasses on the kitchen table and unnerving everyone, including the horses outside in the stable.

Grandmother's father was the one who noticed that Elias, a young cowboy, was missing. Another cowboy, Alberto, mentioned he had seen Elias riding his horse towards the river early in the afternoon. Doña Antonia pulled out her rosary and sat in a corner of the room to pray for Elias's safety. Grandmother went into her room and lit a candle to Saint Barbara, the saint of thunder and lightning, for protection. As she gazed at the flame, she became fascinated by the glowing dance of the orange, yellow, red and blue colors—a dance that pulled her into the heart of the fire. Grandmother told me that she had seen Elias being hit by lightning and thrown from his horse by the electrical charge. She could see that he was about a mile away from the house, near the cornfield.

Trusting her intuition, Grandmother Patricia went back to the room where everybody was gathered and told them about her vision. The men jumped on their horses and went in search of Elias. When they brought him back, he appeared to be dead, he was so pale. But Patricia could tell he was alive by the slight movement of his chest. She heard a voice inside her head, guiding her to place her hands above his heart. She did as she was told, and her hands became very hot. Energy coursed through her body. It was how she had felt with Doña Mariana. Both Elias and Patricia were shaking intensely, as if the storm had descended from the sky into them.

Slowly Elias opened his eyes. Everyone, including Grandmother, was surprised by the miracle. At that moment, young Patricia began to understand Doña Mariana's words. She became aware of the existence of a force bigger than herself, a force of energy she could bring into her hands for the purpose of healing.

"I called it espíritu divino, the medicine that heals the soul and the body." These were Grandmother's words as she finished her story, and I noticed that the wrinkles around her eyes and along her cheeks looked deeper than ever. I asked her if she was okay.

"Yes, cariño. My body is all right, but . . . my soul aches with the thought that you'll be leaving soon. You'll be so far away from me, from this land. I worry that your spirit will get lost in this new place, among people who speak a different language. I'm sad that you might forget these stories."

I tried to comfort Grandmother by promising to write letters every week from my new home in El Norte.

"It will never be the same, Negrita. We're running out of time. I am an old woman now, my life is almost over, but Negrita . . . Negrita, you have a long road ahead."

"Abuela, what about you?" I interrupted. Grandmother looked out the window. She appeared to be lost in her thoughts.

"I will be here. Like that old tree." She pointed at the mango tree in the backyard. "Like that tree, I had to bear fruit for many years. Now it's time for me to sit still in my home. That tree, Negrita, has seen and heard many who come to rest under its shade. It doesn't need to go anywhere because the stories are brought to it." Grandmother paused and took my hand into hers a final time. "Negrita, I'll be here with my roots deeply grounded in this Cuban soil. I'll be the anchor that holds while you travel and change."

Grandmother's words sent waves of sadness through my chest. She could smell the bitter scent of my impending departure in the air. She could feel the blow coming towards us like the sweeping winds of a hurricane. Our time together was coming to an end. When I left, the teachings she was supposed to pass on to me would eventually dry up inside her, like the caked milk in the swollen and sore breasts of a mother who has suddenly lost her child.

2

LA REVOLUCIÓN

"VIVA LA REVOLUCIÓN!" Those words droned in my ears like the buzz of angry bees whose hive has been disturbed, like a twisting tornado, its long black tail just ready to touch the ground. Though I was very young when the Cuban Revolution began in 1956, it has had a lasting impact on my life. Four decades later, I still freeze when I hear the sounds of a helicopter. The deafening noise of the engine, the thwack of the blades evoke images of terror I can't control, even today. *That sound! They're coming back!* In an instant, I am a small child covering her ears to shut out the terrifying noise. My stomach forms knots thick as a rope, my eyes search for a place to hide . . . my heart pounds against the walls of my chest and I begin to sweat. My legs shake so hard I feel any minute I may drop to the floor and be swallowed up by my terror.

My early childhood unfolded in the swirling storm of political change. The nation was weary of money-hungry politicians and their broken promises. All around me, revolutionaries dreamed of creating a new Cuba free of dictators. I was a year old in December 1956, when Fidel Castro and his brother, Raúl Castro, along with Ernesto "Che" Guevara and seventy-nine other revolutionaries disembarked from the cruiser Granma in the province of Oriente to start a revolution.

Most of these guerrillas were soon killed by government forces.

The group that survived escaped to the mountains and established a base in the Sierra Maestra. From there, they launched a campaign of insurrection against Fulgencio Batista, the dictator who had controlled Cuba since the 1930s. Radio Rebelde was inaugurated, from which Fidel spoke to listeners all over the country. From his distant and isolated territory, Fidel, a charismatic leader, was able to move people deeply with his speeches of hope and promises of changes that would transform our island for the betterment of all.

I can still recall snippets of intense conversation that floated around me like soap bubbles when I was three and four years old. Fidel Castro was going to help poor children and their families. He was going to let black people go to all the places where the whites went. Fidel had his two best friends helping him—Ernesto or El Che, and Camilo Cienfuegos. The tension in the air was no less than if a hurricane were about to hit the island.

At that time, Fulgencio Batista was widely despised—even the wealthy wanted him out. But many people felt uncertain about Castro and his band of revolutionaries. Like my father. He said Castro made too many promises. Our neighborhood was equally divided in its opinions. During the evening domino games, loud arguments could be heard from the street. Occasionally these heated discussions were interrupted by Radio Rebelde, with a special broadcast of Fidel Castro direct from the Sierra Maestra. All activities would immediately stop, and even the children would gather around the radio to listen to Castro's speech.

Towards the end of 1958, the winds of this so-called hurricane gathered intensity, and the domino games were stopped by frequent blackouts that left the town in darkness for hours. I overheard the adults say that the blackouts were the work of Castro's men so that they could pick up food supplies and weapons from their allies.

During one of those long nights, my father was almost shot by the Batista militia. As my father told the story, he was walking home around 9:00 p.m. after a game of dominos when the lights went out. Aware of the danger, he began to hurry, but as he turned a corner, a soldier shot at him. Father ran towards a tall brick wall that surrounded an old convent, and with the swiftness of a cat, jumped over to the other side, landing on the tall grass of an unkempt garden.

Unfortunately, two soldiers posted along the tall columns of the building went after my father and captured him. Father was accused of being one of Castro's allies and was sent to jail, where he was interrogated. I was not quite four years old at the time, but my memory of the night remains vivid. Mother and a group of neighbors went from door to door, asking if anyone had seen my father. These conversations were conducted in hushed tones. My mother was thinking the worst. During those times, it was not unusual to find people dead on some abandoned road or on the outskirts of town.

Mother tried very hard to keep calm, and she reassured me that "Papi was coming home soon," but I knew something very serious had happened. Then I heard Uncle Manolo say, "If Pepe is dead we should find him soon, but if he is in jail we might not get any information for a while. They'll torture him, especially if they think he's involved with the Revolutionaries." I was terrified. I couldn't imagine my Papi dead, alone somewhere. *Papi . . . Papi, come home soon.*

Two days later, a pair of well-armed Batista officers appeared at our door. They brushed us aside and began searching the house. I was so frightened by their rudeness that I moved into a corner of the playroom and hid behind an old brown leather chair. From my hiding place I could hear things being thrown on the floor, drawers and doors being opened and then slammed. I could hear Mother's voice asking, "What are you doing? Tell me what you're looking for! Where is Pepe?" She had Jose, my two-year-old brother, in her arms as she followed them around the house. There were no answers.

The soldiers poked into our things till they had searched every room and every corner of the house. Finally, I heard them say to my mother, "Listen, lady, if you have any guns in the house, you better tell us now. Your husband is in jail under suspicion of involvement with those rebels in the mountains." Mother cried, "Oh, thank God, he is alive! Look, I don't know who you are, but my husband is no revolutionary, and we have no guns in our house."

When the soldiers finally left, I ventured out of my hiding place. The house looked as if a tornado had upended it. The contents of our closets, cabinets and night tables had been emptied out on the floor.

Mattresses had been pulled from the bedframes, pillows were cut open and their stuffing strewn all over the bedroom. I walked around, picking up some of my toys, and found my mother standing in the middle of the living room. She held Jose in her arms wearily as she cried, "Teresa, come here, my baby, your father is going to be home soon. Come . . . come, my baby, don't be scared!"

Father came back home that same day. He was pale, with dark circles under his eyes. The white shirt he wore was torn and stained with brown dirt and blood, probably from his bottom lip, which was swollen and purple. The right side of his face was badly scratched. He hugged and kissed Mami and then lifted Jose with one arm and came towards me. Kneeling on the floor, he put his other arm around my shoulders, holding the two of us close to him. He wept. I'd never seen my father cry.

"I thought I'd never see you again, my little children, pequeños de mi corazón."

After my father's disappearance, I was constantly worried about my parents. I didn't want to leave their sides. Any time they went out of the house, I feared they would be killed. I began having stomachaches and developed chronic constipation from my anxiety.

For weeks my mother had to give me painful enemas. The minute I saw her coming towards me in the morning with that horrible red rubber bag, I ran and hid under my bed. Mother would beg me to come out: "This is for your own good, Teresa. You're constipated, and this will make you feel better. Come on, don't be scared. It won't hurt as much this time." Lies! I knew it was going to hurt—the terrible cramps doubled me over and sometimes left me crawling the bathroom floor. The ordeal would last for almost an hour, leaving me exhausted and limp. I hated that red bag, much as I came to hate Fidel Castro and his red Communist insignia years later.

During the next few months, as the Revolution moved closer to our town, new fears were added to my world. One morning, we were awakened by the staccato of machine-gun fire. My mother came rushing into my bedroom, holding Jose in her arms.

"Come, Teresa . . . come, get down on the floor!" Her voice sounded harsh and shaken. Mami pulled me down with her and Jose and covered both of us with her body. Jose was screaming, terrified by the noise of the gunfire. I curled up and held my breath, thinking if I remained quiet, a stray bullet wouldn't find us.

The shooting went on and on. Then, everything was silent, the only sound a fly buzzing somewhere in the room. We were all still trembling but Mother got up and turned the radio on: Batista's army and Castro's revolutionaries had skirmished. We were regaining our composure when a loud siren sounded down the street. Jose ran and hid behind my mother.

"Felicia, Felicia!" A neighbor called my mother from the street.

"Qué pasa?" my mother asked, walking to the door.

"Felicia . . . Miguelito was killed on his way to work just around the corner from here."

"Oh, por Dios, qué desgracia!" My mother put her hands to her head. Miguelito was the son of Carmela, my mother's best friend.

From that morning on, I became very familiar with the refrains of "so and so was killed" and "so and so is in jail." Terror hung thick in the air. It became the monster under my bed, sneaking out at night and chasing me in my nightmares. Death invaded the fragile world of my childhood games as my dolls got "shot" and were rushed to the hospital.

One afternoon, Jose and I were playing with his wooden blocks in the living room when, again, we heard the sound of helicopters followed by machine-gun fire. We automatically stopped our games and Jose crawled towards me, seeking the protection of my arms. The shooting continued. Through the large window that faced the street, we could see people running in all directions, seeking refuge wherever they could. I saw one woman hide with her young child under a milk truck. Bullets hit the asphalt, the trees, the trash cans in front of the houses. Suddenly, there was a break in the fire. The streets became silent, so silent one could almost hear the pounding hearts of those hiding.

The sound of a motorcycle and then an explosion unexpectedly broke the silence. Our whole house shook. At first, I thought we had been hit by a bomb. But out the window, I saw a ball of flame racing down the street and then drop to the ground. After a few moments, I

17

realized in horror that the burning mass was the body of the motorcyclist being consumed by fire.

Pieces of the motorcycle were scattered all over the street. The pungent smell of burned rubber and of incinerated flesh filled our nostrils. The woman who was hiding under the milk truck dragged herself out and ran to the scene. Her young child, left behind, began to scream. The woman didn't look back. She took off her skirt and tried to stop the fire from destroying whatever was left of the motorcyclist. A neighbor from across the street came outside with a big white blanket to cover the remains.

My view was blocked by the neighbors as they formed a circle around the dead man. But it didn't matter. The image of the scorched body was forever fixed in my mind. Jose, poor Jose, he was still holding on to me, his little arms wrapped around my body so tight I could hardly breathe. I pulled him closer. I don't remember if we cried. With our eyes closed, we stayed entwined and rocked each other back and forth. After that, every time we heard a helicopter we ran and ducked under our beds.

On the morning of January 1, 1959, revolutionaries under the command of Che Guevara invaded Santa Clara, the province where we lived. According to my father, we never went to bed that New Year's Eve. Our traditional family dancing and arroz con pollo dinner were interrupted by a bulletin on the radio. The voice vibrated with excitement as it informed us that General Fulgencio Batista had deserted and left the country.

Glasses of wine went up in the air, toasting the long anticipated freedom from Batista's rule. Family and friends gathered around the television to watch images of an island in a state of euphoria over the victory of the Revolutionaries: People were out in the streets celebrating, waving Cuban flags and posters of Fidel Castro, Che Guevara and Camilo Cienfuegos, singing the national anthem and shouting, "Viva la Revolución!"

As I grew older, I heard the details of that day from my mother. Her recollection always begins: "Neighbors were coming and going from one house to the other, drinking coffee and talking about how many Cubans who didn't like Castro were rushing to the airports with the hope of getting to Miami." During one of the quiet breaks between visitors, Mother was in the kitchen while Father sat in the living room, glued to the radio. I was playing with my set of plastic army soldiers next to Papi when our next-door neighbor and friend, Nena, came rushing through the front door.

"Felicia! Innocent people are getting killed by the milicianos."

"What are you talking about?" my mother asked as she dried her hands on her apron.

"Right by the big wall at the entrance to the cemetery. They're killing all those who don't like Castro, anybody under suspicion for counterrevolutionary activities."

When describing this part, Mother never forgets to mention how Nena's hands trembled as she held the tiny cup filled with coffee that Mother had handed to her friend.

"Oh, Felicia, you should have seen how those poor men were lined up, blindfolded and then sprayed with bullets from the machine guns of those criminals. Oh, my God!" Nena broke down in sobs. "The white wall turned red with their blood. I couldn't believe what my eyes were seeing."

Afraid for our safety, my mother and father decided it was best for us all to go and stay at my mother's parents' farm until things settled down in town. Without wasting any time, she packed a small suitcase with clothes and we started out on the eight-mile walk. "It is not safe to travel by car with all these crazy shootings," she said firmly. She thought the Revolutionaries were targeting the "fugitives" driving to the airports to escape to the United States with their fortunes and families.

As we set out, Mother and Father took turns carrying Jose, while I held one of their hands. To me, our walk was an adventure at first, but as we reached the edge of town, the scenery changed. What had been a sugar cane plantation was now a cluster of still-smouldering ruins. A rain of dark gray ashes began to drift down on us and the air smelled of burned grass and cane juice. "There goes Luis's fortune. This year he won't need to worry about finding cutters; the fire took pretty good care of his plantation," Father said. We continued walking down the main road, occasionally meeting other people on their way to town who greeted us with "Viva la Revolución."

About a mile from my grandparents' farm, as we approached an orange grove, I saw the bodies of two men, each hung from the long branch of a big ateje tree on the side of the road.

"Papi, look! Those men are swinging from the tree," I said, not quite understanding what I was seeing.

Both Father and Mother stopped and I realized something was very wrong. The men's faces were swollen and purple, their features twisted, their tongues hanging from their mouths. Each man's head was tilted somewhat to the side, the eyes wide open, looking up at the sky.

"Oh, God!" I heard my father say.

"Pepe, please let's go," Mother pleaded, and with her free hand she pulled me to her side. Father didn't respond but walked straight to the men.

"Poor souls," Father said, and he took his hat off.

One of the men wore gray twill pants and a shirt, with a wide leather belt around his waist that held a machete on the right side, the dress of a local farmer. His white straw hat had fallen to the ground. My father commented that the man was no older than forty. The other man was younger, maybe twenty. His white guayabera was stained with blood that was still dripping from his nose.

"Don't look, Teresa," I heard my mother say, but I couldn't pull my gaze away from the men. All I could see was their faces, the strange look in their eyes. I wondered if the men had children like Jose and me. My heart withered with the thought of a little child waiting for her Papi to come home, as I had waited for my father the night he was thrown in jail. Young as I was, I knew these men would never return home.

My father stood motionless beneath the men for a moment. Then he pulled his knife from his pocket and tried to reach the rope from which the older man was suspended, but it was too high. He looked around for something to step on but finally had to climb the wide trunk of the tree and crawl out on the big branch from which the men hung. Holding on to an upper branch with one hand and the knife with the other, he cut each rope and one by one, the bodies dropped to the earth, hitting the ground with a dull thud that still echoes in my ears.

"Mami . . . are they really dead?" I asked. It took her a few seconds to find her voice. "Yes, mi hijita, they are dead." I wanted to go and touch them, but my mother's arms held me fast.

Father kneeled down in front of the older man. He lifted his right hand and, with a slow and tender motion, closed the man's eyes. Then he did the same with the younger man. During the years that followed, I comforted myself with the thought that these men had been tucked in their death beds by my father, and that, perhaps, he had helped them not to be so afraid of whatever dark places lingered near the stars.

Father picked up his hat from the ground and walked back to where we were waiting. Silently, he reached out for my small hand, and we began the final mile to the farm. Behind us, the dead men were no longer hanging from the tree. Thanks to my father, they were at rest on the warm Cuban earth.

But to me, they are always there, hanging in the darkness of my nights. I can see their tongues, long and purple, and their eyes, wide open to the sky.

3

LA FINCA

*T*HAT AFTERNOON, New Year's Day 1959, Grandfather José and Grandmother Petra were not surprised at all to see us arrive at their home. Sweaty and exhausted from the trip, we drank tall glasses of icy lemonade and ate fresh chunks of juicy papaya by their beautiful garden, where tropical plants—hibiscus, bird of paradise, orchids, petunias, ferns, azaleas and roses—grew under the magical touch of the sun and my grandmother's fingers.

My grandparents' farm was truly a place of magic. Named Villa Petra by my Grandfather José in honor of his wife, this beautiful piece of land—la Finca—was rich and vibrant, its golden-green valleys bordered by cañaverales, royal palm trees, with voluptuous hills, like rounded breasts, in the distance.

At Villa Petra, I felt safe and far removed from the turmoil I had seen outside la Finca. There I could play and dream again. The farm was like a sturdy tree that held me in its branches, its roots grounding me in the Cuban soil, its shade protecting me from the burning heat of the Revolution.

We stayed at la Finca for only a week that time, leaving when it was safe for us to return to our home in town. But with all the uncertainties and sudden small terrors of the Revolution, Villa Petra became our refuge, a place where we could hide from the dangers of the post-revolution.

At la Finca I learned to listen to the land and find sustenance in it. As my Grandfather José said to me, "When one lives with the land, one is blessed by the perpetual gift of life and death: Seeds sprout in the darkness of the night; leaves die and join the soil." Villa Petra taught me about the intimate relationship between the spirit and the daily experiences of life. God was there in the fields. She sang to me with the voice of gentle winds that made the palm tree leaves dance and sway. She talked to me through the calls of the birds on early summer mornings. I felt her presence every time I walked among the rows of sugar cane and corn and smelled their strong, sweet fragance in the warm air.

I was five and a half years old when in April 1961, the Cuban militia was called to defend our island from a large group of U.S-backed Cuban expatriates from Miami who had landed at Playa Girón in the Bay of Pigs. As I heard it, these mercenarios had come to wrest Cuba from Castro's hands, but before they had a chance to fire their arms, they were captured and thrown in prison. My family went to la Finca until the familiar war planes and helicopters had gone away.

During the U.S.-Soviet-Cuban missile crisis in October 1962, my mother once again packed our bags, and Father drove us to the farm. Around the country, organized protests were being held on the streets. People were calling the U.S. president John F. Kennedy a "capitalist," an "imperialist dog." At age seven, I didn't know exactly what those words meant, but I understood enough to figure out that the Soviet and American missiles could mean the destruction of our island. We left Cabaigüán as the town began to prepare for an attack by the United States. The government was mobilizing our neighbors and the local militia to dig trenches and play out war games.

At Villa Petra, we sat together in my grandparents' living room to watch the evening news. My stomach tightened as I watched the large green trucks filled with soldiers and their machine guns heading for the Havana waterfront. To me this was the end of the world.

"Are we going to be safe here, Grandmother?" I asked, cuddling closer to her. "Shouldn't we be building some of those trenches for us and the animals to hide in?"

"Not yet. We should wait to see what's going to happen."

I was surprised to hear Grandmother say that. Wait, wait for what? It was clear to me that we were in great danger. I got up from my chair and walked to the room where my brother Jose was playing with his new set of army men. I joined in, thinking this could be a way to practice our "strategies of escape," in case the farm was attacked by the "Yankees."

The Yankees, the Soviets and Castro settled their dispute without a war, and we returned to our home in town. But the farm continued to be my safe haven. In moments of fear, knowing la Finca was there was as comforting to me as my old threadbare blankie. Throughout my childhood, I was constantly reminded of how la Finca was born and grew like the roots of our family tree, our raíces. Villa Petra, I was told, was the fruit of my grandparents' dreams. Here, in the fertile Cuban soil, they cultivated not only the seeds of crops, harvested year after year, but a new generation of Spanish-Cuban children—twelve total. One of them was my mother, Felicia.

My grandfather had arrived in Cuba around the turn of the century at the age of seventeen. He had left his native Canary Islands off the northwest coast of Africa in search of fortune, like many other young Spanish people. After its conquest by Spain, Cuba, "the beautiful pearl of the Caribbean," gradually became "the land of promise," and large groups of immigrants from the motherland poured out of sailing vessels onto Cuban shores.

When José Maria Barrios landed in Cuba with a vision as his only fortune, he went to live in the province of Las Villas, where he knew a relative who employed him as a cowboy on his cattle ranch. He worked long hours for little money, and whatever he was able to save, he invested right away in a cow that a few months later gave birth to a strong calf. It was not long before he had made enough money selling animals to purchase his first piece of land.

Around this time, Petra Alvares came to visit the ranch, accompanied by her Uncle Antonio. She was only fifteen and on her first vacation to Cuba from Tenerife, one of the Canary islands. José and Petra fell in love and married in less than a year. She never went back to the islands.

Grandfather built their first home on the land—a modest bohío, Cuban style, with a frame and walls built from local palm tree boards, painted bright white both inside and out. The roof was made of woven ash-colored leaves from guano palms. Foot-square light-gray tiles, baked inside earth kilns and glazed by the hands of artisans, covered the floors. A wood-burning stove, built with round stones gathered from the riverbed, was the centerpiece of the kitchen. It sat right next to the window facing the valley, a small but thoughtful detail, considering the long hours of the day and night young Petra stood there cooking meals for José and the farm workers, and for the children that quickly arrived.

Their living room was small, perhaps twelve by fifteen feet. A large clay tinaja with a stone filter gracefully rested near the entrance door, a convenient place for everyone to reach out for the refreshing drinking water as they came in from the fields after a hard day of planting or harvesting rows of sugar cane, tobacco, malanga, sweet potatoes and corn under the hot Cuban sun. There was only one bedroom, but its large window opened to el palmar, an area where tall, slender palm trees swayed under the skies, serenading the young couple with their gentle murmurs during the breezy tropical nights.

A black and white photograph of José and Petra taken shortly after their marriage hung in our family room when I was young. Grandfather is a very serious-looking young man with dark eyes, a round face, strong angular jaw, long Spanish nose, thin lips and piel morena. His five-foot-six, stocky but muscular body is dressed in a white guayabera and light cotton pants. He emanates passion and firmness of intention.

Next to him Grandmother Petra has an almost virginal appearance. With her long hair braided and rolled at the nape of her neck, the soft lines of her oval face and her light hazel eyes are accentuated. Her skin is fair with the texture of porcelain; her features, delicate. Despite her youth, there is a look of wisdom, unsophisticated elegance and distinct majesty about her. She is wearing a white embroidered cotton dress of simple lines, the collar low enough to disclose the gentle, sensuous lines of her neck. But I knew from family stories and my own experience that

25

beneath Petra's superficial fragility, her small and thin constitution—maybe five feet three inches tall, 110 pounds—had been a core of strength.

Life on the young couple's farm was hard, with long working days from sunrise to sundown. José and Petra worked side by side, sweating, feeling their backs burn under the hot tropical sun. They ploughed the land with the help of an old ox and a metal arado, and planted rows and rows of banana, plantain, boniato, malanga, corn, yuca, potatoes, rice, beans. The dark soil of the island was fertile and generous. Everything grew fast, as if touched by God's hands.

It was not always easy for the Barrios couple. Petra's strong personality frequently clashed with José's desire to maintain control over his developing empire. Astute and sharp-minded when it came to business transactions, Petra voiced her opinions without reservation and even fought her husband whenever she felt he was not making the right decision. Petra's intuitive hunches frustrated José tremendously. He couldn't understand why his stubborn wife demanded, without much explanation, that he stay away from certain influential local farmers who wanted to join efforts with him.

"That man is a vulture! He will eat you alive," she would say.

"How can you say that, woman? You don't know the man."

"I don't need to know him. It's written all over his face."

"There you go again. When are you going to stop reading people?"

"Never! You'd better get used to it," Petra would say and then walk away, leaving José perplexed and angry.

Petra was the kind of woman que no tiene pelos en la lengua, as we say in Cuba; she didn't waste words when it came to telling people exactly what she thought. She called workers on their laziness if they tried to steal time from work during the hot afternoons, or a bag of fruit, potatoes or rice from the storehouse before they went home at night.

"Señor Carabia, next time you need food for your family, all you need to do is ask," Petra would say to the man the next morning when he returned to the farm to work. "Sí, señora, thank you. It will never happen again. I promise you," Señor Carabia would reply, lowering his eyes to the ground.

"Why did you say that to Carabia?" José would shout at his wife. "He may not come back tomorrow. You know how hard it is to find good workers these days! It's not a big deal if he takes a bag of beans home!"

"Well, José, last night, it was a bag of beans. Tomorrow it could be something else, and soon you won't know. I'd like to be around people I can trust," Petra replied.

The birth of Grandmother and Grandfather's first child, Tomás, took the young couple by surprise. Petra began her labor pains before sunrise. José was concerned about leaving his inexperienced wife alone, but finally, Petra sent him out to get the local midwife, Camila, who lived twenty minutes away. José jumped on the bare back of his white horse, Azucre, and took off down the valley.

All alone in the house, Petra began to pray Padre Nuestros and Ave Marías. Not a practicing Catholic, she had difficulty remembering the prayers her mother had taught her as a child, so she filled in the blanks with her own words.

I knew the story of my Uncle Tomás's birth because I had overheard Grandmother share it with my mother and my Aunt Juana when I was young. They had been seated around the large kitchen working table, peeling yuca to make almidón, or starch, a tedious process that requires hours and hours of work. After the brown skin of the root is removed with a knife, the root is ground and the pulp placed on a large cheesecloth. Water is poured over it and squeezed out by hand till the fluid comes out clear. This mixture of water and yuca milk is kept in a large metal (usually aluminum) container for a day or two, till all the starch has settled at the bottom. Then the water on top is poured off carefully and the remaining soft creamy paste is left to dry under the sun. The three women were so involved in their work and their conversation, they never noticed me playing nearby.

"I couldn't remember how to pray," I heard Grandmother say. "I was too scared. I kept saying to myself, 'Don't panic, Petra, don't be such a weakling. Women have given birth from the beginning of the world. Try to remain calm!'"

"I can't imagine being alone in such a situation," my mother said.

"You were so young, Mamá," Juana added.

"Not only was I young, but I knew nothing . . . nothing at all about having babies!" said Grandmother, grabbing another yuca from a pile on the kitchen floor. "Mamá delivered five children, all at home, with the help of midwives. I was the youngest, so I missed all the action." Grandmother became quiet. A few seconds later, she put her knife on top of the table and looked at her daughters.

"How I wished Mamá were there with me!" Slowly she took off her dark-framed glasses and cleaned them on her white apron. Then, putting the glasses back on, she picked up her knife.

"The pain—well, you know, you both have given birth—the pain, as if someone had taken a knife and stuck me with it all over my belly."

"Tell me about it . . . when I had Teresa, I spent twenty-four hours in labor," my mother said.

"I lost any notion of time," Grandmother said. "All I could think of was . . . I was going to die, my baby was going to die, if José didn't show up soon with the midwife. I cursed him for taking so long. I was screaming and crying at the same time, and in between the pain and the fear, I was calling for my mother—'Mamá . . . Mamá . . . Mamá querida.' I could feel the muchacho moving and pushing inside me. The contractions were getting stronger, but I had no idea what to do. If only Mamá were there to tell me. I knew I was supposed to push, push hard, but every time I tried to push, it hurt even more." Grandmother paused and looked at her daughters. "You girls were lucky to have your kids the way you did, with all the comforts of modern hospitals."

"Sí, Mamá, but the pain is the same, no matter what," Juana replied.

"Well, as time went by," Grandmother continued, "I couldn't tell how long, I was feeling weaker and weaker. It was then . . . it was then that something inexplicable happened. Something that has puzzled me all the years of my life. Ay carajo, las cosas que tiene la vida. I was so tired that I think I dozed for a bit. Then I heard Mamá's voice, so clear, as if she were there with me. 'Petra, hija, relajate.' I saw Mamá placing her hands on my belly, calming me, and then she said, 'Push . . .

push hard, coño!' And as I gathered all my strength and pushed, I felt the child coming out, followed by a great relief from my misery."

As my Grandmother Petra told her daughters, José and Camila, the midwife arrived at the house almost an hour later. Petra lay on the bed exhausted, her face paper white. The bed linens were soaked in Petra's blood, some of it still oozing in a fine stream from the raw opening of her vagina. The dark purplish colored baby was still connected to his mother by the umbilical cord, peacefully resting between Petra's legs, which lay open. Camila took the child in her arms, relieved that he was breathing.

"Hurry up, José, get some water boiling!" Camila shouted across the room. "Petra has lost a lot of blood and she is still bleeding."

The midwife found the scissors in her straw bag and disinfected them with José's alcohol.

"José . . . come here." Camila handed him the pair of scissors and took the newborn in her arms. "José, cut the umbilical cord of your first son."

Grandfather's hands shook as he took the scissors. He moved slowly under Camila's instructions and finally severed the cord connecting child and mother. Tears ran down José's tanned face. Going to his exhausted wife, he took Petra's hands in his and kissed them many times. "Petra, mi querida Petra, look at me, look at me."

From the depths of her weariness, Petra smiled at him and then closed her eyes to rest.

"He is a handsome and strong boy," José said.

"Just like his father," Camila said to the happy young man.

After a short pause, during which Grandmother appeared to be lost in the past, she continued her narration.

"My dear José told me that Camila turned to me. I was between two worlds—you know how it is . . . you feel as if you are floating in the room. The midwife held the child near me so that I could look at him.

"'Petra, Petra, can you see your child? Can you see his beautiful face?'

"I wanted to touch my baby, but I was too weak. I mumbled a few words. I think Camila was a bit psychic, because she placed the newborn next to me on the bed so that I could feel his little warm body. She was a kind woman. After so many years, I can still hear her words: 'Your baby is fine, healthy, complete, no missing fingers or toes. He is fine. You can rest now. Rest, my dear, you are going to need your strength.'"

Tomás's birth was the beginning of a long chain of births. A total of fifteen children were born to Petra and José. Twelve survived. Twin boys were stillborn, and a girl was strangled at birth by the umbilical cord. The midwife had again arrived too late.

There was very little time for grieving the dead or for recovery. As soon as she was strong enough to be on her feet, Petra was back in the kitchen. Often she cooked while breast-feeding a young one. In the same way that the family was growing, so was the farm under the care and management of José, who kept buying land and expanding the boundaries of his property. With money no longer a problem, José decided to build a bigger home closer to the newly developed highway, or carretera central, and to the nearby town of Cabaigüán.

Grandfather José took modern comforts into consideration when designing every room of the new house. The expansive bathrooms had large windows that looked out to the gardens, and beautiful marble tubs. There were long corridors with tall columns and tiles imported from Spain, eight bedrooms, a very spacious kitchen, and two dining rooms, the formal one used only on Sundays and special occasions when the whole family gathered or when guests were invited.

My favorite part of the house was the living room, where a crystal chandelier hung from the ceiling. I would lie on the cool tile floor on hot summer afternoons and watch the crystals refract the light from the window, forming little rainbows. I thought of these crystals as the home of the angels watching over us.

Every Sunday, the entire family gathered at Villa Petra. The Barrios children with their own children and spouses began arriving early in the morning for a day of leisure, work and play. After lunch, Grandmother Petra and her daughters—Ana, Juana, Mensa, Caridad, Linda, Felicia, and Nelda—and her daughters-in-law sat on one end of the long, wide porch in front of the house. The women of the family enjoyed the tranquility of this spot surrounded by the colorful garden. There, as they quilted, needlepointed and crocheted, they talked, laughed and even cried, reminiscing about old times.

The sisters' favorite stories were always about their trips to Santa Lucia, when as young teenagers, they rode their horses to visit relatives twenty or thirty miles away from the farm. The journeys were anticipated for days, with elaborate preparations that included baking cakes and canning fruits that were taken as gifts, or making new dresses for the occasion—often the celebration of someone's birthday, a wedding, a baptism or simply a family gathering.

On the other end of the porch, Grandfather and his sons—Tomás, Victor, Antonio, Osvaldo and Manuel—sat together with their brothers-in-law and talked about the harvest, politics, horses, boxing, baseball . . . while smoking big Cuban cigars and drinking coffee from tiny porcelain cups. At age seven, I went back and forth from one group to the other, till finally, bored, I joined the boys, who would usually be playing cops-and-robbers in the orange and guava orchard. The girls were, more often than not, inside the house looking at fashion magazines and talking about school and boyfriends.

In the fall of 1963, I turned eight. My family and I had gone to Villa Petra to visit my grandparents for the weekend. On Saturday, before sunrise, we were awakened by loud knocking at the front door. From my room in the back of the house, I could hear the alarmed voices of Grandfather José and Grandmother Petra; then I heard my father say, "They have surrounded the house. They have guns!"

I went to the window and saw a group of uniformed men with machine guns standing around the west side of the house, near the orchard. It was the militia. Scared, I ran to the living room where I heard the voices of my grandfather and my father. I was shocked to find one of the officers with a gun pointed at my grandfather, demanding the keys to the office where all the records and papers concerning the property and farm were kept. Three other officers were searching the living room, opening drawers and emptying the contents onto the floor, breaking things and kicking the furniture out of their way.

My mother, still dressed in her nightgown, was standing next to Grandmother, who somehow had managed to get into a skirt and blouse. I was shaking with fear. In my mind, these men were going to shoot us or perhaps hang all of us, like those men we saw hanging from

31

the ateje tree the day after the Revolution. Grandfather kept asking them to put their guns away. A miliciano with a black moustache and piercing dark eyes laughed disrespectfully. "Viejo estúpido, your time is over. Forget about this house and your sugar plantation. It is all ours now." Grandmother tried to confront him, but when she grabbed the man's gun, she was pushed away and thrown to the ground.

"Qué buscan? What are you searching for?" Grandmother asked from the floor. Her face was pale and contorted with rage.

"Armas, we know you have weapons in the house . . . and money. We want your dirty money."

"There are no weapons in this house," Grandfather said. "I have never owned a gun in my life. I never needed one because I have no enemies. Please, leave us alone."

"Alone? No, viejo. We are here to stay for a long time while we make an inventory of the property. Haven't you heard about the Agrarian Reform? It went into effect two days ago. Our comandante, Fidel Castro, has ordered us to take this land from your hands. Kiss it good-bye!"

What was to have been a weekend visit to the farm lasted for two weeks. Given the situation at Villa Petra, my mother decided that she and the children would stay and help her parents. On Sunday, Father went back to town to work. For ten days, the eight militia men lived in the house, demanding to be fed while they figured out what to do with my grandparents' land. They went through my grandparents' papers and bank accounts, stamping everything with the government seal, while Grandfather and Grandmother watched all their dreams and their fate thrown into the hands of people who had never worked the land in their lives.

The milicianos called us gusanos imperialistas—imperialist maggots. Then came the final crushing blow: The militia men announced the farm was to be repossessed by the government except for five caballerias of land and the house. After that, Grandfather José scarcely spoke. He stopped riding his Arabian horse. He made no more trips to town. He was like a ghost—there but not there. Grandmother Petra retreated into her room. There she spent long hours in silence, staring out at the fields.

I never told my grandmother in the years that followed that I saw her cry. Perhaps, in my own way, I understood her struggle. Nor did I tell her how angry I was to see her so defeated, and how lonely and scared I felt, not knowing how long the nightmare was going to last.

4

PETRA AND ALAZANA

My MEMORIES of Grandmother Petra are always connected to the period I spent growing up on the farm. She was to me a symbol of strength, a source of quiet wisdom. It was Petra who taught me to love the land. When I think of her, I always remember the strong woman I knew before the Agrarian Reform took away her dreams. After the repossession of the farm, Grandmother aged quickly. She began to walk more slowly, and her back became hunched by the weight of her losses.

By the time I came into her life, Grandmother Petra was in her sixties and tired from giving birth to and raising so many children. Still, time and a hard life had not erased the beauty and kindness of her soul. Grandmother was as sturdy as the wide trunk of the ceiba tree that grew by the riverbed. She had strong legs with veins that popped from the skin, just like roots wrapped around the earth. She was a woman who could easily wrestle a man down with her wiry arms, but those arms could also be gentle and protecting, like the tree branches that shelter one from the storm. Grandmother's long white hair, rolled into a bun at the nape of her neck, gave her the appearance of a flamenco dancer and the wise look of an old gypsy.

Occasionally, Grandmother would allow me to comb her unbraided silky mane, which ran all the way down her back and legs to below her knees. She had her favorite comb, what we call in Cuba a peineta, a small half-moon-shaped comb made from the shell of a kaguama, a big sea turtle. Grandmother Petra's peineta had been a precious gift from her mother. When Grandmother wanted me to comb her hair, she would pull the peineta from the small pocket on the side of her dress and hand it to me. This was a very special time. Grandmother was never, in my experience, very talkative, but during our combing ritual, she would relax and share some of her memories.

"I always wanted to go back to my native Tenerife," she might say, followed by a long, pensive pause.

"Why didn't you go back, Grandmother?"

"Well, I'm not sure I know that myself. All I know is that time passed so quickly. So quickly . . . I didn't see myself getting old. One day, when I was in my late forties, I got a letter saying Mamá had died . . . and then, two years later, another letter, Papá had died."

Silence. I looked at Grandmother's face, expecting to see some tears. Instead, I met the stillness of her hazel eyes. Memories of those loved ones left behind were all Grandmother had left of them, and in the quiet darkness of her sleepless nights, she would savor those memories. "After Papá's death, I didn't care to go back there. I cried and cried many nights. Oftentimes José would wake up and say, 'Basta, mujer, que te vas a secar de tanto llorar. If you keep going like this, you're going to get sick.' Like many men, my beloved husband couldn't understand my pain. Men don't suffer as women do. I never saw him lose sleep over anyone's death, not even when our children died. Instead, he worked and worked till he dropped exhausted in bed at night, like a dead horse."

Grandmother worked as hard as a man. She didn't believe in having servants, and even when Grandfather hired two people to help with the cooking and housework, Grandmother did most of the work herself. Every morning, without exception, she was out of bed before five to help fill the huge metal cantinas with milk the men brought in from the barn. I would be awakened by the clanking of the containers in the kitchen, sounds that meant it was time to get up and get a taste of the foamy, sweet, warm milk, fresh from the cows.

Sometimes, Grandmother sat with me, and we would enjoy the

slow sipping of our café con leche while the rest of the household slept. Once, she told me these early hours were her favorite time of the day—when everything was quiet and one could still smell the minty scent of the morning dew. "Get ready, Teresa, soon as breakfast is over, we are going to pick guavas for marmalade," she might say.

Grandmother taught me how to choose the best guavas for my favorite Cuban dessert, casquitos, a simple recipe in which the guavas are peeled and seeded and then simmered in a kettle with water and plenty of brown sugar till tender. "Here, Teresa," she'd say, "this is what you want. Look at the skin, feel it. It feels thick and juicy. That's what we need. Remember, not too ripe, not too green. Look here! This one has the perfect color." And then she would be quiet for a while, totally absorbed in the job of picking the fruit.

I was eager to learn from Grandmother and I experienced a certain pride in being able to do the things she did. At the age of six, I enjoyed the kind of attention she gave me and would follow her around, to the corn fields to pick fresh corn for lunch or when she went looking for the eggs of wild hens hidden in the tall grass. One afternoon, she and I went out to dig some malangas, a root similar to a potato. On the way home, we walked across the potrero, where the golden grass intermingled with dark green patches of dormidera weeds and some tiny yellow and brown wildflowers, making the valley look like a handmade quilt. I was fascinated by the way the dormidera's feather-shaped leaves coiled into a small bunch under the light pressure of my foot or finger.

I was busy stepping on the plants and magically making them go to sleep—dormidera means "sleeper"—when I heard what sounded like a horse in pain or distress. Grandmother immediately stopped and put her bag of malangas on the ground, listening for the next call. A few seconds later I heard her say, "It's the pregnant mare—Alazana! Something is wrong with her!" Grandmother began walking fast toward an area maybe thirty yards away, and I followed. Right in front of some tall bushes, I could make out the figure of an animal lying on the grass, next to an old tamarind tree whose large, thick branches extended themselves like the ribs of a gigantic umbrella, providing protection from the hot sun. The mare was making attempts to get up, but every time she tried, her left leg would buckle. Alazana was a beautiful horse with a dark-amber coat and a golden mane and tail, but now her dark round eyes were filled with fear.

"Her left leg is broken!" Grandmother said as she moved closer to the animal. "Stay where you are, Teresa!"

"Grandmother, can we help her get up?"

"No . . . no, don't move any closer! We don't want to scare her."

I watched as my grandmother walked closer and closer to the mare, her movements slow, her voice gentle. She looked like a dancer, totally focused in her dance. Her eyes were fixed on Alazana's as if some sort of exchange were happening between the two of them. I was amazed to see the mare becoming more relaxed as Grandmother approached her side. Taking her time, making no sudden moves, Grandmother knelt next to Alazana to examine the broken leg. As she touched the area right above the hoof, the animal arched back and kicked in the air with her front legs, barely missing Grandmother. When the mare settled down, Grandmother signaled for me to come closer. "Teresa, go back to the house and get your Grandfather or one of the workers. Tell whoever you find what happened, so he comes prepared."

"Yes, Grandmother. I'll be back soon," I said, not wanting to leave but I knowing I'd best not contradict her.

"And Teresa, bring the wooden box that is next to the door inside the utility room."

I ran as fast as I could. On my way, I met Manuel, an old cowboy who spent most of his time in the barn, making sure the animals had plenty of water and food. I told him what had happened and asked him to go help Grandmother. He began complaining about some arthritic pain in his right hip. Manuel was around seventy, but with his unshaved face and missing teeth, plus heavy tobacco stains on the remaining ones he looked much older.

"Manuel, just go! She needs help with the mare."

"Ay carajo! I'll go, but that mare is not worth the hassle!" he said, spitting a wad of chewing tobacco into a pile of hay.

I couldn't find Grandfather, but Matias, a young farm worker coming back from town, offered to help. I found the box, and Matias offered to give me a ride on his horse. When we arrived, Grandmother and Manuel were trying to bind the mare's broken leg with a two-foot-long stick and some strong fishing line Manuel had brought with him. Matias joined them, while I stood a couple of feet away, watching.

"Hand me the box," Grandmother said.

She took a roll of black electrical tape out of the box and began to wrap the tape around the mare's leg bound with the stick. I moved back a few steps so that I wouldn't block the light as Grandmother worked. It was then that I noticed a red bubble coming out of what looked like the mare's rear end. This bubble looked just like a balloon being blown up, gradually getting bigger. "Grandmother . . . Grandmother . . . look!"

"I can't look now. What is it?" she asked, without taking her eyes from the tape she was wrapping around the leg.

"Grandmother, there is a funny-looking balloon growing from Alazana's pipi."

"Oh no! Not now!" she said, getting up from her place. "Here, Manuel, go ahead and finish this. Let me take a look back there. If it is what I think it is . . . " she said with a frown on her face.

"What is it, Grandmother?" I asked, thinking the worst.

"What a day! I wonder where the hell is José? Just when we need him the most, he turns into smoke," Grandmother said, her hands on her hips, her face tilted, looking down at the horse.

"What is it, Grandmother?"

"She is giving birth, está pariendo," she said to me as if it were the most natural thing in the world.

"Is she going to be okay?"

"Sí, Teresita, but because of her broken leg, it's going to be difficult for her," Grandmother said, kneeling down and taking a closer look at the bubble, which was getting bigger by the minute.

"Look, Teresita . . . the head is beginning to show!" I had never seen Grandmother so excited. She was like a little girl, her eyes two big sparks of light. I was thrilled, too. I'd never seen a horse giving birth before.

"Matias, go and bring some water for the mare," Grandmother ordered, while gently petting Alazana for a few seconds. Then she moved away from the animal. "Ven, Teresa, let's leave her alone for now." Grandmother pulled me by the hand towards the shade of the tamarind tree. "These things take a little while, so we better get comfortable," she said, lowering herself to the ground and signaling me to join her.

"Is Alazana in a lot of pain?" I asked, thinking about the times I had heard my aunts talk about their labor pain.

"If yeguas are like women, I'm sure she's in lots of pain." Grandmother pulled a white cotton handkerchief from her dress pocket and dried the sweat from her face.

"Is there anything we can do to help her?" I was worried something could go wrong.

"Uhm . . . not really . . . this is the mare's job."

I didn't know how serious the situation was, but I was afraid for the animal. I tried to figure out the kind of pain Alazana was in. I thought about the time I became very ill from eating too many green guavas. My stomach hurt all night. Maybe Alazana was having the same cramps in her swollen belly.

Time went by slowly. The afternoon sun was beginning to soften, but the temperature was still in the high eighties at four o'clock. Three hours had passed. Manuel decided he was going back to the barn. He didn't seem to be interested in the birth. Matias brought us cold lemonade and coffee. Grandfather José came looking for us and lightened the tense mood with some of his jokes. I kept my eyes on Alazana, afraid that I'd miss the birth if I didn't.

Sometime around four-thirty, the mare became somewhat restless. She moved her front legs as if she wanted to get up, but her hurt leg wouldn't respond. A few minutes later, the transparent sac increased in size. I could see the shape of the foal, cushioned by the fluids inside the bag. "What a miracle!" I said to myself, and I heard Grandmother say, "That's it, José, el potro is coming!"

With a final push, Alazana forced out the entire sac, and without wasting any time, began licking the foal, cleaning away the thick membrane covering its body till its dark nut-colored coat shone. The long, thin legs of the little foal were already moving in an effort to stand up. The mother mare encouraged the colt's efforts, nudging him with the steady touch of her tongue and nose.

"What a shame!" I heard Grandfather say.

"Yeah," Matias replied. I couldn't understand why they were talking like that about such a joyful situation.

"Grandmother, what are they talking about?" I asked.

"Nothing that you need to worry about now." She got up from her place, shaking pieces of grass and dirt from her dress, and then walked towards Grandfather and Matias, leaving me puzzled.

"Do you think Alazana is going to be able to stand up?" she asked the two men.

"The injury is bad, but I think with a little help . . . " said Matias.

"Let's do it! Let's see if we can get her to the stable," said Grandfather, grabbing a rope from the side of his saddle. He walked to the mare with determination and tried to place the rope around her neck. Alazana began to kick and moved her head away from him. "Come on, Alazana! I'm not going to hurt you." Grandfather tried again and one more time met with resistance.

Then Grandmother moved into the scene. "José, give me that piece of rope," she said, looking into the eyes of the mare with the same intense gaze I had seen earlier. Alazana didn't move. As Grandmother patted the animal on her long neck and rubbed her narrow forehead, she talked to the mare in a low voice. I couldn't hear what she was saying, but whatever it was, it was working, and the new mother relaxed. It was then that the young foal, perhaps inspired by the moment, pushed and pulled his body up, straightening his hind legs while resting some of his weight on his front legs. The little one tried once more and was able to straighten all his legs. Grandmother tied the rope around Alazana's neck and slowly pulled while urging the mare to stand up.

"Come on . . . come on, come with me. You can do it, my brave Alazana. You can do it!"

Alazana tried, but as soon as she put weight on her broken leg, she dropped back to the ground.

"Come on, you guys, come and help. Don't move too fast, just come from the other side and help her lift her body while I pull the rope." Grandmother was in charge.

Finally, Alazana was up, and we all cheered and laughed. The young foal stayed close to his mother, taking small steps with his trembling legs.

"Now, let's take this easy. I don't want her to fall down again," Grandmother said, walking right beside Alazana.

"Yes, capitán. I'm surprised you were not at the Bay of Pigs. Those Cubans from El Norte could have used your help," Grandfather teased.

Alazana made it to the stable, where she was kept in the shade with plenty of water and food. Sitting on top of a pile of hay by the entrance, I watched the little colt suckle his mother's teat. After making sure everything was fine, Grandmother and Grandfather joined me.

"What do you think the name of this colt should be?" asked Grandfather, putting his arm around my shoulders.

"I don't know . . . maybe . . . uhm . . . what about Almendro, since he's the color of an almond?" I said, looking at the colt.

"Petra, what do you think? Should we let Almendro be Teresa's horse?" Grandfather looked at Grandmother with a smile.

"I don't know, José. Maybe we should wait and see if she stops arguing with her little brother." I saw Grandmother wink at Grandfather.

"Grandmother, please . . . I promise I will be good! Please let me have Almendro," I said, and I put my arms around her waist.

"Está bien . . . Almendro is your horse . . . but you must take good care of him. I'll ask Matias to teach you, in time, how to groom him and keep him healthy."

I was so happy, I couldn't believe the colt was mine. My own horse that I could ride any time. "Thank you, Grandmother! Thank you, Grandfather!" I hugged each one of them and then ran to the house, so I could tell my mother and brother.

Later that evening I overheard a conversation between Grandfather and Matias. They were sitting out on the porch. The scent of gardenias and wild jasmine perfumed the air. Rain had fallen earlier, cooling the ground and leaving puddles of water all around the flower beds in the garden. I was busy chasing a tiny green frog. The smart creature kept jumping on top of the flat stones of the walkway. I held my flashlight firmly, moving fast, trying to keep the trickster in the spotlight.

Soon I found myself a few yards from the two men. They were talking and smoking their cigars. My green friend disappeared into the bushes. Disappointed with myself, I turned off the flashlight and began to walk away. Then I heard Grandfather say to Matias, "We'll have to see how Alazana does."

"She is such a good horse. It is a shame to have to sacrifice an animal like her," Matias lamented.

"I know. I wish we could do something."

I didn't know the meaning of the word "sacrifice" but whatever it was, it didn't sound good. I went inside the house and found Grandmother in her sewing room, mending some socks and listening to the radio. She lifted her eyes and looked at me over the thick lenses of her glasses.

"Come in, Teresa, what kind of trouble have you gotten yourself in?"

"I haven't done anything, Grandmother, but I heard Grandfather and Matias talking about sacrificing Alazana."

"Come and sit here." Grandmother pointed at a chair next to the window, by her side. "Mira, hijita, there are things in life which are painful . . . and this situation with the mare is one of those hard pills to swallow." Grandmother got up from her place and put the sewing kit away. "There is no way around this. Sacrifice means that we're going to have to kill Alazana." She paused, looking for a reaction, but I was in shock. Grandmother took my face into her hands. "We don't want to do it, either, but we have to."

"Why . . . why do you have to kill her?" I cried.

"Because her leg is not going to heal. Alazana is in a lot of pain."

"Why don't you call a vet? Ask him to come and fix her broken leg."

"It will be useless, hijita . . . believe me, there is nothing anyone can do."

"Not even God?" I asked defiantly.

"That . . . I can't answer. That's for you and God to discuss privately."

I was angry at her. I wanted a different answer. I wanted Alazana to stay alive. I couldn't imagine how anyone had the guts to kill such an animal—so kind and beautiful. I was sure we could find a solution to the problem.

"Teresita, hijita . . . listen to me," Grandmother continued in a soft tone. "It is not that we haven't thought of things to do to save the animal. Your Grandfather and I have talked all day long about what to do but . . . ," she paused. "That mare will suffer if we let her live."

I ran out of the room slamming the door on my way out. I didn't want to hear her anymore. I went to my room, where I threw myself on the bed, hiding my face in the pillow. I expected Grandmother to follow me, but she never came. That night I fell asleep, crying about Alazana and feeling sorry for Almendro, who soon would be an orphan.

I woke at sunrise to the sound of voices in the kitchen. I could hear Manuel talking to Grandmother about something that had gone wrong while he was milking a cow.

"Vea aquí, Doña Petra, that cow threw me in the air, with the chair and everything. I almost broke my leg."

"You are just a weak old man, Manuel. I can't believe you let that stubborn cow get the best of you." As usual Grandmother and Manuel were teasing each other. Even though they were close in age, Manuel was always complaining of all his aches and pains, while Grandmother never said a word when she wasn't feeling good. I was used to their daily bickering.

"That cow is more stubborn than you, Doña," said Manuel.

"How much do you want to bet? I'll show you who is more stubborn," I heard Grandmother say.

"I don't want to bet anything. If you do what I think you're thinking of doing . . . you are out of your mind, lady."

"Grab that cantina, old man, and come with me. I'll show you how to milk that cow."

When I heard Grandmother say that, I jumped out of bed. I threw on some clothes and shoes and in less than a minute I was following the two of them down to the barn. Grandmother was in the lead; she walked fast with firm steps. Manuel was behind her, trying to catch up without much help from his limping left leg.

Grandfather was tying a couple of big kettles on top of his horse and saw us coming. "Hey, what's going on? Petra, what are you doing here?"

"I'm going to show this viejo how to milk a stubborn cow," Grandmother said as she grabbed the milking stool that hung from the corral fence. As she turned, she saw me right behind Manuel. "Teresa, you're supposed to be in bed," Grandmother said with surprise.

"I want to see how you milk the cow. Please let me stay." She didn't answer, which I interpreted as her silent way of saying okay.

"Deja eso mujer! Leave that cow alone. You'll get hurt," screamed Grandfather from the other side of the barn.

Grandmother stepped forward, like a soldier walking towards the enemy. A few yards ahead was the stubborn cow, light gray in color, with sharp horns and an udder full of milk, so full it gave the impression of a balloon about to pop. The animal mooed, sending the message "Don't get any closer," but Grandmother didn't pay any attention. Before the cow had a chance to react, Grandmother positioned herself right next to the swollen udder and began to squeeze the milk out into the bucket. The angry cow began to kick in the air with her hind legs forcing Grandmother to move around as fast as she was able. The dance lasted for a few minutes till one of the cow's hooves found its target in Grandmother's right side. She was thrown into the air with the stool and the bucket. For a moment I thought she might be hurt, but no sooner had she hit the ground than she got up.

I could tell Grandmother was upset by the way her jaw was clenched. Grandfather ran to her, but by the time he got close, she was already standing up with the stool and bucket in her hands.

"Please . . . please, Petra, leave that animal alone. I beg you," Grandfather yelled at her.

"You're wasting your time, José. I want to milk this cow," she said and put the stool on the ground.

This time the cow started to kick before Grandmother had a chance to touch her. Doña Petra, like a matador ready to place the banderillas, moved closer to the animal and grabbed it by the tail. From then on, it was a wrestling match between cow and woman. Several times, the cow dragged Grandmother to the ground. Then, as if charged with supernatural powers, the old woman grabbed on to the horns of the animal and held its head in a position where she and the cow were eye to eye. There was silence in the corral, as beast and woman measured their forces. Finally, Grandmother let go of the horns, and the cow remained motionless. Grandmother picked up the bucket and the stool and went back to milking. This time the cow had met its match.

I saw Grandfather laugh nervously as he wiped the sweat from his face. Manuel stood, frozen, in the middle of the corral, with no expression on his face. It took at least five minutes before he was able to speak. "Coño, qué mujer! You are a mad woman!" And he walked away, spitting balls of the chewing tobacco he had been turning over in his mouth.

Grandfather José came and sat next to me, and we watched Grandmother milk the cow. She was seated on the small wood stool, enjoying her victory. Holding one of the cow's teats in each hand, she squeezed and pulled, forcing the white fluid out of the big udder. I could hear the milk hitting the side of the metal bucket.

"That tiny woman you see there," Grandfather said, pointing at his wife, "that woman has more courage than a battalion of men, and not only is she strong but she knows . . . she knows more about animals than all the ranchers of this area." He shook his head, uncrossed his arms and picked up a stick from the ground. "Your grandmother knows about the way animals think. I've seen her talk to horses, cows, even chickens, as if they were people." He paused. "She can look at a sick cow and know exactly what ailment is there. She has been more accurate than the town veterinarian. She can talk animals into getting well."

I thought of Alazana. If Grandmother was so good with animals, why couldn't she help Alazana?

"Grandfather, why can't Grandmother talk Alazana into getting her leg healed?"

"Ay cariño, that's a different story." He got up from the wood box he had been sitting on, trying to end the conversation.

"Grandfather, why is that a different story?" I insisted. He sat back down on the box.

"When a horse breaks a leg . . . "

"Yes, I know, it never heals!" I interrupted, upset with the same story. He was surprised by my reaction.

"It is true, Teresa, it is true! We don't want to kill Alazana, but we have to, for her own good. You know, sometimes when these things happen, when a horse breaks a leg, we are able to fix it . . . but in this case . . . ," he paused and looked into the distance. "The fracture is quite big. Something like that never heals."

"I don't want you to kill Alazana. What's going to happen to Almendro?" I cried.

"Almendro will be fine. We'll make sure he is fine."

"I don't believe it. He is going to be sad . . . very sad without his mother."

Grandfather put his arm around my shoulders and pulled me towards him. He didn't say any more. He let me cry while he ran his fingers through my long dark hair, combing back the rebellious curls falling on my forehead. I could feel the rough skin of his hand brushing my forehead, a hand calloused from working the land for so many years.

"How did it happen? How was she hurt?"

"Well . . . we think that somehow Alazana got scared by something. She ran and maybe stepped in a hole in the ground and fell. Since the train goes through here at least twice a day, there is a chance that the sound of the wheels on the track, or perhaps the high whistle, sent Alazana into a panic."

I saw Grandmother coming towards us with the bucket full of milk. Grandfather was quick to get up from his seat, ready to take the load from her hands.

"You always get your way," Grandfather teased her.

"Not always," she replied in a grave tone, leaving the bucket with Grandfather.

Years later, I realized the truth in Grandmother's words. She had not always gotten her way. Life had been tough. She lost her homeland and was never able to return to the Canary Islands. She lost three of her children. Then, Fidel Castro took away the land she had claimed as her second home.

"Come on, Teresa, let's see how Alazana is doing," Grandmother invited.

We found Alazana and Almendro lying next to each other in the hay. Grandmother frowned and shook her head.

I looked at Alazana's swollen leg. It was hard to tell whether she was in pain, but the leg had almost doubled in size. Grandmother examined the broken limb carefully, trying not to cause any more damage.

"There is some sort of infection," she said, almost to herself. She patted the mare, and Alazana lifted her beautiful head and looked right into my eyes. A chill ran up my spine. Alazana's eyes were like two black marbles, with tiny sparks of light in them. She was trying to tell me something, and I could feel images forming in my head. I saw Alazana galloping above the hills, like Pegasus flying in the sky, opening her wings wider and wider, getting higher and higher . . .

"Grandmother. Grandmother . . . "

"Yes, Alazana needs to go," Grandmother said before I had a chance to say anything.

"She had wings, and she was flying!" I said, with a mixture of joy and sadness but not knowing why I was feeling that way.

"You saw her spirit. She is going to be okay." Grandmother stroked the mare gently along her neck. Alazana appeared to be soothed by this because she allowed her head to rest on Grandmother's lap. Almendro came closer to me, and with his little nose, he sniffed my right arm. I had a sense the colt needed attention as well, so I rubbed his face with my hand. I felt an immediate connection with Almendro—a feeling of warmth and laughter inside my heart.

That was the last time I saw Alazana. The next morning after getting up, I ran to the stable looking for her and Almendro. I had some brown sugar cubes to feed them both. I was surprised to find only Almendro, and Grandmother feeding him milk from a baby bottle.

"Where is Alazana?" I asked, somehow afraid of the answer.

"She is gone," Grandmother said without looking at me. "Here, feed Almendro." Without taking the bottle from Almendro's mouth, she gave it to me. "Life goes on, mi hijita. This little one needs care now that his mamá is gone. I'm too old to do all this work by myself. Do you want to help with Almendro?"

"Oh sí, Grandmother. I'll help you!" My eyes met Almendro's, and I saw Alazana flying away with her golden wings. At that moment, I knew, in the way children know, that though Alazana was dead, some part of her was there with us, watching her young Almendro.

Almendro finished the bottle. Grandmother took it from my hands and put it in her pocket. "You can stay here if you want to play with Almendro, but don't let him out of the barn." Grandmother began to walk towards the house. I noticed she was limping a bit, probably from the previous day's battle with the cow, but of course, she would never say a thing about her pain. Grandmother was tough as cowhide.

When the day came for me to go back to town, I was sad to leave Almendro behind. Early that morning, I went to feed him as I had done for almost two weeks. I knew he was in good hands with Grandmother, but I was going to miss him. I wondered if this was how Alazana felt when she had to leave behind her little baby. "Grandmother, does Alazana miss Almendro?" I asked later as I packed my bags.

"Yes, mi hijita," said my grandmother. She turned away, then told me in an unusually quiet voice that Alazana was watching Almendro from her new home in the sky. I thought that was okay, but I knew that Alazana wanted to reach down and nuzzle his soft almond-colored coat.

5

CARMEN

A FEW WEEKS after the death of Alazana, the Agrarian Reform took away most of the farm. The sturdy roots that had held my world in place were being severed, one by one. Suddenly the adults around me were too busy with their problems to pay attention to me. My parents worried about what was going to happen next. Grandmother Petra was lost in her sadness. Grandfather José spent his days out on the porch, sitting in his chair and rocking himself to sleep. Villa Petra was no longer the haven I had once counted on.

I began having nightmares. I would wake up in a cold sweat, still shaking from the images of milicianos with big machine guns chasing me. In my dreams the soldiers chased me out of the house and into the fields, their bullets hissing by my head. I ran as fast as I could, but the soldiers kept getting closer and closer . . .

"Niña, niña, wake up!"

I opened my eyes to the brown and loving face of Carmen, my Afro-Cuban nanny and faithful ally.

"Carmen, they're back!" I cried. Carmen sat down on the side of my bed, and I crawled into her arms.

"The milicianos?" she asked.

"Yes, Carmen, the milicianos, with their machine guns!"

"Hmm. We must do something about that."

"Like what?"

"Listen to me, niña. I am going to tell you about an important lady orisha named Yemayá. She loves children, and she knows about their fears. Yemayá's skin is the same color as mine. If you pray to her she won't let anything bad happen to you. With her by your side, you're very, very safe, niña."

From that night on, Carmen and I lit a candle and called for Yemayá's help before I went to bed. Carmen was herself like the flame of the candle, giving light to the dark and difficult moments of my childhood. She was there for me the day I returned home after the confiscation of my grandparents' farm. She sat by the side of my bed and quietly explained that it was not all gone. "Niña," she said, "your grandparents will be able to stay in their house. Don't worry niña, nothing is going to happen to your Almendro."

"But, Carmen, I heard the milicianos when they told Grandfather that his land was now Castro's property."

"Most of it was taken away, but they left your grandparents the house and five caballerias of land, so your grandfather José will have enough acres to grow food for the family."

"What about the animals?"

"Well, not many. Maybe a few chickens, pigs, some cows for meat and milk, and the family horses."

I was very confused about the government's Agrarian Reform. I couldn't understand how Castro could just take land from people. And I was still angry about the way those soldiers had treated us.

"Carmen, how can Castro get away with all this?"

"Oh, niña, he is a traitor. It happens all the time in this big world. My own ancestors were kidnapped by the Spaniards from their home-land, Africa. They were brought to Cuba to work in the sugar planta-tions and mills. As slaves, they had no rights! Castro is like those Spaniards—he doesn't care." Carmen paused and looked at the clock on the table next to my bed. "Come on, niña, it's past your bedtime." She kissed my forehead and walked out of the room.

For a moment, I wanted to call Carmen back, to ask if she would sing me to sleep as she had when I was a young child. Arru ru mi niña, arru ru mi amor, duermete pedazo de mi corazón. While Carmen sang,

50

she would rock me in her arms, holding me close. It was like being embraced and rocked by the Caribbean sea.

"Niña," she used to say, "you'd better go to sleep now, because if you don't, the moon is going to be upset, and she is not going to come around tomorrow night with her silver beams. It will be very dark, very dark."

In addition to her lullabies, Carmen loved to tell my brother, Jose, and me stories about the slaves who had worked so hard on the sugar plantations, and how they had survived the difficult times by drumming and singing at night. She also told us scary stories about ghosts and spirits that haunted the old Spanish houses in Cabaigüán, and how people had heard voices and seen strange things inside the houses.

"You are not supposed to disturb those spirits. People who go inside those houses get sick! They have terrible accidents!" Carmen would say to us every time she told us the stories. "Like the man who went in one of the houses looking for hidden money. He found an old ceramic jar with many gold coins. He took them, and a few months later he became very ill. The doctor in town was never able to say what was wrong with him. The man lost lots of weight, and his skin turned yellow like the gold coins. He died slowly in great misery and pain. Ghost illness!"

In our town, Carmen was well known for her divination and healing powers. As a santera, a priestess of Santería, the ancient Afro-Cuban religion in which the orishas, or deities, of the Yoruba people are worshiped, she was able to diagnose illnesses, heal the sick, cast spells and perform magical rituals for those who sought her help.

Carmen had a special room in the back of our house for her practice. I used to love going in there when she was away and exploring the different magical herbs: plants, roots, leaves, flowers—all carefully gathered in bundles and kept separate from each other on shelves on one of the walls. Occasionally, she would come in unexpectedly and surprise me as I was touching and smelling her medicinal treasures. "Niña, don't touch mis yerbas!" Then, with great patience, she would take the time to answer my questions.

"These yerbas here are for despojos, for the cleansing of negative influences and evil spirits," Carmen explained, and she went on to name each plant. "I have marjoram, sage, spearmint, rosemary and verbena."

"What about this one here?" I pointed to a dried bunch of mixed herbs.

"Escoba amarga. It's good for cleansing baths and to scare away bad spirits who might make you sick." She grabbed the bundle of herbs and brushed me with it from head to toe. "This will take care of your mischievous spirit for a little while." She laughed and playfully hit my buttocks with it.

The altar Carmen had created in one of the corners of her healing sanctuary was as fascinating to me as the herbs. On a small table covered with a white tablecloth she had placed seven glasses with water, dedicated to African powers, or orishas, next to the images of their Catholic counterparts. For the orisha Elegguá, or Saint Anthony, a white candle. Oggún, or Saint Peter, had a little bag of salt. Orúnla, or Saint Francis of Assisi, was offered a cooked yam. A red apple was for Changó, or Saint Barbara. A small jar of honey for Oshún, or the Lady of Charity. Sugar cane syrup for Yemayá, or Our Lady of la Regla. A coconut for Obatalá, or Our Lady of Mercy. In addition, a large Cuban cigar and a cup of rum rested near Babalú-Ayé, or Saint Lazarus, who was Carmen's favorite.

I first saw Carmen practice as a santera when I was nine years old. A woman from our neighborhood named Francisca came to visit Carmen one morning. She had worry on her face and was very pale and ill-looking. She was also coughing a lot. My brother and I were playing on the patio, near the water fountain outside Carmen's room, and I could see Francisca and Carmen engaged in deep conversation. I heard Carmen say something like, "The spirits will help us find out." That was more than enough for me to leave our game of army soldiers to try and figure out what was going on between the two women. Jose was disappointed and wanted to hide with me, but I sent him away with the promise that I would play with him later.

The spirits! I said to myself and hid behind the gardenia tree close to the window, being careful not to make any noise. My heart beat fast from anticipation and fear. Carmen had warned me many times not to go near her when she was doing her healing work, but this time my curiosity was stronger than my fear. I wanted to find out once and for all what she was doing in there with the so-called spirits.

From my hideout I could see Carmen seated in front of the altar, with Francisca seated next to her. Carmen took one of the cigars from the altar and, after lighting it, proceeded to blow puffs of smoke around the room and over Francisca. Then she sat down across from Francisca, closed her eyes and softly sang words I couldn't understand—they were from another language. Soon Carmen sang louder and called out names. Her face began to change, as well as her voice. Her mouth twisted, and she looked angry. She got up from her chair and moved around the room again, puffing on her big cigar and blowing out smoke. Then her voice became softer, and she passed her dark hands over Francisca's body without touching her, as if she were cleansing something in the air.

Abruptly, Carmen's body started shaking and her words grew loud and unintelligible, like the roar of a wild beast. She was sweating. She dropped to the floor, her body shaking all over.

At the same moment that Carmen fell, Francisca began to cry intensely, almost hysterically.

"Oh, my god!" I whispered to myself, and I thought, *What should I do? Should I call Mother?* I was ready to run to the house when I heard a voice from within me say, *Stop, and be quiet.* I immediately felt very serene, almost as if Carmen's big arms were holding me and rocking me to sleep. At that moment, I realized that Carmen knew I was there and had known it all the time! Why hadn't she sent me away as she had other times? Having no answer, I stood there with my eyes fixed on the two women inside. Now things were quiet. Francisca was seated in her chair, and Carmen rose from the floor with a kind expression on her round face.

"Tell me, Francisca, how do you feel?" asked Carmen, looking into the eyes of her friend.

"Ay, negra, I thought that I was going to die, but now I feel as if the whole world has been lifted from my shoulders."

Carmen picked some of the dry herbs she had placed inside a clay pot at the altar. She gave a little bundle to Francisca. "Mira, Francisca, make a tea and drink it in the morning and at night before going to bed, and come back and see me in a couple of days."

Francisca thanked Carmen, and when she left, I could see a lightness in her steps. Carmen turned and walked over to the window. Standing there with her hands resting on her wide hips, she looked right out at me. For a second I thought I was going to faint from fear.

"Teresa," Carmen called to me, "come inside."

I walked slowly to the door, my legs shaking.

"Teresa, what were you doing spying on this negra from that window?" she said sternly.

"I'm sorry, Carmen," I said in a very low voice. "I'll never do it again, I promise. I was just trying—" Before I could finish Carmen interrupted me.

"You are a very curious child." I was surprised she wasn't angry with me. "Come sit down, child."

"Aren't you mad at me, Carmen?"

"No, but if I ever catch you again . . . "

"No, please, Carmen," I begged, knowing now she was not really going to do anything. Carmen adored me, and she had a heart the size of Cuba.

"Mira, Teresa, what you saw today is nothing to play with. These things I do are very sacred. You never want to upset the spirits who come to help me do my work. They don't like to be disturbed or annoyed in any way," Carmen said, without taking her eyes off me.

"What would happen if they got upset? Who are they, anyway?"

"They would come to your room at night and pull your toes while you're asleep. They would hide your toys and play tricks on you."

"Who are these spirits, Carmen?"

"They are ancient ones. They're santos. They are good spirits who continue helping us on this earth when, and only when, we need them."

"What was happening when you had your eyes closed and you were talking in that strange language and making scary sounds?"

Carmen shifted in her chair as if she were getting impatient with my questions.

"Teresa, when I close my eyes in front of my altar, it is like when you white people go to church and pray to your favorite saints. I'm asking the spirits for help. They come and talk to me."

"How?"

"Just imagine my body being like a drum or a guitar. When they come, they play with my vocal cords, making the sounds I need to hear, or sometimes they even talk to the person I'm helping, like in the case of Francisca."

"How do you know when the spirits come?"

"You want to know everything, don't you?" Carmen patted me on the head. "Most of the time it's just a feeling. When they enter the room, it feels like a cool breeze has blown in. Other times, the vibrations of their essence are so strong that my body shakes."

Carmen told me that she had learned much of what she knew from her mother and her grandmother, who learned from their own people, Africanos, who brought to Cuba their spirituality and religion.

"My people," Carmen said, "were strong and wise. They found ways to disguise their spirits—their Yoruba deities—by giving them names from the Catholic church. That way, they were able to continue practicing their rituals."

I thought about the way Cubans call the name of Saint Barbara after seeing lightning in the sky. But in the practice of Santería, Saint Barbara is known as the orisha Changó, who brings thunder and lightning.

One day, soon after my experience watching Carmen in her Santería shrine, she called to me from the kitchen, where she was preparing to make tachinos for lunch. Carmen was, as usual, having a good time, singing along with the songs on the radio and dancing around as she got out the plantains and heated the oil for frying. Her hips were like the ocean waves coming and going, like palm trees swaying to the gentle wind. She smiled at me and waved me into the room.

Since the confiscation of the farm, I'd noticed that, more and more, Carmen was talking to me about her orishas. I welcomed her attention. With everything that had happened around me, I was feeling quite lonely. I no longer looked forward to my visits to the farm. Grandmother Petra was not interested in leaving the house or going on our usual fruit-picking outings. Almendro was now my only pal there. I rode him across the fields, and together we watched the people from the new cooperative ploughing the land that was no longer ours.

"Sit down, niña," Carmen said as she handed me a knife. "Help me peel and slice these plantains while we talk." She turned off the radio and sat next to me. "First of all, I want you to promise me to behave. I don't want you to be wandering off and disappearing from my sight."

"I promise, Carmen," I said, wondering what she was talking about.

"Niña, I am going to take you to a special bembé at Rufino's house. This bembé is a party with drums in honor of the orishas. You're going to see people drumming and dancing for the orishas. I'm telling you this now so that you won't be asking all kinds of questions in the middle of everything." She got up to check the rice she was cooking.

"Now let me tell you about the drums. They are played to call the orishas. Each orisha has a special dance movement and drum rhythm or toque. This is how people, drums and deities converse with each other." Carmen paused. She looked me in the eye and proceeded in a very solemn tone. "You must not talk to anyone about this bembé. The Committee for the Defense of Revolution, the CDR, has given Rufino permission to have a simple birthday celebration. Nothing about a bembé, so you better seal your mouth, niña, otherwise we will all end up behind bars."

"Why Carmen? What's wrong with having a bembé?"

"Mira, niña. That barbudo doesn't want any kind of religion in this country," she said, referring to Fidel Castro and his nasty beard. "Bembé is part of the Afro-Cuban religion. Ese desgraciado, he has declared that religion causes *antirevolutionary* attitudes among the people. So we are back to the times of slavery. Once more in the history of this country, we have to keep our orishas well disguised. But enough of this. Let's fry up these plantains."

I could hardly contain my excitement when Saturday finally arrived and Carmen and I walked down the street towards the outskirts of town. Rufino and his family lived in a modest white brick house surrounded by palms and orange, avocado, lemon and plantain trees.

There was an atmosphere of celebration in the house. Rufino and his wife, Caridad, greeted us warmly at the door. Several of Carmen's friends had already arrived and were talking about the fiesta, expressing their hope that the orishas would descend and that the milicianos would stay away from that part of town.

Rufino had invited thirty or so guests, mainly family members and friends. On the patio, the drummers were already tuning their drums. I was fascinated by the beauty of the drums, their different sizes and shapes, and the smoothness of the wood and the skins. I was wishing deep inside I could play them. Carmen came up behind me and seemed to read my mind: "These drums are very special. It takes many years of training to play them. Each drum has a job. See that big drum there? That's the mother drum."

I walked to the mother drum and touched the stretched hide with my hands.

"Mother drum," Carmen continued, "does all the talking while the smaller drums keep the basic rhythms."

The drummer who sat behind the mother drum, a toothless black man with white hair, maybe fifty years old, winked at me. "This batáa is called Iyá, and those two are called Itótele and Okónkolo," he said and made a signal to the other two men to get ready. Carmen pulled me away from the drums to the other side of the patio, and soon, just as she had said, the mother drum began to talk, followed by the penetrating beat of the two smaller drums. Rufino stood beside the drums and began to sing a song from Africa:

Ibarago moyuba
Ibarago moyuba
Ibarago moyuba Elegguá Eshulona.

Carmen lowered her mouth to my ear and whispered, "The drums are asking Elegguá to open the path for us. Elegguá is the messenger, the Lord of the Roads, the gatekeeper. It is important to call Elegguá first; otherwise he may get upset and not open the doors to the orishas."

The drums continued calling the different orishas, the rhythm or toques changing, according to the saint being called. In the midst of all the pounding sounds and loud voices, Carmen tried to let me know what was going on.

"Now, they're calling Oggún, the warrior of iron," and she went on to name each deity as the drums changed: "Obatalá, the orisha of calm and clarity; Oshún, the goddess of the rivers; Babalú-Ayé, Saint Lazarus the healer; Yemayá, the goddess of the sea."

The dancers were moving their feet, hips and shoulders rhythmically. Finally Changó, the spirit of thunder, was called, and some started to dance frenetically, as if they had been struck by lightning. They jerked their bodies and threw their arms into the air. Other dancers were rolling on the ground. Rufino shook a rattle and chanted in a deep voice. Carmen explained that he was greeting the orishas in the ancient Yoruba language.

An older black man, pretending to have a machete in his hand, moved across the patio as Oggún, clearing his way through the forest. Next to him, a woman danced as Oshún in a sensuous rhythm of love. By her side was Yemayá, the orisha of the sea, whose undulating hips were both inviting and provocative. I was especially fascinated by Yemayá's movements. I asked Carmen if I could dance and when she said it was okay, I moved shyly out among the group.

The more I danced, the more I felt my body taken over by the music. I pretended I was Yemayá, floating in the clear, warm waters of the Caribbean. I felt safe and happy. I closed my eyes and heard Yemayá singing the ancient Yoruba songs to me, and saw her beautiful white and blue dress decorated with shells.

I am the mother whose children are the fish. I am Womanhood. Soon, you'll be a woman, and you must learn the ways of the waters. If you come to me, I'll teach you. This is the place where you can find me, I'm always dancing on the waves.

Yemayá paused and pulled one of the shells from her dress, a tiny conch, which she placed in my hand. I pressed the precious gift against my heart.

Yemayá's lyrics were echoing in my mind when I finally opened my eyes. I found myself in a corner of the patio, still dancing to the beat of the drums. There were people all around me dancing and singing to the orishas. I was confused by my experience with Yemayá. Had I fallen asleep? What had happened? All I could remember was that I had wanted to dance and then . . . nothing made sense. I ran away from the crowd and into the house, where I stayed until it was time to go home.

As Carmen and I walked back to our house, I could tell that somehow she was aware of my experience, but knew not to ask any questions. For the first time, I was happy to keep a secret. Yemayá had given me a taste of initiation into the mysteries of the spirit world. I was eager for more.

One evening about a month after the bembé, Carmen excused herself from the dinner table, saying she was going to visit her friend Graciela. I didn't think much about it, since Carmen went to Graciela's home at least once a week.

Graciela claimed to be eighty years old, but most people believed her to be closer to ninety. Judging from her appearance, I thought one hundred was more like it. She was tall and skinny like a bamboo cane, and her face was as wrinkled as a dried plum. She had a solitary brown tooth left to chew her tobacco. She was unable to cook much because of her poor vision, and didn't trust anyone to fix meals for her, believing that evil-intentioned individuals might poison her food. People who knew her said that she lived on coffee and tobacco.

Graciela was a fervent practitioner of Espiritism, in which spirits are invoked by mediums, that is, by intermediaries between humans and the spirits. She was consulted about health ailments, money problems, romantic concerns and just about anything else that troubled people.

After Carmen left that night, I went outside while Mother sat by the radio to listen to her favorite music program. As it happened, Maria de la Caridad was also outside and invited me to come over and play in her backyard, right next to Graciela's house. At age ten, Maria was a year older than I and a lot more adventurous. She was always getting in trouble with her parents and picking fights with other children, including me.

"Mira," Maria said to me as we walked to her house. "All those people are going to Graciela's house."

"What do you think they're doing?" I asked.

"I think they're having one of those meetings where the spirits come and talk." I wondered whether the CDR would be checking on them. "Hey, Maria, who is doing rounds tonight?" Maria was always well informed.

"Guess who?" She pointed to the corner of the street where someone was sitting on a chair with a rifle between her knees. It was Julia, an older woman from the neighborhood who always fell asleep during her watch. "That's probably why they're having their meeting tonight. Julia will sleep through the whole thing."

"I have an idea," continued Maria, with a mischievous look in her olive-green eyes. "Oh, come on, don't be a chicken." Maria pulled me by my arm, and we ran to the big mango tree in back of her house and climbed up it. We were both sweating from the effort and Maria's curly golden hair was decorated with tiny twigs and leaves.

"Now," she said, "you better stay put and not move around, because any small noise could upset the spirits and terrible things could happen to both of us."

"Like what?" I knew Maria de la Caridad had a tendency to exaggerate.

"Come on, Teresa. Doesn't Carmen talk to you about these meetings?"

"No," I said, surprised.

"Well, she should. That way you'd be more informed," Maria said with authority, making me feel dumb. "Look, there's Carmen!" She pointed to where Carmen sat on one of the tauretes, chairs made of oak and cowhide, right next to Graciela. Maria signaled me to stay quiet.

Men and women arrived and slowly took their places in seats arranged in a circular fashion on the patio. A young woman, her black waist-length hair set off against her white cotton dress, was greeted by Carmen and brought to the center of the circle, where a table covered by a white cloth stood. The young woman kissed Graciela on the cheek before she sat down.

"What's going on?" I asked.

"Hush," Maria ordered me.

The circle was quiet. The young woman asked Carmen to light the tall white candles, one at each corner of the table. Carmen took her time and prayed in a low voice, as if to herself.

"Welcome, Rosa Eugenia, welcome!" Carmen finally said and went back to her place next to Graciela.

Rosa Eugenia sat absolutely still, her dark eyes fixed on the bluish-orange flame of one of the candles for a few seconds, and then closed her eyes.

As I found out later, Rosa Eugenia, although only fifteen years old, was a well-known medium on the island. She was able to channel the spirits of two eminences, an herbologist from France and a physician from Germany. When in a trance, she was able to diagnose and prescribe herbs and medications for those who sought her help.

"Teresa, watch carefully now," said Maria, poking my shoulder.

Rosa Eugenia opened her eyes and signaled for a pregnant woman to come and sit on the chair across from her. Briefly, she shook hands with the woman. Then she closed her eyes again and, in a few seconds, began writing on a notepad. Rosa's right hand moved so fast, and I watched in amazement as she diagnosed more than ten people, one after another without taking a break, and sent them home with prescriptions and instructions.

Tired, I shifted my position on the branch as an old woman, dressed in black, came to sit at the consultation table. I felt a sudden chill, though there was no breeze. Rosa Eugenia stopped writing, her hand motionless on top of the paper. Finally, the medium opened her eyes and said, "Go home, and wait for your time to die. There is nothing I can do for you."

I felt very sad for the woman. Now she knew that her time to die had come, and even the miracle and magic of Rosa Eugenia's healing couldn't save her! Part of me was angry at Rosa Eugenia. How could she let the old woman go like that?

That night when I got home, both my mother and Carmen were waiting for me. Mother had gone out looking for me, but none of the neighbors had seen me. When Carmen returned to the house, she had found my mother in tears. Maria and I had had to wait up in the tree for a long time, until all of Graciela's visitors had left, so we wouldn't be noticed. By the time I was able to get home, my mother and Carmen were very upset.

"Where were you?" my mother demanded, followed by Carmen, who repeated the question as if I didn't have ears.

"Bien, bien, don't panic. I was visiting with Maria de la Caridad."

"That's a big lie!" Carmen said, looking at me suspiciously. "I checked with Maria's mother, and she didn't know where her daughter was either. So, where were the two of you? It is almost ten o'clock."

"Okay . . . okay. We were up in the big tree in Maria's backyard." I stopped, hoping neither would ask any more questions, but I knew I was not going to get away with this.

"Muy bueno, I suppose you were just playing?" Carmen gave me the look she wore every time she caught me in a lie. With her hands on her hips, she asked, "Did you by any chance see a group of people having a meeting at Graciela's house . . . from your tree?"

There was no point in trying to hide the truth from Carmen. "Yes, Carmen, there was a group of people meeting in Graciela's backyard and . . . "

"Don't tell me any more! You were spying again! You were sticking your nose in somebody else's business. I'm very upset with you, niña! With your mother's permission, I'm going to prohibit you from going to Maria de la Caridad's house for a week as punishment for your behavior." My mother nodded in approval and I went straight to my room.

That night, the images of the evening kept dancing in front of me. When I finally managed to fall asleep, I had a nightmare about the old woman Rosa Eugenia had sent home without a cure. The old woman—emaciated and deathly white—was lying on a bed alone inside a dark room.

I tried to back away but her bony hand reached out and grabbed my arm. "Look at me, look at me!" she screamed. Then with her other hand, she twisted my face towards her, forcing me to look. Her flesh was decomposing in front of my eyes and maggots crawled in and out of the purplish patches of skin. Soon only the naked bones were left: a laughing skull with brownish teeth. I struggled till I was able to free myself from her grasp. As I was running away, I could hear her laughter echoing in my ears.

I woke up screaming and sweating in my mother's arms. I was

relieved to see my mother's beautiful face instead of the old woman's hideous skull. I knew the woman in the dream was going to die very soon. I didn't tell my mother about the dream, but went back to sleep, comforted by her arms.

The next morning, I looked for Carmen to tell her about my nightmare. I found her drinking her coffee out in the garden. She enjoyed sitting on the bench by the dolphin fountain, surrounded by roses, lilies, gladiolas and her favorite wild orchids. Carmen pretended not to see me at first, a sign she was still upset with me, and as I got closer I saw her frowning.

"Well, well, what do you want from me this morning?" She searched her pockets for matches to light her thin handmade cigar. Carmen was not a heavy smoker, but she delighted in her morning, afternoon and evening cigars. She couldn't find any matches, so she sent me to the kitchen to bring her some. I figured it was her way to buy time and think about what she was going to say to me.

"Here are the matches, Carmen," I said, sitting down next to her on the bench. "I know you're upset with me, and I'm really sorry. Carmen, I had a dream last night about the old woman. I saw her flesh rotting and maggots eating her face. It was terrifying, and . . . "

Carmen nodded her head and pressed her lips together tightly. Moving closer to me, she placed her hand on my hand, gently squeezing it. "Niña, niña de mi corazón, you are too young to understand what happened there. It has taken this negra years and years of learning to be able to handle that world. Niña, this is nothing to mess around with. Otherwise you'll turn into a big fat sponge filled with garbage from other people's worlds." Carmen took another sip of her coffee. "You are curious, my child, and need to learn patience. I promise you that when the right time comes, I'll teach you all I know about the spirit world. Now you need to listen to me." She shook her finger at me. "Stay away from Graciela's meetings."

"Yes, Carmen, I hear you. But . . . please, can we talk about my dream? Do you think that old woman is going to die soon?"

Carmen appeared to be troubled by my question. "Well . . . " She paused and frowned, as if she were searching for words.

"Carmen, I don't like it when you lift your eyebrow like that.

What's the matter?"

"Well, that woman you saw in your dream died last night—this morning when I went to the store, I heard the news."

I felt goosebumps rise all over my body. "Carmen, why do you think I dreamed of her?"

"It is hard to explain, niña. Let's say that sometimes when people are dying and they are not ready to make the journey, they fight and fight. They don't want to go, so they hang on to anything—usually relatives, friends or someone who cares about them. That woman didn't want to die. Last night when Rosa Eugenia saw death in her aura, that woman was stricken by anger. And you, my darling child, picked up on those feelings. You have always been very sensitive. You got caught in her web."

"Her web?"

"Her web of emotions. Anger and fear can form a web that traps other people if they're not careful. You opened your heart without protection, and you got trapped in that old woman's despair. While you were asleep, her dying spirit, like a spider, pulled you by a thread in her effort to stay alive. Fortunately, you have a strong spirit."

I thought of the woman's bony hand grabbing me and not letting me go. I shivered. Carmen put her hands on my shoulders.

"See what I meant, niña? That's why I don't want you to be wandering around those meetings. It's not safe. Promise me you won't do it again."

"I promise, Carmen," I said reluctantly.

But though I had given my word to stay away from the world of spirits, it proved too difficult. I found myself praying and lighting candles to the orishas. Every night before I went to sleep, I lay on my bed with my eyes closed and quietly chanted the names of Yemayá, Oggún and Changó. I knew they were watching over me.

6

PATRICIA

CARMEN WAS NOT the only person who mentored me in the ways of the spirits and the world of healing. My paternal grandmother, Patricia, was well known for her healing work in her hometown of Guayos and the neighboring towns. People consulted her for all kinds of health problems and maladies such us mal de ojos and empacho, even people whom doctors had given up on and sent home without hope.

One afternoon when my father and I went to visit Grandmother Patricia, Grandfather Victor greeted us at the door with "Patricia is in her room with a woman from out of town." Then both men disappeared into the kitchen. I stayed in the living room, sitting in one of the comfortable rocking chairs and listening to the muted voices of Grandmother and her client. I was very curious about the healing work Grandmother did and hoped I would be lucky enough to catch some of her advice to the client.

I heard Grandmother say authoritatively, "This is not about your heart as the doctor told you. These palpitations you have been suffering from are due to a weakened spirit. Your husband's jealousy is like a death trap for you. That man needs to take care of business from the past."

"But Berto doesn't believe me. He's convinced I have a lover."

"Cariño. This is 1964, and Cuban women have their own revolution going. You better go home and set your Berto straight. On your way back, get a good supply of candles, and make sure you keep one lit for seven days and seven nights."

I knew that Grandmother Patricia would not want me eavesdropping, but I stayed in my quiet spot, picturing her talking to her client. My grandmother was tall and strong, with wide shoulders and hips and muscular arms and legs, which according to her were from years of hard work on the farm where she grew up. She cut her gray wavy hair short and combed it back, parted in the center. She had lively almond-brown eyes, high cheekbones and a few wrinkles stretching across her face. Although she was sixty by then and her skin showed some age spots, I thought she was beautiful and ageless. As I rocked in my chair and listened to her voice, I thought about the many times I had spent with my grandmother, watching and learning.

Like Carmen, Grandmother Patricia had a small room with an altar. This was her sanctuary, a place where she prayed and worked with those who came to her for healing. Located in a corner of the room, her altar was a simple wooden shelf—three feet wide by four feet long—covered by an embroidered white cloth. On the shelf stood several little statues of saints: the Copper Virgin or la Virgen de la Caridad del Cobre, the patroness of the Cuban island; Saint Lazarus; Saint Barbara; Saint Francis of Assisi, and Jesus on a silver cross. A black rosary that had passed through the hands of my great-grandmother to my grandmother hung from the cross.

La Virgen del Cobre was my grandmother's favorite virgin. She had strong faith in the powers of this beautiful mulata with her copper-colored skin and long black hair, and loved to tell her story to us children. Grandmother always began the narration with the same words: "Children, this is the true story of the appearance of la Virgencita to the three Juans. It is said that in the 1600s two Indians known as Juan de Hoyos and Juan Moreno, and a black slave known as Rodrigo, were in the Bay of Nipe, near the mining province of Cobre, to look for salt. They were rowing their canoe against the swelling waves when they saw a small wood carving of what looked like the Virgin Mary floating in the waters." Grandmother's voice became louder at this point in the story, and she moved her arms as if she were inside the canoe with the three men, rowing and rowing. "In one arm the Virgin held the child Jesus and in the other a golden cross. 'Oh,' one of the men said, 'There is something written by her feet! It says: *Yo soy la Virgen de la Caridad.*'

"The three men brought the carved image back with them to the town of Varajagua in the province of Santiago de Cuba, where a small chapel was built in honor of the Virgin." Grandmother paused and took a deep breath. "Many miracles have taken place among the hundreds of people who have gone to pray to la Virgen de color canela. I can account for her powers myself, because she has answered my prayers in very difficult times, like when your Grandfather Victor was very ill with pneumonia, and the doctors said he was not going to make it . . . well, he made it, thanks to la Caridad del Cobre."

Every morning, Grandmother placed fresh flowers on her altar. She preferred white roses, gardenias and orchids, but when they were not in season, she made an arrangement of any flowers she found in the garden—daisies, lilies, bird of paradise and even orange blossoms from the tree that grew next to the house. A tall white candle was kept lit until bedtime. This candle she placed right next to the black and white photographs of her dead grandmother and parents. According to Grandmother, this was how she kept them alive in her heart. The flame also helped the deceased's souls stay near the light and not get lost in the darkness of the other world.

Of her grandchildren, I had always been Grandmother's favorite, and she made it a point to let me and everyone else know that I was her chosen one. This predilection made it hard on my brother, Jose, and my cousins, Reinaldo and Maria, who tried in all sorts of ways to please Grandmother, to no avail. She preferred my company, and I spent endless hours of my visits listening to her stories and working with her in the garden. Though she lavished attention on me, Grandmother never spoiled me or let me get away with any wrongdoing. She was tough on us children, and we never dared to challenge her authority for fear of a stern lecture.

Once, when I was eight years old, I decided to do a good deed for the neighbors and with that same deed take revenge on Don Eufemio, who was always complaining about how much noise we kids made when we played near his house. Everyone in the neighborhood thought of Eufemio as a greedy guy who lived a bitter existence without a wife or friends. So I really had no qualms about taking the big green peppers from his garden and distributing them among the neighbors. I prepared myself for my mission with a big brown bag I took from Grandmother's kitchen and went off to gather the ajíes. I stripped the old man's plants, leaving just two peppers for him to eat.

After I delivered all the peppers to the front doors of the lucky neighbors, I returned to my grandmother's house, feeling great. A few hours later we heard a furious knocking at the door. When Grandmother opened the front door, there was Eufemio puffing like a steam train, ready to run us over with his anger. He was holding some of the liberated peppers, which, after making sure Grandmother saw them, he threw forcefully on the floor.

"Look at that, Doña Patricia! That is what your querida niña has done with my ajíes. She's a little devil!"

As soon as Don Eufemio was gone, Grandmother sat me on a chair by the kitchen door. "You sit here and think about what you've done." She came back a half hour later. I could tell she was still upset with me by the knitting of her eyebrows. Grandmother handed me a grocery bag filled with peppers she had gathered from her own garden, and with a stern voice, she ordered me back to Eufemio's house to apologize for what I had done. I begged her to come with me.

"No, you go and face the consequences of your own doing!"

Doña Patricia, as everyone in town knew, was a temperamental woman of unpredictable nature. When talking to people, she cried and laughed, even about mundane experiences such as what happened to her women friends in the food-store lines. Grandmother had a sensitive and generous heart—as Cubans say, she would give away her own clothes to those in need.

With the constant scarcity of food, Grandmother always saved the best food for our family visits. If one of her patients brought her a chicken in exchange for her services, she waited to kill it till next Sunday's family gathering. Her chicken soup was the best I ever tasted, mildly spicy and with plenty of cilantro fresh from the garden. Grandmother always said at the dinner table, "This soup makes the dead rise in their tombs, so eat till I can see the shiny bottom of your plates, children."

Grandmother Patricia had another side of her that oftentimes surprised me. Like Grandfather Victor used to say, "All coins have two faces, and so does your abuela, Patricia." She could be stern and incredibly critical of little things and of people, especially my mother. I learned from an early age that when Grandmother Patricia was in a bad mood, she had a tendency to pick on my mother. She blamed a lot of the problems my parents had on the fact that my father had married a woman from a wealthy family. Cuban mothers spoiled their sons, and Grandmother was no exception. Father could do no wrong in the eyes of my grandmother.

I knew she was having a good day when she didn't say anything about the cleanliness of the clothes I wore and when she didn't bother to check my fingernails, which were usually filthy from playing in the dirt. For Grandmother, appearance was extremely important. That combined with my grandmother's critical nature drove my mother away from her house on many occasions. "Felicia, these children look like pordioseros," Grandmother would say while inspecting us for mud stains, "little beggars."

Most people forgave Doña Patricia's moodiness and admired her healing gifts. Some even said that this kind of temperament was part of being a sensitive healer. For whatever reason, she got away with it and was always the Doña, a woman with an incredible don to bring life through her hands. To me she was a mystery: One moment she was my dear abuela, warm and nurturing; the next, she was the curandera and teacher—distant, even lost, in another reality.

As her favored grandchild, I occupied a special place in Patricia's world. When I was six months old, a neighbor, an old man who lived a few houses down the street from Grandmother Patricia, stopped to say hello to my mother who was rocking me to sleep on Patricia's porch. My mother noticed that the old man fixed his gaze on me and repeated more than twice, "Qué bonita niña!" When he had left, Mother got up from the rocking chair to put me in my crib. It was then that she noticed that my face was very pale and that my small body felt cool and limp in her hands. My mother shouted for my Grandmother Patricia, who was in the kitchen.

"Patricia, Patricia, something is wrong with Teresa. Please, come quick. I think she is dying."

Grandmother immediately took me into her healing room, put me on the bed and started praying aloud while making circular movements with her hands over my small and pale body. A few minutes later I was back to my normal rosy color.

"Maldito viejo!" said Grandmother. "Every time that old man comes around the children, he gives them mal de ojos. That old man is a brujo. He has evil eyes, and he knows it. He almost sent our Teresa to the land of the dead. She was very close to the other side. Thank all the spirits that I was nearby."

Throughout my childhood, there were incidents of mal de ojo, or the evil eye. One day, I was playing with my cousin Reinaldo in Grandmother's garden when the same old man walked by. He smiled at me, exposing his toothless purple gums. Then he doffed his straw hat, said a brief hello and walked away.

A few minutes later, I felt dizzy and nauseated. I ran inside, getting to the bathroom just in time. Grandmother heard me throwing up and came knocking. I didn't have a chance to say much to her because I fainted. When I came to, I was on the bed in the healing room, and Grandmother was saying prayers and moving her hands in the air just above my tummy as if she were brushing something away from my body. Then she motioned with her hands as if pulling some kind of invisible cord attached to my belly button. I felt something like a current of air blowing across my body and I drifted off to sleep.

An hour later, I woke up, and Grandmother sat me on her lap and brushed my hair with a soft bristle brush.

"Negrita," she said, "You got sick from mal de ojos again. This is the second time that old man has gotten to you with his evil eye. He has real bad thoughts going on inside his head, thoughts that make people sick, especially young children like you. Grandmother is going to teach you some prayers for protection. Next time he comes around, you must say these prayers to yourself, so he won't hurt you anymore."

I listened carefully and learned the prayers.

A few weeks later, I was outside, playing by myself, when I saw the old man coming around the corner. I started saying my prayers immediately. The man did not stop to say hello. Several hours later, a neighbor told us that the old man had been rushed to the hospital suffering from severe diarrhea and vomiting.

Grandmother's response was to the point: "Never try to harm anyone, not even with your thoughts, Negrita, because whatever bad wishes you have for someone could come around and hurt you. Also, keep those prayers in your mind for when you need them, but only if you need them."

Grandmother taught me more than prayers. She was very knowledgeable about herbs and their healing qualities, which was a valuable gift in those economically hard times, when even aspirin had long disappeared from the stores. Luckily for my family, Grandmother always had a cocimiento or herbal tea ready for colds and stomachaches.

Almost every time I visited, I found Grandmother bent over the large beds of herbs in her garden, a large woven straw hat protecting her from the hot Cuban sun. Though she always wore her hat, she didn't like to wear gardening gloves because she wanted to be able to feel the essence of the flowers and plants.

"Come on, Negrita . . . come and help me pull these stubborn weeds," she might say, looking up at me while holding a bunch of herbs in her hands. "Negrita, I want you to learn the names of these herbs. They're medicinal. When I was growing up on the farm, there were no doctors around, so when someone was ill we treated them with home remedies.

"See that eucalyptus tree back there? When your father was a small child, he used to suffer from asthma, and I treated him by using the leaves of the eucalyptus . . . " She paused again, looking around, searching for new things to teach me. "Look, look!" She pulled me by the arm and pointed at a plant. "Here, smell this. That's anise, very good to treat colic, especially in babies. I give this sweet tea to you and your brother for stomachaches. You love it! Now look at these chamomile blossoms. Everybody should have a bag of these at home. They are good for so many ailments—stomach problems, insomnia, you name it—it works for almost everything."

These were special moments with Grandmother Patricia. She never failed to show me some new plant in her garden and teach me about its healing properties, and sometimes she allowed me to witness her healing work. One afternoon, we were interrupted by Grandfather Victor, who was calling Grandmother to come back to the house. She had visitors waiting for her.

"I knew it!" Grandmother said, somewhat disappointed at having to leave her garden. "I knew it, Negrita; it never fails. Since this morning I've known visitors were coming, bringing a young child." She dropped the herbs in my hands—"Take these in the house"—and then walked away, cleaning her hands on the white apron she wore around her waist.

I was dying to see if Grandmother's predictions were right, so after taking care of the herbs, I went to the living room, where Grandfather was talking to a young couple, who looked to be about twenty-five. The woman was holding a small girl, about a year old, and the man had taken his straw hat off and was twisting it nervously on his lap. Grandmother took her time washing up and changing into clean clothes while Grandfather Victor tried to keep some conversation going with the couple. They were guajiros, farmworkers from near Rio Sasa. The woman was quiet and shy and kept her eyes on the child. The man said a few words about the tobacco harvest, but did not seem to be interested in saying much more. Twice, he checked his daughter's temperature by touching her forehead with the palm of his hand.

I saw Grandfather breathe a sigh of relief when Grandmother finally made her appearance. She had changed into a comfortable beige camisero, a simply cut dress buttoned in the front, and had brushed back her silver-gray hair, which dignified her appearance. She greeted the couple with a humble and polite "Good afternoon" and waited for them to initiate their request. There were a few seconds of awkward silence, and Grandfather Victor took this opportunity to excuse himself and left the room.

The peasant woman slowly got up from her chair, and the shy husband immediately followed. He reached out and shook Grandmother's hand with a short introduction of their names—Ana and Emilio.

"Our child has been very ill," Emilio said, holding his wife's left elbow.

Grandmother moved closer to Ana so that she could see their child.

"What is her name?" Grandmother asked, taking the little girl from her mother's arms.

"Adela. She is our only child. Please, señora, do something for her. She has been vomiting and . . . "

"Come with me. You too, Emilio. Come this way." Grandmother walked towards her healing room. I stood there waiting for some sign as to whether to follow them or stay out. Grandmother turned to me and said, "Come on. You're old enough now."

Grandmother placed the young infant on the small bed, right next to her altar. She asked Ana and Emilio to sit on chairs near their daughter. I stood by the door, waiting for directions and worrying that I might be sent out. Grandmother lit a tall white candle in a porcelain candleholder and placed it in the center of the ritual table. She faced her altar and began to pray in such a low voice that I couldn't distinguish the words.

Adela was fidgeting on the bed as if she were in some sort of pain or discomfort. Ana was holding one of her tiny hands. Emilio was quiet, observing every move Grandmother made. Grandmother finished her prayers and turned to me. "Negrita, go to the kitchen and bring me some aceite de olivo."

I went as fast as I could; I didn't want to miss anything. I came back with a pint-size bottle of olive oil imported from Spain. Grandmother was bent over, examining Adela's distended belly. She touched the area with the tip of her fingers and applied light pressure on some of the spots. Adela cried.

"Here, Negrita, feel this." Grandmother took my hand and placed it on the center of Adela's abdomen. I felt a hard lump under the skin.

"Your little girl has empacho," Grandmother said to the couple. "See how she's bloated? Adela's intestines are blocked in this part." Grandmother pointed with her finger to the area where I had touched the swelling. "This is nothing to worry about. She is going to be well, as soon as I finish my work," she said. Taking the bottle of oil from me, she poured some of the thick golden-green liquid into her palm and then rubbed and massaged the child's belly, sometimes with her fingers, other times with her palms, as if she were kneading dough to make empanadas.

"Mira, Negrita, pay attention to what I'm doing. That's the way to learn. Watch my hands. See how the mass inside the intestine moves. I'm dissolving the empacho, so that whatever is there is destroyed."

Adela was no longer crying; she looked relaxed, as if she were enjoying the experience. As a final touch, Grandmother wiped the oil from Adela's body with a clean white handkerchief that she kept folded in a corner of her altar. Then she blessed Adela in the traditional way, "Dios te bendiga," and made the sign of the cross, though Grandmother did not practice Catholicism in the traditional sense; that is, she never went to church except for special occasions such as weddings and baptisms. "God is God, with or without church," she would tell me.

Grandmother Patricia and the woman from out of town came out of the healing room. Caught by surprise, I didn't have time to run out of the living room. I waited to be reprimanded, but instead Grandmother turned to her client and with pride said, "This is my granddaughter, Teresa. She has a don, like me."

After the woman left, Grandmother invited me to sit with her in the kitchen. As usual she put a pot of water to make coffee on top of the kerosene stove. In those days, kerosene was a luxury and tightly rationed. Each time the golden liquid came in to the stores, the entire neighborhood ran to the stores to stand in line with their empty bottles. Grandfather Victor was always alert and prepared when he heard the neighbors yell, "Petróleo."

Coffee was also disappearing fast from the stores. Cubans, being great drinkers of sweet cafesito, were willing to pay very high prices per pound on the black market. Grandmother Patricia was lucky; she had friends that lived in las lomas, in the mountains where they were able to grow some coffee for their own consumption. They were kind enough to share their precious harvest with Grandmother, who in turn augmented the amount by mixing it with roasted garbanzos. Even though it didn't taste as good as one hundred percent coffee, something was better than nothing.

We sat in a couple of tauretes near the stove, waiting for the water to boil. It was our afternoon ritual. As soon as the bubbles began to form on the surface and steam was rising above, Grandmother poured a couple of tablespoons of the finely ground coffee grains into the kettle. She waited a few seconds till the dark brown foam began to rise and then she ran it through a funnel or colador into a small aluminum coffeepot. This was my favorite time, when the black liquid dripped down and its aroma filled the house.

Cuban coffee is served in small porcelain cups and is very sweet. Cubans don't think much about diets when it comes to sugar for their cafesito. One big teaspoon is the usual, sometimes two. Grandmother was an exception in that respect. She liked her coffee unsweetened, and as she said to me while pouring coffee for both of us, "Negrita, el café amargo es lo mejor"—coffee tastes best without sugar.

There was always an air of importance during these meetings in the kitchen. We sat and sipped our coffee while Grandmother talked to me about curanderismo as well as other topics, such as problems in the country. I preferred hearing her healing stories to her lengthy lectures on social problems, but today Grandmother started with the theme of a "woman of honor." I braced myself, as I could tell she was in a serious mood and ready to deliver one of her sermones.

"Negrita, una mujer honrada stays home and doesn't give the neighbors any reason for them to gossip or question her behavior."

"Like what?" I interrupted.

"Well, a Cuban lady doesn't go places alone with a man unless he's her husband."

I knew that well enough because, in my neighborhood, the older girls talked about how they lied to their mothers all the time. Since they were not allowed to go on dates without a chaperone, they made up excuses—a trip to the library, a study group at a friend's house, and then they would go to meet their boyfriends.

I crossed my arms and pretended to be listening to Grandmother.

She went on with her lecture, "Virginity and honradez walk side by side." I looked out the kitchen window. Grandfather Victor and my father were fixing the fence around the backyard. I wished I could escape from my grandmother and join them.

"Listen well, Negrita. When a woman loses her honra, she becomes basura, trash! She's like a rock that rolls and rolls downhill and that no one wants to catch."

That's not fair! I wanted to shout, but I said nothing. Men and boys always get to do the fun things. Grandfather and Papi were out there having a good time. At age nine, I couldn't have cared less about losing my honra.

"Negrita, when you grow up, I want you to remember that a clean house is an open home for the good spirits."

At this, I nearly threw down my coffee cup in disgust. Yes, I knew all about the fact that girls and women were in charge of cleaning the house. At home, my brother was never expected to clean up after himself or do any household chores, and my father would make a big fuss if the collars of his shirts were not ironed exactly the way he liked them. I sat there sullenly while Grandmother collected our empty cups and washed them efficiently, oblivious to my thoughts.

It was not till many years later that I understood the deeper meaning and wisdom of Grandmother's admonition to keep one's life in order and clean of unwanted clutter. But by that time, we were oceans apart, strangers who spoke different languages, not only of words but of hearts. And I had become a woman in a foreign country, where I forgot about the meaning of the word honra.

7

STORIES FROM MY HOMETOWN

CABAIGÜÁN, my hometown, is located near the south coast in Cuba's central province of Las Villas. Mostly flatlands with some sparse hills inland, Las Villas's fertile soil and valleys are ideal for sugar cane, tobacco, and cattle grazing. Cabaigüán is about forty-two miles from the provincial capital of Santa Clara and two hundred and twenty-six miles from Havana.

The town's architecture is a mixture of old Spain and practical Cuban sentiment. Only the main street, called Masó, and a few others in the downtown area and adjacent neighborhoods were paved when I lived there; the rest were cobblestone or dirt. The central park, named after José Martí, the Cuban poet and revolutionary, was then a tranquil sanctuary where people sat to read or rest under the shade of the royal palm, the lustrous reddish-brown mahogany, and the ebony with its jet black bark, while multicolored bougainvilleas embraced the tree trunks and the park benches. In the early morning, the gardenias and lilies sweetened the air.

In the evening, people would gather around el Paseo, a long paved strip in the middle of town dotted with benches and trees. Young lovers hid in quiet, dark corners, their bodies entwined, enjoying their secret kisses. Other less fortunate young men and women were allowed only to hold hands under the strict vigilance of the girls' mothers, who pretended to be distracted, but in reality were keeping close watch on the couples' movements.

Old men gathered in small groups, reminiscing about the past, occasionally expressing nostalgia for the freedom to utter political opinions in public, something that Castro did not allow for fear of counterrevolutionary activities. That left the elders only literature, soap operas and neighborhood affairs as subjects for passionate discussion.

The women in my neighborhood would yell to each other from their windows or doorways: "Hey, Julia, do you have some sugar I can borrow?" Or, "Can you watch my kids? I'm going to the doctor." We were a big family of families, with walls that separated our houses as thin as the skin of an onion, or when conflicts arose, as thick and high as mountains. There were no secrets—everybody knew everybody. Even more so after the organization of the CDR, the Committees for the Defense of the Revolution, which kept strict vigilance on the activities and whereabouts of every household and every person in the household.

By the time the sun settled behind the horizon, the women of Cabaiguán were ready to sit outside on their porches. In Cuba, porches are the centers of most social gatherings. The tropical climate of the island invites people to be outdoors, where they can enjoy the warm air saturated with the scent of flowers and of coffee brewing on top of the stove in every home. After the dishes were done, the ladies of my town would gather at a neighbor's porch, in small groups of "best friends," who gossiped while doing their embroidery, needlepoint or crocheting till bedtime, around eleven or twelve. In those extended sessions, los trapos sucios, or dirty laundry from the neighborhood, were brought out for a heavy wash of chismoteo, a Cuban way of not just reporting the daily news around town, but a nasty gossiping. The topics ranged from future weddings, who was or wasn't pregnant, births, baptisms, and wives sleeping around with other women's husbands, to creative recipes for Russian canned beef, how to mix scarce coffee beans with garbanzos to stretch the coffee and, of course, the black market and sex.

These nocturnal gatherings were also a convenient way for mothers to keep an eye on their daughters as they sat with their boyfriends, either inside the living room with the windows and doors open or outside near the entrance. Throughout the night, the chaperone, mamá, would put her needlepoint aside, with the excuse of going to the bathroom or making coffee, and walk right past where the young lovers were seated, holding hands and trying to sneak a kiss. Though the whole neighborhood was watching them, most couples came up with ingenious ways of touching each other without being seen.

One evening, Susana, my neighbor from across the street, was caught by her grandmother touching her boyfriend's rabo, which he had covered with his jacket. The old woman pulled the jacket off the young man's lap, exposing the strongly erect organ. She screamed so loud that a gaggle of curious ladies ran to the scene, still holding the sharp instruments they used for their needlepoint. Ernesto had just enough time to get up from the sofa and run off, his rabo still dangling outside his fly. A month later, Susana's father forced Ernesto to marry Susana to save the honra of his daughter, but for weeks after the incident the women enjoyed talking about the size of Ernesto's "beast." Every time the story was told, the beast grew. Soon it was close to a foot, and Ernesto had become el Caballo. From then on, any time he walked by a group of people, someone would say "There goes el Caballo."

I asked my mother if Fidel Castro had a large penis like Ernesto's, since Fidel was referred to as "el Caballo." The answer my mother gave me did not clear up my confusion, but a few days later, while I waited in line to buy milk, I overheard a conversation between two women. One of them whispered, "Fidel has a big pinga." The other woman turned to her friend and said, "I heard he's twelve inches." I imagined his pinga, another slang word for penis, the length of my school ruler with disbelief. How could he possibly keep a big rabo like that inside his pants?

The oldest man in our neighborhood was Salvador Gutierrez. The ninety-eight-year-old used to tell stories about the turn-of-the-century war of independence against the Spaniards. In the evenings, we children sat around him with great anticipation, waiting for another colorful tale of the old days. Salvador's repertoire seemed unlimited, and every night he had a new story for us. He was much more interesting than the television programs, which were all about politics and news;

besides, there were only a few televisions in town.

I learned more about Cuban history from Salvador Gutierrez than from any textbook. His stories were filled with anecdotes and vivid images of the people who gave their blood for the freedom of our country and people, our patria cubana and mestiza (the mix of African and Spanish traditions and races). The old man's raspy voice transported us to the battlefields, capturing our attention with imaginative sounds and images: I could hear the old shotguns and the machetes of the Cuban independence fighters, and see the morros and the cañones firing at the enemy.

One of Salvador's favorite subjects was Mariana Grajales. "She was a courageous mother and revolutionary," Salvador would say, raising his right hand to his heart. "What a lady she was! I was a young child, maybe seven or eight, just old enough to remember the cuentos I heard about Doña Mariana. She had nine children by her husband, Marcos Maceo. These children, she raised them all to become mambises and to fight till the very end against slavery." Salvador would pause to take a big puff of his cigar; then, turning the brown havano in his long bony fingers, he would watch the red ashes burn.

"Mariana was quite a woman. Yes, she was. After the Creator made her, He probably tossed the mold away so that there wouldn't be any replicas. My father told me that Mariana singlehandedly ran a bush hospital in the mountains. But she had many sorrows: First came the death of her son, Justo, then her beloved husband, and then her son, Antonio, the Bronze Titan, was wounded. Misfortune only pressed Mariana to continue the struggle against oppression in Cuba. When all the older sons were dead or wounded, Mariana looked to the youngest, a boy still, and said, 'You go now. It is time to fight for your country.'"

Salvador was highly respected in our community. He had once been a farmer and knew how to predict the weather, so sometimes in the afternoon, farmers from the area would gather around him and discuss the possibility of rains and hurricanes. They trusted the old man's advice implicitly and referred to him as el viejo cedro, the old cedar tree. They said he knew so much because he was deeply rooted in the earth.

To me, Salvador was the wise old man, the one who remembered the link to the ancestors and to the soul of our town. I felt comforted by his dignified presence. Tall like a palm tree, he looked like a strong cacique, a Taíno Indian chief, with his angular face, prominent cheekbones and black eyes. Salvador was the anchor that held the line between the worlds of past and present.

Graciela was the other elder and storyteller of the barrio. In addition to her spiritualism sessions, she enjoyed telling us stories about ghosts and haunted houses where jars of old gold coins and precious stones had been buried more than a hundred years ago by wealthy Spaniards and pirates. According to Graciela, these people, even after death, kept guard over their hidden fortunes.

After a night of listening to Graciela's spooky tales, my brother would be afraid that the ghosts were going to sneak into his room, and he would come to my bed and hide under my covers. Any little noise or shadow was enough to terrify both of us. Shivering, we prayed together, promising the lost souls we would never do anything to disturb them.

One night during the summer of 1965, Graciela, as usual, was sitting on her porch in her old rocking chair, sipping sweet coffee from a tiny tin cup and smoking a cigar. That was her ritual preparation for storytelling as she waited for all of us eager children—and some grownups—to gather around her.

"Well," Graciela began, in her deep voice, "you know . . . " She took a long pause, leaving us in suspense while she sucked on her cigar. "One of these days, you won't see me come out of the house anymore. I'm getting old, and my body is tired." She stopped and smiled at us craftily. "But my ghost will be here to tell stories, and if you don't show up, I will come and get you. I will pull your toes when you are asleep." Then she laughed, displaying her worn-out gums and her one rotting tooth. There was a moment of silence, and then we all laughed nervously.

"Well, well, enough of this. I am not quite ready to go in the box, but I warn you, I want the best cedar coffin ever made in this town, and I want to be buried with the proper rituals an old woman like me deserves. I don't want a cheap pine chest, like the one they got for Juanito Belmonte when he died last year. That wasn't fair for old Juan.

81

After all, he was quite a character, in his own way, even though he had a bad temper and didn't like to be around all of you. He had his reasons. He told me about all the bad tricks you played on him, like pushing his car off the street so that he had to go looking for it. And I know about the time you put frogs on his porch knowing he was terrified of those creatures! You kids better learn to show respect to the old people—if you don't, their ghosts will haunt you forever when the old people die. With this, I'll tell you the story of Benito Jimenez," Graciela said, shifting her position on the rocking chair.

"Benito Jimenez!" several of us exclaimed in unison. We all knew a little bit of this story, of the two ghosts that hung around the big ceiba tree that grew on the side of the road about a mile from Benito's farm on the outskirts of town. Many people claimed they had seen these lost souls—a man and a woman—walking and holding hands at night.

"When I was a young girl, many, many, but not too many, moons ago," Graciela began, "I lived with my parents on the farm owned by Benito, la Paloma. El Gallego, as Benito was called because he was a native of the Spanish province of Galicia, traveled to Cuba with his pockets full of pesetas. Enamored with the beauty of the island and its women, he decided to buy some land to grow tobacco. At the beginning la Paloma was just a small plantation, but slowly it became one of the largest in all Las Villas province. He employed many workers, whom he paid poorly and treated very badly. He was harsh and had no compassion. If someone got ill and couldn't work, he threw him out like a sack of potatoes and immediately replaced him with a healthy and strong campesino from the area. He was a greedy man and a very ambitious one, with aspirations of becoming the greatest tobacco producer of the island and, someday, of the whole world.

"Benito married Irma Serrano, the daughter of a wealthy neighboring farmer, also an immigrant from Spain. Five beautiful and strong children were born to the couple. Four boys and one girl. The girl Vasilia grew up to become a beautiful young woman and fell in love with Geremias, a black man from Jamaica who had come to Cuba to work in her father's tobacco fields.

"The strong handsome negro and the lovely golden-haired Vasilia met secretly every night inside an abandoned barn. Misfortune struck them one night when Benito, unable to sleep, saw his daughter sneaking out of the house past midnight. He followed her to the barn and discovered the young lovers, their naked bodies entwined like braided sweet bread.

"Enraged, Benito decided to clear the honor of Vasilia and his family by killing the 'sinful negro.' He hung Geremias from a ceiba tree near the road, where everybody could see him. He was left there for days while the buzzards cleaned the bones of flesh bit by bit. Benito prohibited anyone from giving Geremias a proper burial.

"Brokenhearted, Vasilia sank into a dark well of inconsolable sadness. She withdrew into her room and refused to see anyone or eat. With time, Vasilia became a shadow, a ghostly figure, who wandered in and out of the realms of the dead in her desperate longing to find her beloved Geremias."

At this point in the story, Graciela paused for the sake of suspense. She took a puff from her cigar and blew the smoke in the air with delight.

"You know?" she said. "I was just a kid . . . but I remember Vasilia's face as if she were here, in front of me now. One night, as I was trying to go to sleep, I heard her screaming for Geremias. It was eerie, really eerie.

"The next day, Vasilia was found dead with her arms wrapped around the wide trunk of the ceiba tree where her beloved Geremias had been killed by her father. Some people in town claimed that, while passing by that area, they had heard the voices of Geremias and Vasilia and seen their ghostly figures holding hands and dancing. Others told of how their horses were spooked and galloped away in a frenzy."

Graciela took a deep breath and another sip of the cold coffee from her tin cup.

"That's the story of evil Benito Jimenez and the lovers Vasilia and Geremias."

That night, I walked home unable to leave behind the thought of poor Geremias hanging from the ceiba tree as buzzards picked off his flesh. It reminded me of the two men I had seen hanging from the high branch of the ateje tree on the morning of the Revolution.

I was aware that the Revolution, with its promises for equality, had not changed the attitudes of whites towards blacks much. In school, the idea that all people were equal was pounded into our heads, but outside, things were different. The Cuban proverb *juntos pero no rebueltos* (together but never mixed) was as real as black beans and rice. Even when all the restrictions on blacks had been removed, white Cubans would still think twice before they sat next to a black person on the *guagua*.

Not only were the blacks seen as different, but Castro himself prohibited them from practicing their religions. Carmen would complain, "That Castro with his golden mask. He is a Spaniard at heart! The two-faced *descarado* has taken away our freedom."

The story of Geremias and Vasilia stayed with me many years, even after I left Cuba. It is a story that captures something about my homeland and my culture, about the merging of the black African traditions, religion and spirituality with those of the white Spaniards. Indeed, all my grandparents were from Spain, but I always thought of myself as a *mulata*. Like Geremias and Vasilia, the seductive African drum and the passionate Spanish guitar were entwined in my soul and spirit.

A few hours after Graciela had told us the story of Geremias and Vasilia, she died peacefully in her own bed. As she had requested, the old woman was placed inside an elegant cedar coffin made by the best carpenter in town. Since Graciela had always expressed a dislike for funeral homes, the wake was held in the living room of her own house.

The entire neighborhood took part in decorating the house and preparing the food. Carmen and my mother agreed to be in charge of serving the rum and coffee that had been bought on the black market. Graciela didn't have any relatives that we knew of, but it was evident that everyone felt she was part of their family.

As soon as the sun went down, groups of people began to arrive at Graciela's house. As in any traditional open-casket wake, the mourners paid respect to Graciela first. The men took off their hats and stood in front of the coffin for a few seconds with somber looks on their faces. The women carried white embroidered handkerchiefs to wipe away their tears. When my turn came up, I froze in my place; I couldn't move my feet. The pale white face in front of me was not Graciela's! I saw only a tightly closed mouth and bluish lips. My mother, who was right behind me, took me away to a corner of the room where I could sit and recover from the shock of seeing Graciela in that state.

The night went slowly. The house was packed with people talking and joking. Sometime near midnight, all the lights in the house went off. I held tightly on to my chair as I listened to the nervous screams and laughter. I tried to call for help, but words wouldn't come out of my mouth. Then, as if in a dream, I saw the ghostly figure of Graciela rising from the coffin. I closed and opened my eyes several times, trying to shake away the apparition, but instead Graciela floated to the center of the room.

Trembling, I waited for Graciela to come and pull my toes as she had once threatened. For a brief moment, I wondered if I was having a nightmare. Just then the lights began to blink, a glass fell to the floor and shattered, a bottle of rum flew across the room and a match lit a cigar suspended in the air.

"Virgen de la Caridad!" I heard someone say next to me.

"Can you see her, too?" I managed to ask.

"The old woman is saying good-bye. She couldn't leave this world without leaving us the gift of a final story." It was the same voice next to me, a woman's voice.

A few seconds later the lights came back on. I turned around to see the face of the woman who had shared my experience, but no one was there. Like the smoke of Graciela's cigar, the woman had disappeared in the darkness.

For the rest of the night all kinds of stories were told. Some said they heard the glass break. Others witnessed the cigar and the bottle of rum. One thing was for sure, everyone present at the wake was convinced that Graciela had visited the house and that she had played some of her old tricks on us. By morning, people were reporting that Graciela had spoken to them and given them important messages.

"Graciela told me that Fidel doesn't have many shavings left," one man declared, meaning that Fidel was going to die soon.

"According to Graciela, we must be prepared for the worst crash of our economy," our neighbor Nena warned us.

Tales grew taller. Ironically, Graciela was more alive in death than she had been in life. I had the crazy thought that Graciela had created all this drama so that she could sneak some cigars and rum inside her coffin for her final journey. As I passed by her house, I thought I heard her say, "Don't forget the spirit of Geremias and the grief of Vasilia. As long as we remember them, there will be stories to tell, great and wonderful tales that can never be silenced." Then I saw Graciela, not inside the cedar coffin, but out on her porch, as usual, sitting on her rocking chair.

8

LA LIBRETA

AT AGE TEN, I would wake up uneasy about the day ahead in school, anticipating the constant brainwashing from my fourth grade teachers. The words "conciencia revolucionaria" floated in my head like noodles in a bowl of hot soup. Borrowed from Marxist doctrine, the model of revolutionary conscience was hammered into our daily experiences with unrelenting monotony, becoming the ruler that measured our behaviors, values and beliefs. Over and over, we were reminded that to be good citizens, we must be dedicated Communists, always obedient and loyal to the Revolution, ready to sacrifice everything for the cause and the country.

Unfortunately for me, I was lacking in conciencia revolucionaria. I had been suspended from school for two days when I refused to write an essay in my political science class on the economic benefits of the Agrarian Reform. The principal threatened me with expulsion if I persisted in such antirevolutionary behavior. She lectured me at great length about my poor attitude, making veiled threats towards my family. After that, I was plagued by the fear of saying or doing anything that might get me or my family into trouble.

This morning was no different from any other. The day was hot and humid. I hated my elementary school uniform, with its gray twill skirt and the heavily starched, white cotton blouse whose stiff collar made my neck itch. Just looking at it in my closet filled me with dread.

I could hear the voices of Carmen and my brother from the other room. As usual, Jose was having a hard time getting ready for school. He had stayed in bed till the last minute and then refused to dress by himself. "Jose! You'll be late for school. Come here. I'll get your shoes on," Carmen said, as she finished polishing the old black leather shoes whose soles were worn to the point of having several holes. This was the only pair of shoes Jose owned, and only thanks to the generosity of an older cousin who had passed them on to him. I could tell by the tone of Carmen's voice that she was getting impatient.

"I don't want to go to school! I hate it!" Jose screamed, running out of his room half-dressed. Carmen followed him to the hall.

"You're going to get big ears like a donkey! Wait till your mother comes home. She'll take care of you. I don't want to argue with a malcriado like you." Carmen walked towards the kitchen, leaving Jose sitting in a corner of the hall with his face buried inside his hands.

Like she did every morning, Mother had left the house before sunrise, armed with an empty paper shopping bag and la libreta, the ration card given to each household by the government. Without this indispensable little book, no one could buy anything. All the stores required customers to present it so that their quota of food or goods such as toothpaste, toilet paper and soap could be marked. There was a quota for everything—bread, milk, sugar, a few ounces of this and that, three pounds of rice per person. People spent most of their days walking from store to store and standing in long lines to get whatever was available, sometimes just a bag of Cuban crackers or a pound of brown sugar. Other times, by the time Mother got to the counter, everything was gone.

Mother hadn't returned home with our breakfast, so I went to the kitchen with the hope of finding something I could eat before going to school. My empty stomach growled with disappointment at what I found: a piece of butter, homemade cheese, a couple of tomatoes and leftovers from last night's dinner: a pot of steamed rice and some picadillo—ground beef cooked in oil, tomato sauce, onions, garlic and green peppers. Carmen walked in as I was cutting myself a slice of the cheese.

"Your mother must be in one of those endless lines," she said as she sat at the kitchen table. Her forehead was covered with drops of sweat. Lately, Carmen seemed thinner and slower to me as she walked around the house. Carmen never told her age to anyone, not even my mother. Even so, I figured she was probably in her forties or older. It was hard to tell because her beautiful, silky dark chocolate skin and bright black eyes were ageless.

"This cheese will do it for me. I've got to go, or I'll be late for school," I said and kissed Carmen on the cheek.

"Take your brother with you."

"Is he ready?"

"Yes, he finally managed to put his shoes on. I just finished combing his hair," she said, with a half smile on her face. I could tell Carmen was upset about our going to school again without breakfast, from those knitted eyebrows of hers.

I shared the cheese with Jose as we headed out the door. I felt sorry for my little brother. I could tell he was having a difficult time with second grade. I knew la bruja he had for a teacher, Mrs. Guerrero. She had been my teacher, too. I hated the way she punished her students by hitting us with a long, thin ruler kept behind her desk. Many parents had complained to the principal, but apparently Mrs. Guerrero held a privileged position in the Communist Party, and nothing was ever done.

My first class of the day was history. The teacher, Eduardo Arnaz, was serious but inexperienced. He had recently graduated from the University of Havana, thanks to scholarships provided by the Cuban government. Mr. Arnaz's lectures were dry and long. When nervous, he stuttered, most often at the beginning of the class. If by chance one of us happened to cough or laugh, the stuttering problem became worse and his right cheek would begin to twitch. He was totally dedicated to indoctrinating all of us fourth-graders on the goodness of the Communist philosophy. More than history, his class was a marathon of Marx and Lenin. As usual, he had already written the title of the day's subject on the blackboard—U.S. EMBARGO.

Quietly, I sat at my designated desk and took out my notebook and pencil from my bag. Mr. Arnaz now stood in front of the class, right hand inside one of the pockets of his blue pants, and white chalk in his left. He was writing in big letters, "OCTOBER 19, 1960." Then he turned to us and began his talk. "The Eisenhower Administration declared a partial embargo on trade with Cuba, prohibiting all exports, except for foodstuffs, medicines, medical supplies and a few items that require special licenses. Vice President Richard Nixon described this policy as an all-out 'quarantine'—economically, politically and diplomatically—on the Castro regime." Mr. Arnaz paused and took a deep breath. He had not stuttered a single time, so perhaps he was enjoying his success. Not for long, though. Miguel, a student sitting in the back of the classroom, raised his hand.

"Yes, Mi . . . Mi . . . Mi . . . Miguel . . . " The face of Mr. Arnaz was red from the effort and embarrassment.

"Is it because of the embargo that we have a libreta to buy things?"

"Mo . . . Mo . . . Mostly be . . . be . . . because of that. Yes. When the block . . . block . . . blockade was imposed, our country began a pe . . . pe . . . riod of scarcity. We were not really pro . . . producers. In the p . . . p . . . past, it was cheaper and easier to import from the States."

Mr. Arnaz went on and on about the importance of all of us sticking together and fighting against imperialistic forces. "The way to win this war against poverty is to increase our commitment to the Revolution and its leaders, especially Fidel Castro," he said, and he hit the top of the desk with his fist, immediately getting our attention. But also, my disbelief. It was difficult to think of any happy endings when I had been listening throughout the class to my empty stomach which was growling louder than a hungry cat's.

That afternoon when I went home for lunch, I found Mother and Carmen in the kitchen, talking and cooking. I began to salivate at the smell of sweet plantains frying in hot oil.

"Mmmm, where did you go to get those delicious plantains?" I asked Mother, while checking the other pots on top of the stove. "Mmmm, black beans! And freshly cooked rice. What are we celebrating?" I asked. Neither Carmen nor my mother answered. "I bet you went out to the country today. That's why you were late for breakfast," I said, grabbing a slice of fried plantain from the plate Mother was holding in her hands. But before I could eat it, Carmen came from behind and took it out of my hand.

"I told you, niña, never to pick at the food we are cooking. Bad manners!" She put the slice of plantain back on the plate.

"Just one piece," I begged. "I'm starving."

"Wait till the table is set. It will be just a few more minutes," Mother said.

"Did you go to the countryside today?" I asked again.

"Yes, Teresa, I went to the countryside." Mother knew that I worried any time she went off by herself to visit small farmers on the outskirts of town. She took with her whatever she could to exchange for food. Mostly these were things Father was able to buy on the black market in Havana during business trips—things such as men's socks, T-shirts, a bar of soap, toothpaste, razor blades and even aspirin.

"Why do you worry so much about my going to the farms, Teresa?" Mother asked, while serving food at the table.

"Because you know they're watching us. One of these days you're going to end up like our neighbor, Juana, in jail."

"Juana was caught smuggling pounds and pounds of coffee into town from the Sierra Maestra Mountains. That's not what I'm doing," she said, putting some extra plantains on my plate.

"Well . . . if the CDR checks your bag, they'll know for sure you didn't buy those things in the store. Besides that, Aurelia is constantly looking out from her window, checking the whereabouts of every person in the neighborhood," I said, trying to convince Mother of the danger involved in her trips to the countryside.

In those days, I was scared of everything. The CDR, with its invasive eyes, controlled every move in my neighborhood. The recent election of representatives to the CDR had placed in top positions a couple of sharks who were more than eager to enforce the daily guardia, or vigilance. Every adult in each household was mandated to participate in and to take turns doing la guardia. In other words, individuals were forced to become spies on their friends, families and neighbors. Each night the person charged with playing vigilante was given a rifle that otherwise was kept at the house of the head of the CDR. The selected vigilante would sit on a chair on the front porch of his or her

91

house to watch the others on the block and their activities—who came in at what time and with whom. Any kind of unofficial gathering in a neighbor's home was suspicious in the eyes of the CDR. Its main concern, of course, was to prevent the formation of counterrevolutionary groups.

My fear that Mother would get thrown in jail was well justified. If the CDR found out that a person had been wheeling and dealing with the farmers or on the black market, a committee meeting would be immediately called, and the person judged right in front of his or her neighbors. Penalties varied from having to work in the sugar cane fields or pick up trash from the streets, to being thrown in jail.

The general paranoia that resulted from this constant surveillance swept through our town like an epidemic. People whispered to one another and, before talking out loud would turn their heads in all directions, checking to see who might be eavesdropping. You could be sent to jail simply for saying a word against Castro or the Revolution.

Mother, however, was willing to risk her safety to feed our hungry bellies. Carmen prayed every time Mother said she was going to the country. "Don't tell the children, and if anything happens to me, you know that you are in charge till Pepe gets back," Mother would say to Carmen whenever she left the house.

"Felicia, ten cuidado, don't trust anyone," Carmen would say, blessing Mother on her way out, calling the spirits Saint Lazarus and Yemayá to be with her and protect her. "Ay Virgencita, when is this misery going to end, when are we going to be free again?" I would hear Carmen mutter while she swept the floors with her big grass broom.

After I finished eating my lunch and asked for permission to get up from the table, Jose followed me. We usually played for a half hour before going back to school.

"Teresa," Mother called. "Come home right after school. Don't hang around the street today with your friends."

"Why not, Mother?" I asked.

"Because I need to leave home early to get in line for shoes. I'll feel better if you're home with Carmen and Jose this afternoon. I'll be spending the night in front of the store till they open in the morning. I'm praying this time there will be shoes your size when my turn comes."

This would be the third time Mother had stood in line to buy our school shoes with la libreta. The other two times, she'd slept in front of the store for two nights, but still she came home empty-handed. She had been so upset that she cursed Castro and his Revolution for days after. The last time, she returned from the store looking exhausted, with dark circles under her eyes and her black wavy hair in disarray. She threw the empty shopping bag on the floor of the entrance hall, took her shoes off and walked to the living room where Father, Jose and I were putting a puzzle together. Then she collapsed in one of the rattan chairs.

"Mami . . . Mami." Jose ran to her, jumped on her lap and hugged her tightly. She held Jose's body close to her and began to cry. Father and I stayed quiet. When I had seen the empty bag, I knew she would be upset.

"Hell . . . This is worse than hell," she said. "I can't believe I wasn't able to get shoes this time either." She dried her tears with the back of her hand. "What are we going to do, Pepe? These kids don't have any decent shoes," she said with a tone of desperation.

"The black market is getting tougher every day," Father replied.

"You've got to do something! I'm just too sick and tired of this basura!" Mother said, raising her voice.

"Don't get so upset, mujer! I'll see what I can do." Father got up from the floor and stood by the window facing the street. He looked at Mother while searching his pockets for the key to his truck.

"That's easy for you to say, but what about some solutions! Or why don't you get in line next time instead of me? I'm tired of being the one running around town every day," she screamed.

"And just what do you think I do when I'm away working! Those things I bring home don't fall in my lap from the skies. I've got to spend hours and hours looking for connections and risking my skin," Father shouted back, his honey-colored eyes turning darker. He turned away from Mother, looking to the street. Then in a low voice he spoke, almost to himself but loud enough so that we all heard it. "This wouldn't be happening if you'd agreed to escape in that boat."

"Turn around, Pepe Fernandez! Look at me, and listen carefully one more time," Mother responded immediately. I could almost see sparks of fire coming from her dark brown eyes. She moved Jose to the side so that she could look straight at Father.

"I'll never . . . *never* risk the lives of my children that way! If you want to go . . . go! But don't ever expect me to put my beloved children in such danger! You know those boats get lost and end up drifting in the currents of the Gulf. You've heard how hundreds of people, including children, have been shot and killed by our coast guard. You know what happened to Cecilia and Ernesto. Yes, they made it to Miami, but their young son died from dehydration on the way."

Mother took a deep breath. Her chest was heaving up and down, and her whole body was shaking. Father was quiet, but clearly angry. His right hand was clenched and pressed against the side of his body.

"I'd rather have them walking around without shoes or clothes than subject them to what you want," Mother added.

"Cobarde! You are a coward! Our children are going to die anyway. Their souls are going to die as soon as they are taken away and brainwashed against us! They are already getting a good dose of Communist crap in school. Wait a few years, and you won't recognize 'your children,'" Father said as he hit the wall with his fist. Then he walked out, slamming the front door after him.

Mother broke down in tears, and Jose tried to comfort her. "Don't cry, Mami, don't cry." He kissed her cheek and with his little hand tried to dry Mother's tears. I didn't move from my place. Mother looked so tired, so beaten by the daily struggle of living. For a moment, I feared losing her, feared something happening to her. I was aware of Mother eating less so that Jose and I could have larger portions. She was getting thinner, her skin was dry, and she had some premature wrinkles around her eyes and mouth. At least that's what I heard Carmen say to her once. Carmen worried about Mother all the time, but I guess we all worried about everybody. The whole country was infected with some sort of worry sickness.

I wasn't sure what to do to make it better for her. I was feeling angry with my father. Every time the subject of escaping Cuba was brought up in conversation, angry arguments followed. For months, Father had been trying to convince Mother to follow him out of the country illegally. He didn't miss any chance to remind her how bad the situation was. Many people were risking their lives in poorly built small rafts, venturing into the Caribbean waters. Father's idea was to go to Havana where he had a contact, an ex-captain who had been planning his own escape. The old sailor had offered Father the opportunity for all of us to leave Cuba in his yacht.

I was glad Mother refused to go along with this plan. I was terrified at the thought of being eaten alive by big sharks. Every day, the radio and TV news gave the names of people who'd drowned or been killed by the Cuban coast guard or by sharks coming from the depths of the turquoise water, ripping apart small vessels and human bodies. These images haunted me at night. I had dreams in which I was swimming desperately against huge waves that threatened to swallow me. I would see myself trying to get hold of my father's hand as he reached out to me from a raft built of bamboo cane. Every time I got close, a wave would toss me away from him. I couldn't see Mother or Jose and I sensed that they had already died.

I couldn't understand why my own father would want to subject us to such danger. But nothing made much sense anymore, not even my parents' constant arguments. It was getting to the point where if I saw them talking, I was afraid they were going to begin arguing again. My biggest fear was that during one of these fights, one of them would walk away and not come back. Carmen never said a thing—she knew how to make herself invisible during the stormy times between my parents. But one afternoon she sat by my side while I was trying to take a nap.

"Teresa, niña, I can tell you're worried about your mamá and papá. I've been watching you, honey. You know, your mamá and papá are having a hard time dealing with all these problems in the country. This revolution is causing lots of pain for people. Life is hard. Castro lied to us, niña."

Carmen ran her hand over my forehead and hair, slowly and gently. She looked into my eyes, searching for a reaction. I stayed quiet. I didn't care about Castro's promises. All I wanted was my family to be happy again. Carmen kept on, almost as if she were talking to herself. I closed my eyes.

"Think about how the stores are empty. Ay, San Lazaro bendito,

I remember going to Carlos's market. I could buy everything I needed for the day. Now your poor mother spends her day going from line to line." I opened my eyes just in time to see Carmen frowning and shaking her head.

Father was not successful in his efforts to get us shoes through the black market. The CDR's vigilance was increasing all over the island. Even people's homes were searched if the committee suspected them of being involved with contraband. Father was scared to call his contacts in Havana for fear that their phones were tapped by the militia.

At that time, I was wearing shoes one of my cousins had passed down to me. Jose's only shoes, the ones with the holes in the soles, were now falling apart. Our hope for shoes was placed on a shipment from Russia that was coming to the town store. Russian shoes were ugly and cheap in appearance, but they lasted for a while, sometimes a year if we were careful to avoid kicking any rocks or balls. They looked like short boots, but it didn't matter whether they were intended for girls or for boys, because in times of necessity you wear what you can get. After all, shoes came to the stores only once or twice a year, and one was extremely lucky to be able to purchase a pair.

The night my mother was waiting in line for shoes, I prayed to the orishas to help her through the hard hours. I thought of her sitting on the cold concrete, outside the store. I knew she was not alone; many other women friends from the neighborhood were there in line, too.

The next morning, Mother came back from the store before we left for school. Once more her shopping bag was empty, and once more she was furiously cursing the Revolution. She walked into the kitchen where Carmen was making scrambled eggs and Jose and I followed her.

"No shoes . . . no shoes!" She opened her purse and pulled out la libreta. She threw it on the floor and started to stomp on it. "This is shit! Mierda! It is good for nothing! You can't buy anything with it! It's all a bunch of lies. We don't need a ration card because there is nothing to ration anymore. This country is going to hell!" Mother kept stomping la libreta.

"Stop that, Felicia!" Carmen said sternly.

"All night . . . all night waiting to buy a pair of shoes, but the shoes never arrived in the store. It was all a lie! One of those desgraciados in uniform came to inform us this morning that something had happened in the port. The shoes were sent to another province by mistake. Can you believe that! They are soulless sinvergüenzas!" She continued stomping on the ration card. Then she bent down and grabbed it, ready to tear it to pieces. Carmen quickly pulled la libreta away and held Mother by the shoulders, shaking her.

"Come to your senses, Felicia! You're a strong woman! You can't let this get to you! The children are watching you. Enough is enough! Basta ya!"

Mother stopped and then broke into tears, throwing herself into Carmen's ready arms. Carmen held Mother close and lovingly stroked her hair. Jose and I stood there and watched as Carmen gently rocked our mother. I thought to myself how lucky we were to have someone like Carmen living with us. Our reliance on her was especially great during moments like this, when the adults in my life turned into helpless children.

9

SCHOOL GOES TO
THE COUNTRYSIDE

*T*HE YEAR OF 1965, like a strong gust of wind, blew new problems and possibilities into our lives. In September, Fidel Castro took us by surprise with his announcement that all Cubans who wished to leave the country could do so from the port of Camarioca. Thousands of people rushed to Camarioca with the hope of catching a boat to Miami.

When my father heard the news, he was working in the province of Oriente, four hours away from home. With his big Mack diesel truck loaded with a shipment of bananas, he was stuck there until he could get rid of the cargo. He called my mother right away. "Get the children ready. We're going to Havana as soon as I can get out of here."

"Are you crazy? I'm not taking any boat with the kids," I heard my mother say. Then, "You go by yourself." And she hung up.

"What's going on?" Carmen asked.

"Pepe wants us to join that crazy bunch of people in Camarioca."

"What are you going to do?"

"No way! I haven't lost my head yet."

"Why not, Mami?" Jose interrupted.

"Because I don't want to see you being devoured by sharks."

Mother had always been afraid of the ocean, so I knew the idea of taking a boat, even when it meant freedom, was not for her. I wondered what made my father think this time was going to be any different. Tired of the same old quarrel, I grabbed my books and left for school.

Two days later, my father returned home from Oriente. He insisted that we all go to Camarioca and wait for the boatlift that was about to begin. My mother held firmly to her position. At night, I covered my ears with my pillow so that I wouldn't hear their heated discussions. Carmen remained neutral, but Grandmother Patricia took my father's side. She visited us every day and tried to convince my mother what a great opportunity this was. My Aunt Nelda, my mother's sister, who lived a block away, became my mother's ally.

By November, so many Cubans were leaving the port that it became a problem for the U.S. Coast Guard. The boatlift was ended, and the United States and Cuba agreed to start the "freedom flights." People who had relatives living in the United States could be claimed by them. Without wasting any time, my father called Uncle Manolo, who resided in California, and asked if he could sponsor us. A few days later, we took a trip to the Swiss embassy in Havana so that we could get passports and visas ready.

We returned to Cabaigüán with a mixture of great hope and some disappointment. We had been told by the embassy official that, because of the large number of Cubans leaving the country, it was going to take a while to get a flight. Nothing was certain. Once you filed papers to leave Cuba, there was an indefinite period of waiting. Who knew that it would take not months, but years.

Back in school, I was presented with a new challenge. A few days after the trip to Havana, I was sent home from school with a letter from the education ministry. It informed my parents about the decision taken by the government "to further coach Cuban youth in the correct ideological thinking and to help them develop a conciencia revolucionaria." The new educational idea was introduced under the name "School Goes to the Countryside." To combine education with productive work in farming cooperatives, thousands of youngsters were to be sent to rural areas, where for a period of forty-five days they would camp with their teachers.

My mother was the first one to read the letter. Her hands visibly shook. "No one is going to take you away from home to work in the fields," she said in an irate voice.

"Mami," I said, "everybody has to go; the teacher was very clear: 'Everyone in this school and many schools across the country.'"

"She can say whatever she pleases, but I'm your mother, and I won't sign this piece of paper. No way! Never in my life would I let you go at your age. You've just turned ten. Ten!" she repeated as she paced the kitchen floor. Mami was so upset that she forgot about the pot of garbanzos cooking on the fire until the kitchen began to fill with the smell of burning beans. Mother rushed to the stove and turned the burner off. Then she stopped and read the note again. Once more I saw her clench her jaw, and then raise her fist and slam it down full force on the kitchen table.

Walking into the kitchen with a brown bag in her arms, Carmen took in the scene in a glance: "Qué pasa, niña?"

Mother handed the note to Carmen—"Here, see what you think of this new idea!"—and immediately went back to pacing and to cursing the Communists. "This revolution sucks! They've taken away our country and . . . and now they want our children. They want to take Teresa away from us, Carmen!" Mother screamed, grabbing Carmen by the shoulders and shaking her. Carmen lifted her eyes from the note. Gently she took my mother's hands and held them in hers.

"Calmate, mí vida. This is a time to be strong and to keep our heads clear. Teresa is going to need our support. I heard from Nena that if you don't sign that paper, Teresa could be expelled from school." Carmen pulled out a chair and gently guided my mother to it. "I'm going to make some tilo tea to calm those nerves."

Mother sat in the chair with her head in her hands. She looked so tired and helpless, I went to her and wrapped my arms around her. Something was breaking inside me.

Seeing my mother defeated reminded me of Bola, one of the many cats Grandmother Petra had on the farm. Bola had given birth to three beautiful kittens, and when the kittens turned six weeks old, they were given away. I was there visiting when a neighbor farmer came to pick up the last one. Bola reacted with loud howling and meowing. The inconsolable mother ran around the house, sniffing corners, floors and walls, the search for her babies continuing for almost an hour. Exhausted, she settled down in the laundry room, next to the now-empty cardboard box that had served as the bed and refuge for her young ones. Like Bola, my mother was feeling pain, but hers was in anticipation of being separated from me. The government was taking me away, and there was nothing she could do to prevent it.

That evening when my father returned home from work, he cursed Fidel Castro and his barbudos. He ate a very small portion of his dinner, the burned garbanzo soup, rice and a salad of tomatoes and avocados. Then he went out to the porch and sat on the concrete floor, his back resting on one of the columns that held up the roof. He usually played dominos with his friends after supper, but that night the mood was different. He pulled a long cigar from the front pocket of his shirt, and then holding the perfectly rolled tabaco in a horizontal position in his right hand, he ran it across the tip of his tongue and bit off the pointed end with his teeth. The final part of the ritual was to light the cigar with the silver lighter my mother had given him on his birthday. I watched him for a few minutes from the window in the living room, feeling sad for him and for all of us.

"Qué pasa, Negrita?" he said to welcome me.

I was aware of other neighbors sitting close by on their porches as well, but for some reason we seemed to be invisible to them. I sat next to Father, inhaling the scent of gardenias on the tree that grew next to the house. He put his arm around my shoulders and as if reading my mind, he said, "Don't worry, Negrita. I'm okay; I just need some time to get used to the idea. I hate the thought of your working so hard in those tobacco and sugar fields. That's a man's job."

"Papi, everybody is going, all the schools in the country," I said, repeating the words I'd heard from my school principal that day. The principal had visited every classroom to talk about the "schools going to the countryside" project as some kind of voluntary and united effort to help the economy. She had said very little of the location where we were going, except that we would stay in a newly built compound situated near a tobacco plantation. The schedule was simple: We would work during the day and go to school in the evenings. Girls and boys would be placed in separate camp sites.

At first, these ideas were exciting to me and my classmates. We imagined the adventure of being together and talking for endless hours at night. But as the day went by and we had a chance to think about some of the details, such as not being able to come back home for a few days at a time, not having electricity or hot water to take showers, having to get up at sunrise . . . we began to feel scared. My friends, Marta, Mariluz and Coki, were worried about rats and lizards crawling into their beds and big bullfrogs jumping on their backs. I was envious of Jose, as he wasn't old enough to go. The cutoff was fourth grade.

"We have to get out of Cuba," Father said, throwing his cigar away. "These Communists are going to destroy us, bit by bit . . . "

"Pssssst, lower your voice, Papi, someone from the CDR might hear you."

"The hell with the CDR, I'm up to my nose with having to whisper. Everybody knows now that this is una mierda!

"I know exactly why they're doing this," he continued, finally lowering his voice. "They want to take you all away from us, from the parents, so that they can brainwash you, drill the communist doctrine into your young heads, morning, afternoon and night. This country was bad when Batista was in power . . . " He stopped when he realized his voice was getting loud again. "Anyway, it was bad. I hated Batista, but Castro is not any better. He betrayed us, he lied to us by promising a revolution and then turning around and selling us to the Russians. We are at the mercy of these antisocial and angry barbudos." He paused and we sat in silence for a few seconds. A neighbor from across the street, Paco, interrupted with an invitation for my father to join them in a game of dominos.

"Tomorrow," my father replied. He turned to me and said, "I promise you, Negrita, we are not going to be here for very long. And if these freedom flights don't get us out of here soon, I'm going to find a way to leave this rotten Communism. I promise!"

My father looked lost in his own thoughts and words. A man of many dreams, he was not defeated. He had a vision, a steady light in the darkness of all our losses. "When we get out of here," he continued, "we are going to go fishing every Saturday, just as we used to do. There are big rivers in El Norte. We are going to catch the biggest trout ever."

That image of catching a huge trout in a free country kept me going during the difficult weeks and years that followed. I would close my eyes and see my whole family fishing together on some emerald-green wild river, surrounded by gentle meadows filled with wild flowers.

When the day came for me to leave home for camp, Mami and Papi insisted on walking with me to the front of the school, where I would join the other students. Papi grabbed my muchila and Mami helped with an additional bag that she and Carmen had packed with food supplies they'd been gathering for days: Cuban crackers, bread, delicious frituras, a jar of papaya slices in heavy syrup and condensed milk. Together, we marched down the cobblestone street. I was wearing the work boots given to us by the government. My toes felt squished inside the stiff leather but I tried not to say anything to upset my parents. I figured that after a day of work and a couple of blisters, the army boots would soften. If not, rain and mud would eventually do the job.

Many children and their parents were already at the school doors when we arrived. The mood was a mix of many emotions. Some parents were trying to get last-minute instructions in: "Don't forget, Julito, to take your asthma medicine." "Arelia, keep a glass of water by your bed at night, just in case you get thirsty." My father stayed quiet, waiting, anticipating. My mother wanted to be reassuring: "We'll visit you every weekend."

Then the green army trucks—the monster vehicles charged with taking all of us girls and boys to our faraway destinations—arrived and lined up in front of the school. Some of the mothers broke down in tears, and the fathers became more somber. Suddenly I realized how serious the situation was. We were not going to summer camp or anything like it. Hard work was awaiting us together with strict discipline from our teachers and supervisors. My stomach began to tighten with fear, worry and sadness. I was already feeling homesick.

The school principal, Mrs. Garcia, a short round woman with a stern look in her eyes, called for our attention. "Compañeros, compañeras, this is a monumental time in our history. This day marks a new cycle of productive and cooperative work for all citizens of our country. Children will learn to understand responsibility and to develop a Communist consciousness for a better future. Our Revolution needs hands to work in the fields, so that we can improve our economy and show our Yankee neighbors that we can do it all alone, without their corrupted support."

It was almost impossible not to be swept away by the patriotic enthusiasm of the speech. For a brief moment, I felt infused with the seductive imagery of our heroic endeavor. I could see our school army as it marched through rows and rows of tobacco. Our beloved country would be saved from hunger and poverty. We, the children of this island, were the heroes.

"We are going to show los gusanos that we can bring Cuba to prosperity and economic stability," Mrs. Garcia continued.

Los gusanos, I thought to myself. What a term the Communists chose to describe those who refused to join their party. Whether I liked it or not, I was a gusana, by virtue of my parents' disagreement with the politics of Fidel Castro. It was not uncommon for children in school to call me and others like me "gusanos" whenever they wanted to pick a fight, or for teachers to use the word freely in the classroom as a form of punishment, like the time Mrs. Olivera, my political science teacher, discovered I hadn't completed an assignment . . .

"Teresa, where is your homework?" I'll never forget the cold look in Mrs. Olivera's eyes as she stood in front of the class with a pile of papers in her hands.

"I didn't do it," I said. My voice was shaky, and all eyes in the room turned to look at me. My face flushed.

"How come? Were the questions too difficult for you?" she asked with sarcasm.

"No."

"Well then, I'm going to read the first question of the assigment to you right now and I want you to give me an answer: During the initial phase of the Revolution, Fidel Castro and his government implemented measures to create a more egalitarian society. Name and describe these."

Of course, I knew the answer. One of those so-called measures was the Agrarian Reform. The sad faces of my grandparents Petra and José flashed in front of me, and my whole being refused to comply to Mrs. Olivera's orders. Perhaps it was my own way of rebeling against the loss of the farm. I decided that this woman, even if she was the teacher, was not going to make me answer.

"Come on, Teresa. I'm waiting."

I could feel Mrs. Olivera's impatience growing with my silence. The room was so quiet that the ticking of the clock on the wall seemed to fill the room as everyone waited for my response.

"Gusana! You're a gusana!" Mrs. Olivera suddenly yelled at me with a fury that left me cringing in my seat. I waited for her to send me to the principal's office, but instead she walked towards me and said, "You gusanos deserve to spend the rest of your lives washing cars for the Yankees." Then she went and sat at her desk.

Mrs. Garcia's emotional "Patria o' muerte, venceremos," brought me back to the present. She had ended her speech with the popular slogan used by Castro's revolutionaries, which means more or less, "Our country or death, we will win." A small group in the crowd shouted in response, "Viva la Revolución!" The rest of us were quiet. Dressed in work clothes—dark-gray twill pants, a light-gray shirt, and a red scarf tied around her neck—our principal commander ordered us to board the trucks by classroom numbers.

In spite of efforts to keep order, confusion took over. Parents and children went up and down the line of trucks, and teachers screamed at the top of their lungs in an attempt to regain control. One mother carrying a heavy canvas pack fell from a truck as she attempted to climb the wood railing around the truck bed. By the contorted expression on her face, the woman appeared to be in pain, but she refused to go to the hospital. "I want to see my daughter go," I heard her say.

Then it was time for my class to board the army trucks. I hugged my father first, a brief but tight hug. He turned away and wiped the tears from his face. Mother held on to me longer and kissed me on both cheeks. Shaking and crying, she managed to say, "Take good care of yourself." I pulled away and ran, knowing that if I allowed a few more seconds of this embrace, I was not going to have the strength to break away. I joined the other girls already standing on the the truck bed. I wanted to imagine this was a simple excursion to the countryside. I didn't want to think about tonight and the many nights awaiting me. My heart was bouncing against the walls of my chest like a ping-pong ball, and a big lump in my throat threatened to suffocate me.

A half hour later, the engines were running and our entire school was on wheels, ready to go on the road. Out on the streets, a mass of parents waved good-bye and cried. Inside the eight trucks, we children were screaming for our parents. Reality was sinking in, and we all were beginning to feel the separation. As soon as we were moving, I pushed through the bodies pressing against me and managed to get my face in between the bars of the railing. There were my parents, side by side, looking defeated. In a moment of despair, I wanted to get off the truck and run to their arms. Inside was a silent scream never to be uttered— *Mami, Papi, don't let them take me.* I waved good-bye, and soon their faces were blurred by the distance between us. A few seconds later I could no longer distinguish them in the crowd. I grabbed my pack from the floor and moved to a corner, where I sat quietly, tears running down my face.

A teacher named Aurora stood up in the very back of the vehicle bed and began to shout, "Viva la Revolución!" and some of the girls responded like a broken record, "Viva la Revolución!" I shrank into my corner, trying to become invisible. I didn't want anyone to see my pain or notice my fear. *It is going to be okay*, I said to myself. I turned the phrase into a mantra, but as time went by, rage began to choke off the words in my throat. I didn't want to be there or work in the tobacco fields. I didn't want to be away from my family.

I wanted to spit in the fat face of the principal and throw her out of the truck. A silent scream of rage was building in the pit of my stomach, just as a hurricane sits off the coast building up its ferocity. I was about to cover my ears so as not to hear any more Communist carajo, when I discovered Mariza, sobbing next to me. Trembling like a little mouse, she sat with her arms wrapped around her legs, her big brown eyes red from crying. I moved closer to her.

"I'm scared, I'm so scared," she said between sobs.

"I know, me too."

A fine rain was falling by the time we arrived at our destination.

The trip had taken at least two hours. We all stood up and watched the trucks lumber through the muddy red soil. From my place in the back, my eyes focused on the deep tire marks left behind in the road. When the rain had washed away the tracks that connected us to our town, there'd be no way for me to backtrack to my home.

A sudden jerk, the sound of grinding brakes and shouts of "We're here!" brought me back to the present. I looked around for the "newly built compound," the principal had mentioned, but saw only some empty barracks with walls built from yaguas, the prickly stalks at the base of palm tree leaves, and roofs of palm leaves. The four long structures had makeshift doors at each end and no windows that I could see. A center house or dining area, built of the same materials, was awaiting us with empty wood benches and tables. *Welcome to the Amazon*, I said to myself as I jumped to the muddy ground. My boots sank at least three inches into the soft clay as I struggled to keep my balance.

"What a mess!" I heard Mariza say right behind me.

"Line up, everybody!" yelled a high pitched voice from the other side of the trucks. I grabbed my pack and walked towards the voice, trying my best not to slip in the mud.

The welcome speech was more of the same revolutionary consciousness-raising. A bowlegged man dressed as a cowboy was introduced by Mrs. Garcia as Benito Cardona. He took his big hat off and said a few shy words about his duty as a field supervisor, meaning, he was going to teach us how to pick tobacco leaves; then he smiled, revealing two dark holes in his upper-front-teeth. His black moustache curved down as he said, "It's not going to be easy work, but I'll be here to help you." After shaking hands with Mrs. Garcia, the middle-aged man stepped to the side and allowed the principal to continue.

"And now we are going to tour the camp," said Mrs. Garcia, and she signaled us to follow her. Lined up like an army battalion, we followed our plump principal to the first barrack. The inside was dim and windowless, and the pungent smell of wet yaguas and moist dirt was nauseating. The dirt floor was muddy and rainwater sat in big puddles where the surface wasn't level. The combination of standing water and weather had spawned a swirling cloud of mosquitoes that eagerly attacked us.

As we walked through the barrack, the principal explained that the parallel beams along the sides were where we would hang our hammocks. I wondered where the hammocks were; maybe they had stored them someplace else. As if reading my mind, Mrs. Garcia added, "You'll be making your own hammocks as soon as we finish the tour." Some of the girls protested that they didn't know how to sleep in hammocks, and their complaint was met with, "You'll learn! This is not a vacation resort in the U.S.A."

Next on the tour were the restrooms and showers located about a hundred feet from the sleeping quarters. No creative architecture here, either, just a line of square outhouses, each consisting of four wood posts holding up burlap walls, the top open to the sky. In the center of each outhouse was a deep hole with a crude-looking seat made of concrete. No sign of toilet paper anywhere. I assumed we would have to come up with our own or find some other way to wipe our tender buttocks. Nothing at all surprising though: Toilet paper was one of those necessities Cubans were now used to doing without. Newspapers filled in for toilet paper under the Revolution.

The showers were no less primitive—a line of small rooms with dirt floors, again enclosed by stinky burlap. I wondered how we were going to keep our feet clean. I didn't see any water pipes or shower heads, which meant we were going back to basics: buckets of water and cans to pour the water over ourselves. The question was, where was the water? Later in the tour, we were informed of a small river running close by and a holding tank near the kitchen area.

Finally, we were directed to an area behind the dining facility where a big pile of wet burlap sacks awaited us. Mrs. Garcia stood there in front of us, looking at the brown stack. She raised her thick, dark eyebrows while grabbing her chin, as if she were trying to figure out what to do and what to say. Two teachers, Mrs. Molina and Mrs. Zanabría, joined the principal. Each grabbed a bag and proceeded to give a demonstration on how to build a hammock.

"First, try to find a sack that is somewhat dry." Smart talk from Mrs. Zanabría. I doubted if there was a single dry sack in that pile— the whole place was soaked in water.

"Then, run a piece of rope through the hemmed edge at each end of the sack . . . " Mrs. Molina took over from there.

The instructions were simple, but we were all too tired to carry them out. Mrs. Garcia and the teachers went around trying to help, but the reality was, no one really knew how to make a comfortable hammock out of such rough material. My father had taught me a different way to make a hammock. I sat there looking at the burlap sack, struggling with whether or not to offer my suggestion.

After a few minutes, I got up and went to Mrs. Garcia, who agreed to let me do it according to my father's instructions. But now I was faced with the problem of not having any tools. I wandered around the camp looking for something sharp I could use to cut off a couple of tree branches. After a long search, I found a rusted machete half-buried in the mud near one of the barracks, and using a piece of rock from the ground, I began sharpening the machete's dull edge.

The sound of the stone on the metal attracted the curiosity of a few of the girls, and almost immediately a circle of them gathered around me. Soon, I was in a position of teaching what I'd learned from my father. I was nervous and proud at the same time. First I cut two strong branches to put through each of the sack's hemmed edges. Then, rope was tied to the ends of each branch to stretch and open the hammock for a comfortable sleep.

I'd never been so thankful to my father for teaching me a skill. He was a practical man, so he had always taught Jose and me what he felt were useful and reliable tools for survival.

I remembered the bicycle he bought me for my fifth birthday. It was the color—blue—and style that boys rode, and it didn't have any training wheels. My mother wanted him to go back to the store and get another one but my father insisted, "Those training wheels can get in the way of her learning; she doesn't need them."

The next day, he and I drove out to the countryside, to a dirt road where I could learn to ride. Father lifted the bicycle from the back of his truck and placed it on the ground. "Here," he said with a smile on his face, "Get on it!" With a mixture of apprehension and excitement, I jumped up on the black leather seat, and grabbed hold of the handlebars. "The key to learning how to ride is not to be scared. If you fall, get up and try again," he said. "Now, let's go!" Grabbing the bike underneath the seat, he pushed it along, and I started pedaling.

For a few rounds, he held the bike with one hand as he ran next to me. When I had learned to keep my balance, he let go, and I found myself riding up and down the dirt road while he watched me gain confidence. Many times I fell, scratching my elbows and knees, but it wasn't a big deal, and my father was always there to help me up and get me back on the bike again.

As I tied the last rope to my hammock, I thought about what was awaiting me in this hellish camp. The reality of my situation hit me hard as I realized there were no training wheels here, no strong father's arms to catch me if I faltered. I looked ahead, far into the distance. My eyes met with rows and rows of green tobacco plants and dark clouds threatening more rain and wind. Never in my life had I felt so small, so alone, as I did that moment.

10

LIFE IN THE CAMP

*B*Y THE TIME we made it back to camp from the tobacco fields, it was close to noon. Exhausted and hungry from a long morning of hard work, I was looking forward to a hot meal. Mrs. Garcia instructed us to march down to the "cafeteria" and line up for food. My feet hurt from wearing the uncomfortable army boots—I could feel blisters eating at the soft skin of my soles—but I tried hard to ignore the pain while I waited my turn to pick up the aluminum tray with lunch at the kitchen window.

Those who had been first in line were already sitting at the tables. I wasn't surprised they weren't devouring their lunch. For days now we had had nothing but spoiled, poorly cooked food to eat. Today a slight commotion added a twist of interest. A girl named Carla, after taking a sip from the contents of her bowl, spit it up and screamed, "Coño, this tastes like pig's slop!" Immediately, she was ordered to eat in silence.

Finally, I was at the window, where a woman with a tired expression handed me my portion. I grabbed the tray and went to sit with my friends, who were picking at their food and complaining under their breath. And no wonder: The garbanzo bean soup had tiny yellowish worms floating on the surface, and the small portion of rice piled in a corner of the plate smelled like wet burlap sacks. In a separate compartment was a solitary piece of yuca, the only edible thing

111

on the tray. Perhaps this is a bad joke, I thought.

I ate the yuca and a couple of spoonfuls of rice, but the soup I couldn't touch. I tried to skim the worms from the top of the soup, but more of the little creatures kept coming up from the bottom of the bowl. I gave up when my stomach began to revolt. "Forget it! I can't swallow this garbage," I said in a low voice.

I closed my eyes to avoid looking at the food on my plate. This could only be a nightmare, and I wanted to believe that, soon, I would wake up to the smell of my mother's delicious fried plantains, and to the taste of black beans cooked by Carmen, as only she knew how to cook them, with a pinch of cumin and fresh cilantro from the garden.

A group of girls began banging their spoons on the metal trays and shouting, "We're hungry, we're hungry . . . " Their courageous act didn't last for long. In an authoritarian voice, Mrs. Zanabría ordered them to leave the dining area and wait outside. After the girls left, not a sound was heard in the dining hall but the buzz of flies above the girls' trays. Mrs. Zanabría punished the rebels by forcing them to wash dirty dishes.

After lunch, Mrs. Garcia gave a lengthy lecture reminding us of the camp rules and regulations. The list went on and on: "You must obey your teachers at all times. Any disobedience will be treated severely. Expulsion from the camp, with no possibility of a future return to school, will be considered in cases of anti-Communist acts or sabotage of the goals and purposes of this program . . . " Mrs. Garcia stopped briefly to look at a yellowish piece of paper, where she had written some notes.

"I have received several complaints of tardiness from the brigade leaders. Many of you are not getting up on time. Your wake-up call is at 5:00 a.m., and you have twenty minutes to get dressed and get in line. I won't accept any excuses. Bedtime is at nine o'clock. Everyone is expected to be in their hammocks with no flashlights on and no talking when the main propane lamp in your barrack is turned off by the designated teacher. Last night, a few of you were heard whispering and giggling. I want to warn you that if it happens again and we can't identify the offenders, the entire barrack will be punished."

Mrs. Garcia ended her lecture with, "Your brigade is now the only family you have, and therefore, you must work together for the best of all."

The day of our arrival, we had been divided into work brigades named after famous revolutionaries. I and twenty-four other girls were in the Ernesto Che Guevara brigade, headed by one of the teachers, Mrs. Elvira Cordoba. Now Mrs. Garcia ordered all the brigades back to their lodges to rest before the afternoon jornada.

I lay inside my primitive hammock, thinking, *If only Carmen could see this place, she would call for all her saints and spirits to help us!* I kept saying to myself, "Don't worry, any minute you're going to wake up and be home." I missed my comfortable bed and the privacy of my room, the large window facing the garden, where my mother spent her afternoons under the shade of the gardenia tree, doing her needlepoint or embroidery in the company of her friends. They would spend hours laughing about the past and old boyfriends, while sipping sweet Cuban coffee and savoring Carmen's delicious guava pasteles. It all seemed so far away now.

I had almost fallen sleep when I heard someone crying. Marta had fallen off her hammock while napping and was sitting on the dirt floor with her face in her hands.

"Marta, are you okay?" No answer, just more sobbing. Before I had a chance to get out of my hammock, I heard the voice of Mrs. Cordoba, our brigade leader, calling us to get in line outside. "Come on, Marta, let's get ready," I said.

"I don't want to go. I hate this place! I want to go back home! I want to sleep in my own bed."

I put my boots on and picked up my straw hat, hoping that Marta would get the message that this was no place to throw temper tantrums, that no one cared about feelings or fears. She didn't move.

"Come on, before Mrs. Cordoba comes back in here. You know she's tough and doesn't care a bit about how we're feeling." As I looked around, I saw Mrs. Cordoba coming towards us.

"What's the matter?" she asked, harshly. Marta didn't respond.

"She's not feeling well," I said.

"Well, what's the matter?" she asked Marta directly. Mrs. Cordoba placed her right hand on her hip and tilted her head so she could get a better look at Marta's face.

"I have a headache."

"How bad is it?" asked Mrs. Cordoba, tapping Marta on the knee with the tip of her boot.

"Pretty bad, it's pretty bad," Marta sobbed.

"Well, Marta, just in case you're trying to avoid work, let me tell you that there are consequences for such behavior." She knelt down and grabbed Marta's chin in her hand, lifting it so that she could look into my friend's eyes. "I want you out there right now, in line with everybody else, so move! And if you continue feeling sick, report to me. Maybe I can find you some kitchen work to do. Is that clear, little princess?"

"Yes," Marta said in a small voice. Mrs. Cordoba looked at me. "You move on, too, before I change my mind." She grabbed Marta by the arm and pulled her up from the ground. Marta didn't resist. I felt the heat of my anger rising, filling my brain and clouding my vision. I wanted to kick Mrs. Cordoba in the face.

As I was walking away, I heard Marta say, "Don't you have a bit of compassion?"

In a second, Mrs. Cordoba had pinned Marta by the shoulders against one of the barrack poles. This time Marta struggled to get away. "You're hurting me, let me go! I don't feel good. You can't force me to go to work." It was useless. For whatever reason, Mrs. Cordoba had to demonstrate her power, maybe as a way to intimidate the rest of us. My body shook with rage, but no one dared say anything, and soon, we were all marching down the road towards the tobacco plantation.

For ten minutes we walked in silence, but then Mrs. Cordoba attempted to lighten the mood by initiating a round of "Cuba sí, Yanqui no! Arriba la Revolución!" The hell with that, I said to myself. I was sick of the Revolution and the red Communist insignia, and sick of the pictures of Marx and Lenin in our history books.

My interest in Communist philosophy was as Carmen would say, me importa un comino, as big as a grain of cumin. All I knew was that the word "communist" meant lack of freedom. Coming to work in these fields was no act of patriotism. I didn't want to be there at all. I wanted to be home with my family, not picking tobacco leaves for the good of the country. Of course, our principal would say: "You are getting a free education." A big lie! Nothing was free, nothing!

At the plantation, each brigade was assigned to a working area. Two compañeros, male supervisors, refreshed our minds on how to pick the tobacco leaves from the four-to-five-foot-tall plants. Only the orange foliage was to be collected, the rest was to be left intact for a later harvest. We were to place the leaves carefully on top of each other and, when the pile was big enough, carry them to the end of the row. Later in the day, trucks would come around to transport the harvest to big barns where the tobacco was hung in bundles to air-cure.

At first, the task appeared to be simple, but after days of the same routine, my lower back ached from bending up and down and from carrying the stacks of tobacco leaves to the the road. And when my fingers rubbed the thick oval-shaped tobacco leaves with their velvety hairy covering, a viscous liquid oozed out. With the heat and the high humidity, my now-black skin itched like crazy. After one or two hours of work, the tarry ooze was all over my hands, arms, face and clothes, and I could feel it in my eyelashes, my ears, my hair, and taste its bitterness on my lips and tongue.

During the ten-minute break, I rushed to the water supply area, where clay canteens were kept. I poured the cool contents all over my mouth and face in an effort to rid myself of the acrid taste, but it didn't seem to help much. Then I ate my portion of a matahambre handed to us by Mrs. Cordoba. Matahambre, meaning "hunger killer," was a somewhat sweet pastry made of leftover dough, but those we got at the camp were often rancid. After a few bites, I was relieved to discover that the bitter flavor from the tobacco juice had disappeared, at least temporarily, replaced by the rank taste of the pastry.

The afternoon went by slowly. My body was about to give out from exhaustion when I heard Mrs. Garcia ordering all the brigades to stop. The long walk back to the camp was painful. My feet were raw from rubbing against the heavy stiff leather of my army boots. Every step I took was torture. Many of the girls were limping. Even Mrs. Cordoba had a weary rigid gait.

Taking showers required patience. Aluminum buckets and empty soup cans were available by the side of the water-holding tank. First we stood in line for the water, and then we formed another line to get in the shower area. Irritation would build, and girls would begin yelling, "Hey, hurry up! Get that line moving!" A large group protested the lack of soap and demanded that their brigade leaders do something about it. I was fortunate that my mother had packed a small bar for me.

In the middle of all this confusion, Sofía came running out of the shower naked, screaming, "there's a snake!" Many of the girls waiting for their turn joined in with their screams. We were not quite settled from this experience when a girl from my brigade came out yelling that a frog had jumped on her back while she was taking her shower. The excitement lasted until Mrs. Zanabría threatened to make us all take second showers if we didn't behave. By that point, some girls refused even to go in the shower area, and at least half of the girls didn't get showers that day.

Dinner was a repeat of the noon meal—the wormy garbanzo bean soup, stinky rice and a piece of yuca. The only addition was a spoonful of the canned beef that Cubans called carne rusa. The meat, packed in a greasy reddish sauce, had recently been introduced into Cuba by the Russians. Rumors on the island were that the so-called Russian meat was horse meat. At that moment, I couldn't have cared less whether it was horse, cow or even cat. I was starving, and the carne rusa was the only portion of our meal that was tasty.

I ate my small ration slowly, savoring it, making it last as long as possible, as if I would be able to fool my hungry stomach. Marta came and sat next to me. She was carrying a small brown bag in addition to her food tray. She read the curiosity in my eyes and said, "Here, take one, but only one." She threw the bag in front of my tray. "Galletas Cubanas!" Cuban crackers—white, round, about the size of my palm— were crunchy and could be eaten with almost anything, including carne rusa.

"Thanks," I said, moved by her kindness. Galletas were worth gold in our starving camp.

"Now, we are even," Marta said. "You helped me build my hammock the way your father taught you. Now my father can return the favor. Every day he manages to sneak a few crackers here and there in his pockets or inside his work-clothes bag."

"That's great," I said, but I felt sad that Marta's father had to risk his own job to bring home a few Cuban crackers for his children.

After dinner was school time. We marched down the dirt road, about a half mile from camp, to an empty tobacco-drying barn. The sixty-foot-high barn was spooky in the darkness. Like the barracks, the barn walls were sheathed with yaguas and the roof was made of the traditional guano yarey, fan-shaped leaves taken from a species of palm that grows only seven to eight feet high.

Inside this monster of a barn, wide beams made it seem even bigger. Waiting for Mrs. Cordoba to light the propane lamp, I couldn't help but imagine the many ghostly entities inhabiting the barn's dark corners. It didn't help any when bats came streaming out of those corners making weird high-frequency pulsing sounds.

Improvisation continued to be the theme: With no chairs to sit on, we searched for substitutes. By good fortune there was a pile of wood that we turned into primitive benches, although some of the girls chose to sit on the dirt floor, rather than trust the strength of our creation. It took us at least a half hour to settle into the evening class. We were tired, and the temperature inside the barn was at least ninety degrees. That, combined with the humidity and the strong smell of the cured tobacco hanging from the cujes, was enough to put a horse to sleep. I, myself, was falling into a light trance. I struggled to keep my eyes open and concentrate, but my mind kept drifting into dreams.

I found myself traveling in my imagination to a foreign land, near the ocean. I was talking, in a different language, with other children, and we were laughing and playing. I figured this place must be California. My father had talked so much about it—a beautiful country across the ocean where people were free to do anything they wanted and where they could talk without fear of being thrown in jail. I thought of my cousins Jorge and Juana living in Los Angeles and attending a regular school, not having to work in the fields like me. Occasionally they wrote letters in broken Spanish and sent us pictures of their elegant home and their new cars and bicycles.

"Hey, wake up Teresa, it's time to go back!" Marta was calling me back from my dream.

By the time we got to the road, it had begun to drizzle. Dense clouds covered the stars and moon, and the air was thick with humidity and the smell of wet grass. Tired. I was so tired, I couldn't think clearly. The thought of my comfortable bed, with its firm mattress and clean, soft white sheets made me homesick.

Back in the barrack, I slipped into my hammock, twisting and turning like a snake to find a comfortable position. Though my whole being felt heavy and tired, my mind was too busy with worries and fears for me to sleep. I wanted to escape into the world of dreams, but I was too keenly aware of the very real smells and sounds around me—the pungent smell of the burlap sacking, the calls of crickets and frogs, the snoring and deep breathing of the other girls, the hoots of an owl.

Rain was falling hard on the roof now; only the cracks of lightning and the rumble of thunder masked its drumming. For a moment I felt the urge to run away from this awful place. I just wanted to run and run under the rain, like a wild horse, to feel free again. It was hard to breathe; I wanted to scream and wake up the whole camp, but all I could do was cry.

But instead, I could feel heavy iron bars against my chest, pressing on me, making me gasp for air. The barrack was turning into a dungeon, filled with the monsters of my imagination and terror. I slipped from my hammock and grabbed the khaki pants and shirt I'd left hanging from a nail on a nearby beam. I tried not to make any noise as I dressed slowly. My boots, covered with mud from the day of work, were still wet and cold. I wrapped them in a dirty shirt and then looked around to make sure no one was awake. I took the flashlight from under my pillow and began to walk towards the door, taking small steps, careful not to bump into anything. Then I realized I needed my bag and some water if I was serious about escaping to the nearest town. I was in the process of packing some food when I was blinded by the bright beam of a flashlight.

"Where are you going?" It was the voice of Mrs. Cordoba. My heart leaped. "Where are you going?" My body shook, and my tongue felt heavy and thick. I couldn't answer.

The propane lamp was lit, and I found myself staring at Mrs. Cordoba, who was dressed in a black-and-white striped nightgown that made her look just like a zebra. If I hadn't been so scared, I would have laughed. By now, most of the girls in the barrack were awake and looking at me with wide eyes.

"Answer me! Where were you going?" Mrs. Cordoba said again, but this time, she grabbed my bag from the floor and began to inspect its contents.

"I was going to the bathroom," I lied, knowing the lie wouldn't work.

"You don't take a backpack full of clothes to go to the bathroom in the middle of the night." She pulled my belongings out of the beige canvas bag and threw them on top of the hammock. "You were running away! Teresa was running away!" Mrs. Cordoba thundered so that everybody could hear. "You little gusana! Everybody wake up, wake up! I want to show you what happens to anyone who tries to run away from here." The teacher walked around the barrack getting the girls out of their hammocks and screaming, "Get up! Come and see what happens to traitors!" enticing them to join her.

I looked around, searching for some small window in time and space that would allow me to escape. Under the light of the propane lamp, the faces of the other girls, maybe fifty in total, appeared distorted, or maybe it was the combined effect of my fear and their fear that somehow cast shadows over all of us.

"Come with me!" Mrs. Cordoba ordered. She walked towards the door, and I followed without protest. All the girls fell in behind me. Walking behind this woman was like being too near an erupting volcano. I felt that the hot lava and ashes spitting from her mouth were going to consume me any minute now. I had no idea what she had in mind, but I was confused by her viciousness and afraid of being the target of Communist rage towards the gusanos.

Outside, the rain had let up some. The air was cool and the night blanketed with clouds. I was comforted by the familiar smell of wet grass and the sweet scent of wild jasmine and tobacco blossoms coming from the fields near the barracks. For a moment all my fears disappeared as my shoeless feet touched the earth. "La tierra es la madre," Grandmother Petra had told me once when we were picking fresh corn for dinner. Thinking of that I didn't feel as lonely. The earth was the mother of all, and therefore I felt protected.

"Take your clothes off!" Mrs. Cordoba ordered. "Can you hear me? Take your clothes off!" I tensed all the muscles in my body, trying to contain my rage and humiliation. Behind me, I heard Marta and other friends like Mariza and Coki protesting. "Mrs. Cordoba, don't do that to her." They were ignored. "Take your clothes off," she ordered. "You're going to run naked around the camp ten times. So come on! Come on! Take everything off!"

In the beam of Mrs. Cordoba's flashlight, with everyone's eyes on me, I took my clothes off—first my khaki pants, then my white panties and finally the blue cotton shirt. It was silent except for an occasional nervous giggle. I hated Mrs. Cordoba so intensely I wanted to rip off her clothes and shred them to pieces.

Standing naked, I looked at those in the group watching me. Those who were my friends had compassion and pain for what was happening to me. Then there were the young Communists who sympathized with Mrs. Cordoba and the system. They were probably enjoying my bad luck, savoring every bit of it. Suddenly self-conscious and vulnerable, I embraced my body in a shy gesture to protect my just-blooming breasts. A few raindrops, like silvery pearls, fell from the sky, refreshing my skin, washing away my sorrow and the deep scorn I felt for Mrs. Cordoba.

From the distance came the haunting sound of an owl. Carmen had once told me, "Owls announce death," but images of the night bird looking right into my eyes quickly replaced the fear, and I saw myself becoming the owl, opening my wings and flying, flying high to the nearest ceiba tree where no one could reach me.

"Okay, Teresa, we are waiting for you to start running." Mrs. Cordoba's voice brought me back from my fantasy. I realized I was no hero changing into an owl, but neither was I going to die. I would not give Mrs. Cordoba the satisfaction of seeing me cry or break down in front of the group. I was going to run, and I was going to do it with dignity. Once more I heard the owl calling, and my feet began to move on the ground like a jittery horse ready for the race.

I started running. Some of the girls cheered me on, clapping and yelling, "Come on, Teresa, you can do it! Go! Go!" For a brief moment, I felt like a marathon runner. The soles of my feet hurt as I stepped on small rocks, stones, twigs, even pieces of wire and nails left over from the construction of the barracks, but I kept going in the dark, hoping not to find anyone in my way. The circumference of the camp was maybe a quarter of a mile, so ten times around made a run of about two and half miles. I was confident I could do it.

I imagined that I was running home from the camp, and a surge of energy and strength filled the muscles of my lower body. Just the thought of seeing my family again was invigorating enough to take me around a hundred times. I could hear Carmen's voice saying, "niña, what are you doing running naked?" I could feel my mother's arms around me and hear Papi's reassuring voice: "Don't worry, Negrita, soon we'll be in El Norte." And Jose asking me to play another game of Parcheesi. Oh, how I missed them!

Running and running, losing track of time and space, it just felt so good to run. My feet no longer hurt, and every step was a leap to freedom. The landscape changed, and instead of the barracks there were golden rolling hills dotted with elegant royal palms, blossoming piñon trees, the tall umbrella-like atejes with their bright red seeds, a delight for the birds. The fragrance of the wild campanillas, white and purple bell-shaped flowers that grew on vines, was sweet to my senses. Out in the distance, coming towards me, I saw a white stallion galloping, almost flying, in my direction. We were moving directly towards each other. Oh Virgencita! I thought to myself, *We are going to collide.* A few seconds later as I looked down I could see my feet were the hooves of the horse. What a joy! My body was as light as a feather. I was the white stallion!

Blinded by a flash of light, I came to a sudden stop. Mrs. Cordoba's face emerged from the shadows. "Ten rounds, that's enough," she said, and handed me my clothes. "That should teach you a good lesson." Then, she disappeared inside the barrack. Marta was the first one to hug me. Lucia brought me some water in a metal canteen, and Coki helped me put my shirt on.

"That bitch, she is going to pay for this!" said Mariza, pointing in the direction Mrs. Cordoba had gone.

Nearby a small group of girls waited for the opportunity to get closer. One of them was Angela Jimenes, the head of the UJC, Unión de Jóvenes Comunistas, in our school.

"Mira, see who's hovering around like a hawk," Marta said, loud enough so that Angela would hear her.

"Leave it alone, Marta, we don't need any more problems," I said, walking towards the barracks.

"Traitor!" Angela yelled at me. "You're a gusana and a traitor, just like your whole family of ricachones." She meant wealthy imperialists.

"Don't listen to her," intervened my friend Coki. "She's trying to make more trouble for you, Teresa."

"Your grandfather is a thief!" Angela screamed, and that did it for me. I ran up and grabbed her by the collar of her sky-blue militia shirt. She was at least a couple of inches taller than I was, but at that moment, with all the anger that had been boiling in me for hours, I was a giant.

"You're going to eat your words. I'm sick and tired of you people attacking my family. Leave them alone!" I yelled, pushing her with such force that she fell to the ground. The other girls in her group tried to defend her, but Angela stopped them. "This is between me and her," she said, getting up and brushing the dirt from her jeans.

Soon Angela and I were surrounded by a circle of silent girls. Without much warning, Angela hit me right in the face with her closed fist. That set me into a hurricane of emotions. Furious, I hit her back and broke a blood vessel in her nose. A stream of blood ran down from her right nostril. Then Angela kicked me hard in the stomach, leaving me gasping. I was ready to punch her again when a strong hand snatched me from behind. It was Carmita, one of the tallest girls in the camp. We had been friends and neighbors since early childhood.

"Stop this nonsense!" she yelled and got between Angela and me. "Do you guys want Mrs. Cordoba to come back and have another round of races around the camp?"

I was still recovering from Angela's kick so Carmita's appearance was kind of a blessing. She had a reputation in school of being a tough fighter and no one ever messed with her.

"Come on you two, shake hands, and let's get some sleep," Carmita said, grabbing my hand and Angela's hand. I pulled mine away as fast as I could. No way would I shake hands with that girl. Angela looked at me defiantly. Then, she wiped the blood from her face with a towel handed to her by one of her friends. I turned my back and walked away.

In my hammock, I waited for Mrs. Cordoba or Angela to come get me. In the quiet darkness of the night, I listened to the drum of my heart, remembering what Carmen had taught me about calling the spirits with the toques, different drum beats. I needed all the help I could get from that other world to protect me. Judging by the way Angela had looked at me, the battle wasn't over. Sooner or later she was going to get revenge. I tuned into the sounds inside and began to fall deeper and deeper into the sleeping-place Carmen had taken me on restless nights. "Breathe, niña, breathe. Yemayá is watching you, waiting for you to take you in her arms," she would tell me. "Don't be afraid, niña, just breathe and listen to your heartbeat, let your own little tumba take you to the watery house of nuestra señora Yemayá."

A flash of lightning illuminated the night; then the sound of thunder came rumbling from the distance. I breathed deeply, feeling comforted by the watery embrace of Yemayá. The rain started up again, the raindrops drumming their own tune on the roof of our barrack.

"Negrita, you have been blessed by thunder." I closed my eyes and heard the words of Grandmother Patricia. When I opened them I saw a tall, muscular black man standing next to my hammock. With a red cape over his shoulders, his face painted with red and white stripes and a long sword hanging from a leopard skin belt around his waist, he looked like an African warrior. The man reached over me and rattled a maraca from my head to my toes. When he finished, he stepped back and began to dance. Not sure whether this was a dream or reality, I rubbed my eyes. When I opened them again, he was gone. The sound of thunder rumbled in the distance as the storm began to move away. I heard the whisper of a voice in my ear saying, "Changó. His name is Changó."

11

LAS CAPITANAS

*I*N THE STILL MOMENTS before the morning wake-up call, I lay awake in my hammock, brooding about Mrs. Cordoba and Mrs. Garcia. They were so different from Carmen, from my mother, from my grandmothers, Petra and Patricia. The mere sight of them walking towards me filled me with anxiety, and my body would tense in anticipation of their orders and reprimands.

The two women, las capitanas, did nothing but berate us, lecture us and remind us of the dire consequences we'd face if we didn't follow their rules. They were like army captains, and we were their soldiers, under their absolute command. We were also their milk cows, their working mules. They moved us around from pasture to pasture whenever they wanted. Locked inside this big corral that was the camp, we had no say about anything. The only things that mattered were whether we were following their strict orders and how much work was getting done in the fields. There was no time to play, to read books, no time even to think. And there was no room to be who we really were, young girls struggling to survive.

The morning after my nighttime run, I was not surprised to find Mrs. Cordoba just outside my barrack, leaning against the door frame, her hands inside the pockets of the olive-green pants of her military fatigues. According to school gossip, she had been part of the Campaña de Alfabetización, during the first year of the Revolution. Hundreds of youngsters had hiked to the most remote places in the Sierra Maestra mountains, with the goal of teaching the illiterate population how to read and write. Now Mrs. Cordoba wore her faded veteran uniform for a different kind of mission.

"Good morning," she said, twisting her lips and frowning, which made her appearance even more forbidding. Mrs. Cordoba was not an attractive woman. Old acne scars pocked her face, and her collar bones jutted out from an ungainly six-foot rawboned frame.

"Good morning," I answered and continued towards the water-tank area. I heard Mrs. Cordoba's steps behind me. At the water tank, I ignored her and focused on washing up.

"Did you sleep well last night?" she asked. I started to walk away, but she grabbed my arm and forced me to look at her. "Didn't you sleep well last night?" she repeated, more loudly. I held her gaze till she pushed me away. "Look, you're not acting very smart. I can get you into a lot of trouble. You and your whole family of gusanos!"

That touched an open sore, and I clenched my hands. "Why are you treating me this way?" I asked, looking into her eyes.

"Because you tried to run away last night, just like all those gusanos escaping to the United States. They're traitors to the Revolution! What do you think is going to happen to you there? Do you think you're going to have it easy in Yankeeland? Is that it?" Mrs. Cordoba's face was red and distorted. I stayed silent.

One of my friends, Silvia, tried to intervene: "Please, Mrs. Cordoba, leave her alone! It's not her fault her parents want to leave the country!"

"Shut up! What do you know!" And she kicked a small rock in the air with her right boot. She turned to me again and poked me in the chest. "You're going to be sorry, because money doesn't grow on trees over there like you gusanos think, and without the language you'll end up washing dishes."

Mrs. Cordoba's hatred cut through my flesh to the bone. I regretted my behavior of the night before; it was a stupid, dangerous move to try to escape the camp.

"Yes, Teresa, I can't wait till I see you all become servants of the

Yankees. It is about time you wealthy rats got a taste of oppression." Her words echoed inside my head.

"Times have changed, and now we are all equal and the land belongs to the people." No one around the water tank said a word. I didn't want to listen anymore. I thought to myself, *I'm a rock, with no ears to hear her words, with no mouth to express my anger towards her.*

"Your grandparents used to own half of the town. When I was a child, your grandfather José went by my house every afternoon. I saw him riding his Arabian horse like a big tycoon, proud, wearing a clean starched guayabera and shiny leather boots imported from Italy. Where was this elegant rich man going?" Mrs. Cordoba laughed. "Later, when I was old enough to know, I discovered that Don José was on his way to see the town's prostitute!"

"Stop!" I screamed, covering my ears. "Stop . . . stop! Leave me and my family alone."

"Yes, Mrs. Cordoba, leave her alone!" several girls pleaded in chorus.

"Mrs. Cordoba, what's going on?" It was Mrs. Garcia, walking towards us. "What's everybody doing here? It's past the line-up time for breakfast." I began to tremble, anticipating more trouble.

"Teresa tried to run away from camp last night. Fortunately, I was awake and caught her in the act."

"There will be consequences for your behavior," Mrs. Garcia said to me but before I could respond, Mrs. Cordoba took the lead.

"Teresa received her punishment last night."

"Without my approval?" asked Mrs. Garcia, with a tone of alarm.

"I didn't think it was necessary."

"Mrs. Cordoba, this is a serious matter. I'd like to discuss this incident in my office." Then, she turned to the circle of girls around us. "You all go to breakfast right now! Teresa, you may go, too."

I figured this might be my only chance to get my side of the story in: "Mrs. Garcia, she made me run naked and without shoes."

Mrs. Garcia turned to Mrs. Cordoba. "What is she talking about? What kind of . . . "

"She's lying! I'll explain the whole thing to you." Mrs. Cordoba interrupted.

126

"I'm no liar, Mrs. Garcia. Ask the other girls. They saw me running naked in the rain."

I heard Coki speak up: "Yes, we saw her running."

"This is embarrassing, Mrs. Cordoba. Let's go into my office. Teresa, I'll talk to you later."

My friends gathered around me at the entrance to the dining area. "Hey, good job, Teresa!" said Coki as she hugged me and patted my back. "That Mrs. Cordoba's a bitch with no heart. She's a bitter old maid," Coki continued vehemently, perhaps remembering the last time she got an "F" in Mrs. Cordoba's class. It was good to have my friends' support, but I was still nervous about having to meet with Mrs. Garcia.

We went in and sat down to our morning meal of watery milk made from powder that tasted like chalk, and a slice of bread. No butter or anything on it, just plain white bread. But I was so immersed in worrying about my meeting with Mrs. Garcia, I ate my portion without saying a word.

Mrs. Lopez, the geography teacher, came and sat next to me. A mulata with cinnamon skin and expressive green eyes, she was soft-spoken, unlike many Cubans, who have a tendency to speak fast and loudly. It was known in school that Mrs. Lopez was not a member of the Communist Party, and that because of her affiliations with "unwanted elements," meaning friends who were out of the country and with whom she kept in correspondence, she had been warned by the Department of Education that she might lose her job. In other words there were to be no more letters with those on the other side of the "red curtain."

"Teresa," Mrs. Lopez said, "If you need someone to talk to, please look for me. I'm in Barrack No. 2." She squeezed my arm gently.

"Thanks, Mrs. Lopez. I'll keep that in mind," I said politely, knowing I would probably never ask for her help.

The way I was feeling, I wasn't sure whom I could trust or who might gossip a little too much and get me in trouble. This camp was no different from the rest of the country, where innocent people were thrown in jail. My uncle Elio was one of them. He'd been sent to Isla de Pinos, one of the biggest political prisons in Cuba, immediately after Castro's triumph. No one in Cabaiguán could believe it when he was given a sentence of thirty years for the "crime" of having been a member of Batista's police.

During his first year behind bars, Elio almost lost his left leg from a severe beating he received from a guard. Not feeling well one morning, my uncle hadn't been able to get up and go to work. The watchdog in military clothes loosed his fury on Elio's body, breaking bones, tearing his skin and flesh. He kicked and kicked till his thirst for blood was satisfied, and then he walked away from the cell, leaving his bleeding prey there for several days without food, water or care.

Well, I was not about to take my chances with Mrs. Lopez, though it was comforting to know someone cared enough to risk sitting next to me this morning. Not all teachers were as bad as Mrs. Cordoba. Knowing that gave me the hope and strength I needed to go and meet with Mrs. Garcia.

"Come in, Teresa. Please close the door after you," Mrs. Garcia said from behind the old table that served as her desk. Though she looked and sounded rather intimidating in her olive-green khakis, black army boots, short haircut and coarse voice, Mrs. Garcia's big almond-shaped brown eyes had a warm expression. It was hard for me to read her, and that made me even more nervous.

The administrative office was a small bungalow built of royal palm tree shingles. Piles of textbooks and boxes were everywhere. Pictures of Fidel Castro, Che Guevara and Lenin hung on the walls. Mrs. Garcia signaled me to sit across from her on a wood bench.

"I've talked to Mrs. Cordoba, and now I want to hear your side of the story. Teresa, I've known you since you were in first grade. You were always an excellent student, never a troublemaker." She opened a beige folder and took her time reading through the pages in it. "Top grades, good in sports . . . Well, I was surprised when I found out the details of last night's incident." She threw the file inside a box and shifted on her chair so that she faced me. "This could have serious consequences for you and for your family."

Here we go again with my family, I thought. She continued: "I care about your family. Even though we have different political affiliations, our families have known each other for generations."

There was something about this woman that truly enjoyed giving speeches even when I was her only audience. I realized she was not really interested in hearing my part of the story.

"You know how important it is, Teresa, for our Revolution and for Cuba that we all share responsibility and cooperate with the process of solving our economic problems." Mrs. Garcia paused and looked at me for some reaction. I didn't say a word. All the "we" this and "we" that irritated me.

"Anyway, you know, we all have choices," she said walking to the window. She took a quick look out in the direction of the dining area, where kitchen workers were cleaning the tables, and then turned back to me. "Do you really want to leave this country, Teresa?"

I was taken by surprise. She didn't wait for my response.

"As I said we all have choices. And you certainly can make your own decision whether to leave this country with your parents or stay here and help our Revolution grow. Your parents don't have the right to make that decision for you." Mrs. Garcia moved away from the window and sat back down on the chair behind the table. "Have your parents told you the truth about what goes on in America? Have they talked to you about the brutal treatment of black people and people of other colors?" This time she waited for my answer.

"No, they haven't," I replied, hoping that would do it.

"Of course," she said with sarcasm. "They don't bother to share the facts, just like all those Cubans who left right after the Revolution. They send color pictures of their new cars, big homes . . . and so on, but what they don't say in their letters or show in the photos is the kind of life they have, working for low wages in restaurants, washing dishes or cleaning floors. Factory work is also a prize for those in exile."

Mrs. Garcia's face was turning red. Her nostrils flared, like those of a bull ready to attack the matador. *That's it, a matador* . . . I was a graceful matador trying to skillfully avoid the sharp horns of the beast. I could even hear the olés from the crowd and see the waving white handkerchiefs.

I knew Mrs. Garcia was probably right about the racial problems in the United States. But after experiencing this camp from hell, I thought any place in the world would be better than Cuba. At least children in El Norte were able to attend regular schools and be with their families. Occasionally at home, when the weather was clear, we could tune in to some of the American television channels in Miami. I was sad when I saw children in commercials playing with new toys. I particularly loved the doll that talked and cried like a real baby. I had never had anything like it, as toys had disappeared from the stores shortly after the Revolution. Sometimes at Christmas we had toys, but our parents stood in lines in front of the store for days to get them.

"Teresa." Mrs. Garcia's voice brought me back from my thoughts.

"Yes, Mrs. Garcia."

"I don't wish to hear any more complaints about your behavior. Is that clear? Any more complaints could cost you and your family the permission to leave the country."

"Yes, Mrs. Garcia."

"You may go now."

I stepped quickly out of the room, scared that Mrs. Garcia would change her mind and call me back.

That evening, outside my barrack after dinner, I saw someone walk towards the restrooms who reminded me of my best friend Mariluz. She'd had to stay behind in town to recover from surgery on her arm, and I really missed her company and her sense of humor. Extroverted and full of energy, Mariluz could always delight us and herself with the most recent jokes and funny stories, or the famous Pepito chistes.

"Pepito" is the stereotypical Cuban character used to make fun of the daily experiences of Cuban life—both the trivial and the painful. Pepito helps Cubans vent their anger and frustration while getting a good laugh. I remembered the Pepito joke that Mariluz told us right before her surgery: A teacher asked her students, "Where do babies come from?" One child answered, "From Paris." Another boy raised his hand and said, "The stork brings them home." When the teacher asked Pepito, he answered, "My family is so poor, my father has to make them."

Mariluz was a gifted storyteller, a good cuentera. So when the girl turned around and I got a better look at her face, I was disappointed to see it wasn't my friend.

"Hey, watch where you're going," I had been so absorbed in my thoughts I'd almost bumped into Julia from Barrack No. 3. As I turned to apologize, I saw a group of about fifteen girls gathered outside Mrs. Garcia's office.

"What's going on?" I asked Julia.

"They're protesting. Mrs. Garcia refused to take Luz to the doctor in town."

"I know Luz. What's the matter with her?"

"Well . . . she's been vomiting and has had diarrhea all day, and she's running a fever." As Julia walked away, she expressed my feelings exactly: "You know . . . this is a crazy place."

I went inside my barrack, lay down in the rough hammock and closed my eyes. The day's events were running through my mind like an endless film, when suddenly the "film" was broken by commotion outside.

"Esa hija de buena madre!"

It was the protesters coming back, trumpeting like a herd of angry elephants as they spit out their anger about Luz.

I recognized Mariza's voice: "These teachers don't care about our health or shit!"

The group got quieter as it got closer, and then I could only hear whispers coming from the barrack entrance. Exhausted from my punishment the night before and the day's hard work, I put the pillow over my head to shut out the whispering and fell into a deep sleep.

Loud screams and laughter startled me awake. As I looked out from my hammock, something that felt like a small pebble hit me in the forehead. Suddenly girls were running around and pillows and shoes were flying through the air. I heard Mrs. Zanabría yelling. "You girls, stop! What do you think you're doing? Stop! Right now!" she ordered many times, without any success.

Abruptly, the propane lamp was turned on, and behind it, glowing red with fury, loomed the face of Mrs. Garcia. Then I heard the sound of broken glass, followed by total darkness. Someone must have thrown a rock at the lamp. The enraged principal roared "Stop!" but was ignored.

Mrs. Garcia ran outside shouting for help, and teachers from the barrack next door came running with their flashlights and propane lamps. By the time the barrack had light again, some of the girls had managed to sneak into their hammocks and were pretending they had been asleep when the uproar began.

"Everybody, get up and line up outside!" shouted Mrs. Garcia. Several of us who had not been involved protested, but it didn't help. In various states of undress we were marched outdoors.

"Girls, this is the worst behavior I've ever witnessed as a school principal." Mrs. Garcia said, and stood in front of us, fists on her wide, round hips. In spite of the darkness, her eyes were like balls of fire, ready to turn us all into ashes. "You should all feel ashamed. A good revolutionary would never conduct herself in such a manner."

Silence. No one dared say a word or make a move.

"All weekend passes are canceled. No one is leaving camp, and no visitors will be allowed," Mrs. Garcia said authoritatively. "You'll use this time to reflect and to do schoolwork."

No complaints, not even a sound. I'd been anticipating the moment—dreaming about it all hours of the day—when I'd finally see my family again. This was so unfair!

"Now, go back to your beds quietly. Any more problems and you'll be up all night doing work in the kitchen." With that threat, Mrs. Garcia stormed into her office and slammed the door.

The days after the barrack incident went by slowly. Heavy rain interrupted our labor out in the fields, but it didn't free us from having to work. We were taken instead to the drying barns, where we sat for long hours running large needles through the tobacco leaves so that they could be strung and then hung to dry. The smell of tobacco and bat guano was nauseating, and frequently I would have to stand at the door for a few minutes and breathe fresh air to clear my head and calm my stomach.

We worked through the weekend, from five in the morning till six or seven in the evening. Pressure mounted to save the already harvested tobacco from the rain damage. Piles and piles of the leaves were brought by truck and dumped at the barns for us to take care of. In my dreams, an avalanche of tobacco leaves threatened to overwhelm me, and I would wake up in the darkness, sweating and frightened from trying to escape.

If I couldn't get back to sleep, I'd lie in my hammock, thinking of evenings back home, when we kids would walk to the park or to the movie theater, which showed old Mexican movies—heroic charros rescuing beautiful señoritas from the hands of los malvados. In these movies, famous singers like Javier Solis and Jorge Negrete sang romantic songs to their girlfriends under the moonlight.

I thought of the farm and of my cousin Ramón, Jose and I riding our horses, pretending to be cowboys and Indians. We'd make bows and arrows from the flexible branches of the guava tree and headdresses from wild turkey feathers. When we tired of that game, we'd swim in the cool waters of the nearby river, sliding on yaguas from the top of a hill all the way down and into the river. When we were hungry, we would eat right from the trees, depending on the season and what was ripe—mangoes, guavas, oranges, the round, yellow pumarosas with their sweet perfume and taste. My favorites were the green-and-white pulpy chirimoyas, but the velvety, sour-fleshed mamoncillos, which grew in grapelike bunches, were a treat during the hot summers.

Mariluz arrived in camp early Monday, just in time to join us for breakfast. Afterwards, bubbly as usual, she ran up and down the barracks, hugging friends and handing us letters she'd brought from our parents.

"I didn't expect you to be here this soon!" I blurted out, hugging her carefully so as not to hurt her arm, which still had a cast on it from the elbow down.

"Well, I was beginning to get bored all by myself in town, so I begged my doctor to sign the permission slip."

"You're crazy! This is the closest thing to hell!" I said, trying not to raise my voice.

"I'd rather be here with all my friends. I was lonely in town. You should see how sad el Paseo looks with only old people sitting there staring at the sky. The entire neighborhood is like a funeral home. No fun! I couldn't handle it anymore."

"But . . . " I pointed to her cast. "You can't work with your arm like that!"

"Who says I came here to work? I'm your entertainer. The mood in this camp definitely needs some uplifting." She moved back and struck a pose, just like a model would in front of an audience.

"Entertainer? Wait till Mrs. Garcia hears that. We have enough problems the way things are. Thanks, we don't need any more," I said and began to walk towards the door.

"Hey! Don't go yet. I have a letter from your mother and some pasteles de guayaba that Carmen sent you." She waved the letter and a small brown bag at me with her good hand. "By the way, later can you help me tie my hammock next to yours?"

"Sure," I said, grabbing the letter and bag from her hand.

She patted me on the shoulder and walked away. I sat in the hammock and carefully opened the envelope. My hands shook as I unfolded the thin white sheet of stationery, and all the emotions I'd been trying to keep down since leaving my mother's arms welled up in my throat when I saw her beautiful handwriting. I kissed the paper and then began to read:

> *Dear Teresa,*
>
> *We miss you so much. Every night before going to sleep, we ask Saint Lazarus and our Virgencita de la Caridad to watch over you, to give you strength. It's been hard for me to think of you, my little girl, working so hard in the fields, under the hot sun, burning your tender skin and tearing your hands with the difficult labor. I wish I could be the one who was there and not you. I can't wait till that day when we can all be together again. Jose and Carmen send you lots of kisses and hugs. They constantly talk about you and remember the good moments. Grandmother Petra is making some fresh cheese for you, and Jose has been saving his share of galletas cubanas for when you come home to visit us.*
>
> *Teresa, mi hija, be careful what you say and do in the*

camp. Every day, we hear in the news about how the government is sending "deviants" to so-called Unidades Militares de Ayuda a la Producción—UMAPs. Remember Matias, Carmen's young nephew? Well, the poor man has been in one of those hellholes since last week when he was caught hosting a religious meeting at his house. UMAP is just another name for jail. People are forced to do hard labor and treated as if they were criminals. So please, Teresa, behave yourself.

    I love you,
    Your mother

Knowing I and my family could get in trouble for that last paragraph about the UMAP, I folded the letter, kissed it again and then put it back in the envelope and hid it inside my pillow case.

"Attention, attention!" Mrs. Garcia was standing on an old Coca-Cola box so that she would be more visible to all of us as we lined up. "This morning, we begin a very important phase of our work here. We need to gather all our strength and work harder than ever. Because of the rain, we fell behind in our goals, and now that the sun is out again we must make more progress."

"Viva la Revolución!" voices shouted from the front of the line. It was Mrs. Cordoba and Mrs. Zanabría, trying to stir up enthusiasm. They were mimicked by a small group, all members of UJC. Mrs. Garcia's face was bright with excitement because of all the response she'd gotten with her speechifying.

"Patria o' muerte venceremos!" she said, thrusting her right fist in the air. Then she motioned the group to quiet down. "We're going to keep track of the rows you've completed every day. By the end of the week, a winner will be selected." Mrs. Garcia turned to Mrs. Zanabría and whispered something in her ear. The teacher pulled a rolled piece of paper from her olive-green canvas bag and handed it to the principal.

"Here is the Che Guevara award." Mrs. Garcia held it above her head with both hands. "This is an award given in honor of our leader

Ernesto Che Guevara, who has greatly contributed to the creation of a new conciencia in the citizens of this country. Che has worked hard, and therefore, we must work hard! This precious award plus a weekend pass will be the prize for the winner of the week."

With those words, I saw an opening in the dark sky—an opportunity to go home. I turned to Mariluz, who was standing in line behind me. "I could win that pass. I'm going to try."

"You can do it! We can go to town together. I have a pass to visit my doctor," she said and pressed my hand gently.

As soon as Mrs. Garcia's speech ended, I set my goal in motion. Rows and rows of tobacco danced in front of me. Up and down I went through the six-foot-tall plants, drops of sweat dripping off me and mixing with the dark soil. My hands pulled leaf after leaf from the hairy stems, undressing each stalk, leaving it naked under the sun. In my mind, I played out memories of the harvest on Grandfather's farm: Men and women carrying heavy baskets rushing through the corn fields. Their faces and mine covered with dirt and dust. Their bodies and mine smelling of the sweet and spicy Cuban land.

As I heard Grandmother Petra once say, "Working the land is the kind of work that makes one older before time and younger as one gets old." Grandmother was always talking to me about the importance of connecting with the elements, with invisible rhythms gentle as the wind, quiet as the grass growing, swift as the flight of a bird. "Teresita," she would say, "one must learn how to read the writing on the sky and to feel within the heart the pulse of the earth."

Grandfather José told me something, too: "When you're bending over, constantly looking at the face of the land, digging, pulling, planting, you don't notice much of the dance, but soon one day you find yourself loving her more and more, even more than your own woman."

Loving these tobacco fields was hard to do, but I thought that if not love, perhaps I could learn to empty my mind and move through the rows as if in a trance, so as not to feel the pain in my lower back, knees, arms, neck . . . my whole body. Carmen had taught me how to close my eyes and invoke the saints when I needed help. "The orishas can give you strength, niña. Don't forget about them," she'd told me the morning I left home for camp.

136

Fatigue ate its way into my muscles, bones and even into my brain. My head felt light, my body heavy. My two main competitors, Celia and Aurora, closely followed my tracks on the fields from the first day of the competition. Celia had a small body like mine, but she was heavier and slower. Aurora was tall, thin and muscular. She was very fast at the beginning of the day, but towards the end I would see her moving sluggishly through the rows and taking breaks. Occasionally, I found myself having a dialogue with the plants, as I had seen Grandmother Patricia do in her garden. After all, these hateful plants were considered medicinal by the Taíno Indians.

In this race for a weekend pass, the days went by fast for me. By dark, I was so tired that I could hardly eat, and I went to bed early. Mariluz and Marta cheered me on each evening; even when I was too tired to talk I was their heroine. Myself, I felt more like a bloody and beaten boxer, ready to fall to the mat.

Friday afternoon, we all lined up in front of the cafeteria, waiting for the verdict. After a long speech, Mrs. Garcia handed the Che Guevara award and a piece of paper signed for a weekend pass home to me. I was told to pack and be ready by six o'clock so that I could get a ride with one of the supervisors who lived in town. Bursting with excitement, I ran all the way to the barrack. To my surprise, I found Celia and one of her friends, Elena, waiting for me.

"Well, well, well, here comes the hard-working gusanita," said Celia, cutting in front of me and blocking the way to my hammock.

"What do you want, Celia?"

"Next time it's my turn to go home," she said and pushed me to the floor. Elena jumped on top of me and hit me with her closed fist. I was just about to return the punch when I realized that a fight could cost me my pass, so instead I just went limp under her body.

"You coward! Aren't you going to fight?" Celia taunted.

"No, Celia, please leave me alone."

"You better slow down next week . . . because if you don't, I'll find a way to get you in trouble," she said and then walked away before I could respond.

I got up from the floor and began to throw clothes into my canvas bag. Afraid yet angry, I didn't want to think about the incident. It was best to put everything behind and try to concentrate on packing. The most important thing was to be able to go home. The situation with Celia and Elena could wait till my return.

The following week, the competition for first place and a weekend pass became the center of attention for the entire camp. Celia and Elena had decided to team up against me. They told me on Monday morning, before breakfast, and on the way to the fields, relentless in their efforts to provoke me. Celia enlisted four of her friends who took turns shouting at me: "Hey, gusanita, say good-bye to the weekend visits," "You better pray to all your saints for help. You're going to need lots of it." At one point, where the road turned, Elena had waited for me. She pushed me to the ground and then threw a handful of dirt in my face. "Here, worms like you love dirt." I tried to grab her leg, but she managed to get away.

Several girls walking behind me stopped and began to yell at Elena. "You coward, come back here!" But Elena ignored them and ran ahead to join her friends.

My friend Coki handed me a piece of cloth to wipe off my face. "Would you like me to be on your team?" she asked.

"Of course."

"Then let's do it! We can beat those two." Coki squeezed my shoulder and then put her arm around my waist as we walked. Coki was about my height, maybe an inch taller, but she had a stocky, strong body—I thought we'd make a tough team to beat.

It was a bloody contest. To work faster, Coki and I took off our cloth gloves and picked the leaves with our bare hands. After a couple of days of intense work, our fingers were covered with open sores. The raw flesh burned, but we kept going as if driven. We moved through the rows of tobacco plants like swift trout swimming up the river. Nothing could stop us. Victory at this point meant more than just a weekend pass. It represented our pride and honor.

The camp was divided into those who supported Celia and Elena and those who were on our side. Even the teachers became involved and organized cheerleaders for their respective teams. Banners with our names were put up on the walls of the cafeteria and Mrs. Garcia kept the daily scores posted on the bulletin board in her office.

By the end of Friday morning, Coki and I were forty rows ahead, but I was dragging my feet. To supplement the poor meals, I had been gulping down large glasses of brown sugar and water several times a day for energy.

That afternoon, on the way to the tobacco fields, Celia and Elena approached Coki and me. They stood in the middle of the road—Celia, with her hands in the pockets of her olive pants, Elena with both hands on her waist. As the other girls saw what was happening, they formed a large circle around us.

"We're going to win," Celia said, stepping forward.

"You'll have to prove that. Remember, we are ahead in the game."

"We're going to win one way or another." Celia moved closer, and Elena followed.

"What do you mean?" Coki asked.

"If you don't slow down today, we're going to break every bone in your precious bodies," Celia said and punched me in the shoulder. I pushed her away, and Coki got between us.

"Stop." Coki grabbed Celia's arm.

"There's going to be trouble if you guys win," Elena said, pulling Coki's hand away from Celia and then twisting it. Coki's face contorted with pain.

The circle of girls egged us on. "Go, Teresa! Go, Celia!" On and on they shouted, fueling an already charged atmosphere. Elena threw the first punch, at Coki's face. Then Celia came towards me, and kicking high in some sort of karate move, struck me right in the gut. I gasped, but recovering, I returned her kick.

We were so involved in the fight we didn't realize the girls had split into opposite camps as well. Girls were pulling each other's hair and wrestling on the ground, and fists were flying. I could hear the teachers in the background shouting, "Basta!" and trying to separate entangled girls, with little success.

A sharp *CRACK*, a shot so loud my eardrums hurt, froze every one in place. I looked over and saw Benito, the bowlegged supervisor, standing on the side of the road, his legs apart and a revolver in hand, like one of those Hollywood cowboys. Mrs. Garcia wasted no time in ordering us to line up and continue walking towards the field.

I was surprised she did not bombard us with one of her classic speeches about conciencia revolucionaria. I guess she and the other teachers felt guilty for instigating the competition and harvesting its fruits—the spirit of the camp was running high, and the job of picking rows and rows of tobacco was getting done, but the competition had gotten out of hand.

As soon as we arrived at the fields, the two teams went into action. We didn't take any breaks, except to get water from the clay canteens on the side of the road. Conversation was limited to checking on how the other team and our partners were doing. Coki's face was as red as the skin of a ripe tomato, and I could tell her hands were slowing from fatigue. I could feel the stiffness creeping into my own aching muscles and lower back.

During one of my trips to the canteens, my vision blurred and my knees began trembling. I knelt on the ground for fear I was going to faint. At that moment, the memory of a neighborhood cockfight flashed through my mind. I closed my eyes and put my head on my knees to quell the nausea, and a vivid image of the two gamecocks fighting in the middle of the circular stage played across my eyelids. The birds ripped at each other's feathers and skin with their sharp spurs, while the crowd shouted "Matalo!" and "Pelea cabrón!" The word pelea resonated in my body and soul. Yes, I needed to fight! As I slowly pulled myself to my feet, I saw the cock named Rojo inflicting the deadly blow to Amarillo, and the cock dropped to the floor flickering his wings. Then his blood-covered body finally relaxed at the silent call of death.

12

TEN MILLION TONS OF SUGAR

"*T*ERESA, TERESA, wake up!" It was Mariluz jolting me out of my sleep.

"What do you want?" I mumbled as I rubbed my eyes.

"My dad is here. He's going to take us to town."

"Why? What's going on?"

"It's your grandmother Petra. She's very ill." Mariluz hugged me and then urged me to get dressed.

Mariluz's father Henry was standing next to his old beat-up Jeep when Mariluz and I came outside. The minute he saw me, he ran towards me, picked me up in his arms and held me tight. He was like a second father to me.

"It's going to be okay," Henry said as he dried my tears with the back of his hand. "I know Doña Petra. She will pull out of this one."

For most of the trip I was quiet. Henry and Mariluz tried to cheer me up but I felt too worried to respond. The images of the last time I'd seen Grandmother were fresh in my mind. About a month before, I had gone to visit her during one of my weekend passes to town. Grandmother had never entirely recovered from the pain of losing the farm: It had been five years since the Agrarian Reform, and she was still grieving. She spent most of her time out on the porch in her rocking chair, silently crocheting or staring out into her garden.

Life had been turned upside down for all of us, not just my grand-mother. What was supposed to have been a forty-five-day "School Goes to the Countryside" program lasted for two years. After that, the schools were permanently moved to rural areas and operated under a work-study system year-round: We worked half of the day and stud-ied the other half, though during the harvest season, we were forced to work all day, from sunrise to sundown. New buildings were built to house our battalion of girls, but the conditions were still inhumane. Food was rationed and of poor nutritional value, and the labor was harsh because of the economic pressures of the time.

When I arrived at Villa Petra, my father greeted me at the entrance. As we walked together, he told me Grandmother had suffered a massive stroke that had left her paralyzed and unable to talk. "She is not the same tough woman you've always known," he warned me.

"Is there any hope?" I asked.

"We don't know yet."

Day and night, Grandmother Petra was tended to by her sons and daughters, part of the extended family temporarily moving into the house. They said prayers, talked and read to the now-fragile matriarch. My uncle Tomás, an experienced doctor, told everyone that if Grand-mother survived, she was going to be bedridden for the rest of her life. When I heard his prognosis, I knew Grandmother would choose to die instead. She was not the kind of woman to settle for such an existence. Like the mare Alazana with her broken leg, for my grandmother to re-main alive yet helpless would have been a pain too difficult for her to endure.

For two weeks, Grandmother wrestled with death. During the few times I was able to visit with her, I sat by the bedside looking at her wrinkled and drawn face. I could see signs of her internal struggle, as she occasionally attempted to mumble words, but her dry lips could only make a contorted gesture. I refused to see my grandmother in such a beaten posture, a ghostly figure against the white sheets. In-stead, I imagined her as the strong woman I had once seen grab a cow by the horns and wrestle it into submission. I thought of death being as stubborn as the cow, trying to throw Grandmother to the ground and I saw myself standing by the barn fence, cheering her on: "Come on, Grandmother, come back to us."

To everyone's amazement, except mine of course, Grandmother began to recover from the stroke. First, she began to say a few words; then, gradually, her legs and arms began to respond to her commands. She seemed well aware of her situation and not at all afraid to ask questions of the doctors.

"Tomás, tell me the truth," Grandmother said to her son.

"Mamá, I told you, it's going to take a while before you can get out of this bed."

"How long?"

"It could be weeks or even months. We don't know yet, but . . . "

"Nonsense! I am not going to lie here for months like a lazy cow," Grandmother protested. "You're the one who went to medical school. What do you mean, 'We don't know'?"

"Don't get upset, Mamá. I'm doing my best to find you a wheelchair."

"A wheelchair?" Grandmother raised her head from the pillow and looked her son straight in the eyes. "You'll never see your mother sitting in one of those things. I'd rather be dead." Then, she dropped her head back on the pillow and closed her eyes.

"Mother, the wheelchair is just a temporary solution till you gain back the strength in your legs."

Grandmother said no more. Uncle Tomás knew not to waste his time trying to talk the old woman into using a wheelchair, so he just shook his head and walked away. I had been watching them while I waited nearby for my turn to spend some time with Grandmother. Now I walked into the room and sat on the chair by her bedside.

"Grandmother, it's me, Teresa."

"Teresita," she said, turning her head towards me. "Did you hear what Tomás said?"

"Yes, Grandmother."

"Can you see me in a wheelchair?"

I took my time to answer her question. "No, Grandmother, I don't think you and that wheelchair will get along very well. I'd much rather see you riding on the back of Almendro."

For the first time in years, I saw Grandmother's face light up. She looked at me with the same eyes I'd seen when I was a young child. Her spirit, like the old ceiba tree, was still standing firm against the winds of death.

"Grandmother, you can do it. You can grab this stroke by the horns and throw it to the ground."

"You're the only one who believes this old woman can win."

"I do, Grandmother. I know you can do it."

"You know, Teresa, I had a talk with God while I was out there floating in between worlds. I told him I wasn't happy with the way he's been handling business on this earth." Grandmother paused to catch her breath.

"Grandmother, you shouldn't be talking this much."

"I also said to God that I was pissed at him and I wasn't ready to go over to the other side with my soul so full of bitter thoughts."

For a moment I had an image of Grandmother standing in front of God and giving him the finger. I remembered what she'd said to me once when we had gone egg hunting on the prairie. "Teresa, mi hija, God is not any taller than you or me." And pointing to the sky, she said, "He doesn't live up there either, or in the church in town. He has many homes in this land—the palm trees, the sugar fields, the flowers—even the pigs and the cows are the sacred temples of his spirit."

"Death and I worked out a deal," Grandmother continued, her voice fading a bit. "I needed to buy some time from that black witch so that I can set some things in order."

"I thought you were talking about God, Grandmother," I said, thinking that perhaps she had gotten confused.

"No, no. God is God, but Death is a tough witch. There is no way to converse with her. She has a stubborn mind. With her, you have to fight and bargain. Death can't be tricked."

One night, not too long after this conversation, my mother caught Grandmother out of her bed. The old woman was standing on her own feet, leaning against the wall to keep her balance, shaky but determined to walk. From then on, she did not go back to bed. Mostly, she sat in her white rocking chair, where she began the process of teaching her fingers how to crochet again.

I returned to my work-study program only to face an atmosphere of further restrictions and pressures. Once more, school had been postponed so that we could help the Revolution uplift the deteriorating economy. The teachers and supervisors had adopted a new militaristic jargon, and in their speeches, they talked about the "war" against parasitism and laziness.

"This is a battle that won't end till those elements who corrode our economy are completely exterminated. We must fight and fight with all our weapons, with dignity and revolutionary consciousness. As a heroic army of courageous citizens, we want to be prepared to do whatever it takes to obtain victory." Of course, these were the words of who else but Mrs. Garcia.

Nothing we haven't heard before, I thought. As a good soldier I picked up my sharp machete and gloves, ready for another day of nasty sugar cane and hot sun. I was now thirteen and was able to keep up my stamina by drinking sugar-water. It tasted like hell, but it gave me the energy I needed to chop down piles and piles of cane.

Early in the fall of 1968, our family received another blow at the hands of Castro. I received a phone call at the camp from my mother, and in our four-minute conversation, she gave me the news that my father was no longer at home either. He had been taken to a labor camp in Canta Rana, fifty miles away from my hometown.

"Castro has sent all 'gusanos' to work for their bread and water," my mother said.

"For how long?" I asked

"Your father was told he has to stay there till our request to leave Cuba is granted."

"But, Mami, that could take a long time. We've been waiting for three years!"

"I know. People in town are up in arms about this, but there is nothing we can do, except to wait and hope we get permission to leave soon. Your father has a friend who works at the American embassy who has offered to check the status of our papers."

Towards the end of November, Mrs. Garcia called out the entire student body for an emergency meeting. Without preamble, she informed us of the most recent measures taken by the government to bolster the Cuban economy.

"This year we won't be going home for Christmas." A moan of disappointment rose from the crowd. "We are going to stay and work. This is the place where our Revolution needs us now. Our country's new goal is to produce ten million tons of sugar in the 1970 zafra."

"Ten million tons of sugar. That's a lot of sweat," Mariluz whispered in my ear.

"Our leader, el comandante Fidel Castro, has prohibited the celebration of any holidays—Christmas, New Year's, Easter—until we have achieved victory." Mrs. Garcia's voice rang out loud and clear.

Christmas Eve that year was both sad and depressing. Mariluz, Coki and I sat on the grass outside the barracks after the evening meal. Though we were tired and our hands hurt from the heavy machetes, we didn't feel like going to sleep. The mood of the whole school was downhearted and charged with emotion. It was the first time any of us had spent Noche Buena away from our families. I tried not to think too much about it, but the faces of all those dear to me kept appearing despite my efforts.

Noche Buena at Villa Petra was the one celebration I looked forward to every year. A lot of energy and time went into the preparation of the food. Ever since I could remember, my father had been responsible for roasting the pig that my grandfather José selected for the occasion. The day before Christmas Eve, the pig was killed, cleaned and marinated in the juices of lemon and sour orange combined with cumin, black pepper and lots of garlic. The next morning, the pit was dug out and a grill was made from branches of the guava tree. By early afternoon, the pig was in place above the slow-burning coals.

In the kitchen, Grandmother Petra led her women's squadron in the creation of the most delicious dishes—congri, yuca, mojos, buñuelos de malanga and ñame. The desserts were made from papaya, coconuts and guavas, and there were sweet flans topped with caramel. Fresh cheese was taken out of the press, and loaves of Cuban bread were baked in the oven. All the wine came from the cellar of my Aunt Ana, who was an excellent wine-maker. With pride, she presented us every year with a variety of sweet and dry wines made from tropical fruits.

"What are you thinking about?" Mariluz asked me.

"Navidad at the farm. I was remembering how much fun it was."

"I wonder what people in Cabaigüán are doing tonight," Mariluz said.

"Probably not much," Coki joined in. "No one is allowed to celebrate."

"Well . . . I'm not sure of that," said Mariluz. "I know that my mother won't be easily persuaded into giving up her Noche Buena. I bet you anything that right at this moment, she's in the kitchen cooking something good. Mmmm! I can smell the cumin, the fresh cilantro, the garlic . . . "

"Stop, for God's sake! You're torturing us with your great imagination," I complained.

"My *great imagination* is all I have! You on the other hand have the hope that, someday, you'll leave this whole mess behind," Mariluz lamented.

"Teresa, maybe at this time next year, you'll be in El Norte, recovering from a severe attack of indigestion. Too much American roast pig!" Coki said, laughing.

It was not till I heard Coki's words that I realized how lucky I was. At least I could dream about the future, but what about Mariluz and Coki? What kind of life was there in Cuba for my two friends? Suddenly, I felt guilty in anticipation of all the privileges I was going to have as soon as I stepped on American soil. No more camps, no more lines to buy things. No more Mrs. Cordoba and Mrs. Garcia to control the hours of my day.

"Teresa, can you imagine what it's going to be like to walk into a store and try on all the beautiful clothes and shoes, anything you want?" Mariluz said. She jumped up and pretended to be modeling a dress. "How do you like this one?" And with an English accent, she continued, "This dress is from the John Ferrier collection. The elegant spring set of pants and top was designed by Paul Jean-Pierre. Look at the bright greens and yellows of this selection." She went on making up names until, finally, she dropped back on the grass. She rolled over on her back, and with her eyes closed, she said in a sexy voice, "I'd give anything to own a pair of American blue jeans."

"I've been dreaming of a pair of tall leather boots," Coki said. Looking at me she asked, "What's the first thing you're going to buy when you get there, Teresa?"

"I don't know," I replied without even thinking about her question. The whole conversation was upsetting me.

"Come on, tell us!"

"I really don't know. I don't want to talk about this anymore."

"What's the matter?"

"I just don't feel good talking about it. I don't want to think about all the clothes and shoes and stuff I'm going to have there. What's the point? You guys are not going to be there with me."

"It sounds as if you don't want to go." Coki moved closer and put her arm around my shoulders.

"I do want to go. I know I must go, but I hate the thought of leaving you two behind. Every time I think about it . . . " I broke down. Coki held me tight. Mariluz sat up and joined us. "What am I going to do without you? You're my sisters," I said, my face streaked with tears.

"It's going to be awfully sad to walk by your house and know you're not there," Coki said, resting her head against mine.

"Well, I won't be able to listen to our favorite music show, *Nocturno*, for a long time after you leave," Mariluz said. With the side of her hand, she wiped her own tears from my face.

"I don't even want to imagine what it's going to be like in this hellhole of a camp without you," Coki added.

We rocked and cried together under the night sky for a long time, talking about the letters we would write to each other, of the dream of my being able to return to Cuba one day. Finally we drifted back to our childhoods together in the neighborhood.

"Remember that night we collected a bucketful of frogs and put them on Lidia's porch?" Mariluz said. "The poor girl freaked out when she opened the door and saw all those green creatures jumping around her. But she deserved it—Lidia was and still is a snob. Remember, she never shared her toys with us? And she wouldn't play outside because she was afraid her pretty pink dress would get ruined. Qué ñoña!"

Then it was Coki's turn. "What about the day during Carnaval that we stole Henry's jeep and you, Mariluz, drove it down the street! You were bragging, saying you knew how to drive and then *boom!* you hit the neighbor's car. Then you put it in reverse for more than two blocks! You scared the hell out of the rumba comparsa dancing down the street. Those poor people left their drums and ran for their lives!"

"Hey, speaking of Carnaval," I said, "remember last year when Mariluz decided to put together a costume show here at the camp? It's the only time we've ever been able to make fun of Mrs. Garcia and Mrs. Cordoba without getting into trouble. That one girl who dressed up as Mrs. Cordoba was hilarious!"

Later that night, as I was falling asleep, I had the premonition that my time in Cuba was coming to an end. The idea of leaving Coki and Mariluz behind was too painful to think about. Our experiences at the camps had made us closer than ever. Alone and without our families to depend on, we had had to learn to take care of each other, to share our food, to hold one another when we felt afraid or homesick. In the absence of our parents, we became like family. If one of us was sick, the others took on the role of watching over her, making sure a fever was not too high or a cough not too serious. We talked about our problems and found answers together.

The anticipation of having to say good-bye to Coki and Mariluz weighed as heavily on me as Castro's so-called ten million tons of sugar could have. And yet, even at age thirteen, I was well aware that Cuba was a death trap for me. My options were clear: If I chose to stay, I could either join the Communist Party and become one of them in order to survive, or I could revolt, with jail and even harsher work camps as my reward.

13

CANTA RANA—WHERE
THE FROGS SING

ONE WEEKEND when I was home on a
camp pass, Mother, Jose and I visited Father at the Canta Rana camp.
Early Saturday morning, before sunrise, we walked to the corner near
the bus station and caught the truck to the men's camp. The old beat-
up guarandinga, as Cubans call it, was packed with women and children, so we were all standing up, holding on to whatever we could, as
the truck jounced down the gravel road at forty miles an hour. After a
half hour of this roller coaster ride, many of us were nauseated and
rushed to the railings to throw up over the side.

We were all screaming at the driver to slow down, but he continued driving like a madman till a rear tire blew out. The guarandinga
almost went off the road, pirouetting at the edge. Jose was thrown to
the floor of the truck, but Mother pulled him back up just before three
women rolled over his spot.

Spare tires were a luxury and hard to find, so we sat waiting on the
side of the road for more than an hour while the driver walked to the
nearest town for help. He returned in a green government jeep with a
young, bearded militia man and a used tire, and after the tire was
changed, we all hopped back in the truck, ready for the rest of the mad
journey—at least two more hours of standing under the hot sun.

An hour later, the truck suddenly pulled to the side of the road and stopped. The driver jumped out and kicked the door shut. "Carajo! This is bad luck. Where are the saints today?" He shouted and cursed and hit the fender with his fist. I climbed the railing, and from there I could see a big cloud of steam coming out of the engine. "Hey, you guys, get out!" the driver yelled. "The engine overheated, so it'll be a while before we can get back on the road."

It was almost eleven o'clock when we arrived at Canta Rana. The fifty-mile trip had taken us five hours, and we were tired, hungry and thirsty. Dozens of men ran to the truck and greeted their wives and children with effusive hugs, kisses, even tears. Our legs still wobbly from the trip, Mother, Jose and I stood side by side, waiting for Father. He was one of the last to arrive. He was limping, and his pants were rolled up to just below the knees. A white bandage was wrapped around his left leg, a little bit above the ankle.

"Papi, Papi!" we called. Jose and I ran to him, and Mother followed us.

"What happened to your leg, Pepe?" Mother asked anxiously, after greeting him. "Nothing major. I cut myself accidentally with the machete."

"Did you have a doctor look at it?"

"There are no doctors here . . . fortunately Idalgo, one of the men in camp, is a nurse; he was the one who took care of it for me. But come on, come on, we're not going to spend the whole day talking about this little scratch on my leg," Father said, putting one arm around Mother and the other around me and Jose.

The place was familiar to me. It was almost identical in design to the camp where I had gone for the School Goes to the Countryside program: It had a central meal area surrounded by rustic barracks built with the leaves and wood from palm trees and the same kind of shower and outhouse facilities. The landscape was different, however: Instead of tobacco there was sugar cane: fields and fields of green cañaverales, and far away in the distance, a sugar mill with its long cylindrical tower.

The men and their families scattered around the camp. Some sat under the shade of the few trees left standing. Others gathered around the tables in the dining facility. My father wanted to show us his living space, where he had managed to keep a small propane stove that he shared with a group of new friends. Here they improvised supplemental meals with whatever their families brought them from home or what they themselves were able to catch by hunting and fishing. Hunger and a common identity as gusanos, plus hard labor under torturous conditions, contributed to the building of strong bonds and alliances in the camp. Drawing from the comfort and support of the brotherhood was the only way to survive.

"Do they let you keep this stove in here?" I asked.

"They do . . . in exchange for coffee and food. Did you bring some coffee?" he asked Mother.

"Yes . . . I was able to get some on the black market."

"Coffee here is like gold dust. Let's make some—my mouth is watering with just the smell of it," Father said as he took the small brown bag of coffee from my mother's hands. Then, with delight, he gently pressed his nose against the paper and inhaled the aroma.

Father was a lot thinner. He had lost at least fifteen to twenty pounds. His face had been burned a dark red by the sun, but I could still see the deep shadows under his eyes and the yellowish tint of his skin, the remnants of a recent bout with hepatitis that he had contracted from contaminated camp food. Father had almost lost his life because of the negligence of the camp officials: He had not been allowed to see a doctor at first, and by the time he was taken to the hospital, the disease was so advanced and his liver so damaged that the doctors told him he might die.

Grandmother Patricia was the only one who hadn't given up hope. She practically moved into the hospital with her bag of herbs and homemade potions, and two or three times a day, she rubbed my father's body with the aromatic oils made from formulas only she knew. The old woman said her prayers, while doctors and nurses watched her with disbelief and amusement. But no one dared remove her from the side of her beloved son.

A few days after, when father began to recover, the doctors gave Grandmother no credit, but being the confident healer she was, she was concerned only about her son's health and didn't leave the hospital room until she was able to walk out with him.

Now I studied my father's face carefully. A ray of light coming through the window revealed tiny cuts and scratches all over his cheeks and forehead. Sugar cane leaves have sharp borders that can cut through the flesh like knives. Having picked sugar cane at my own camp, I knew both the cuts and the almost unbearable itching that followed.

I could tell shaving for my father had been painful—patches of irritated skin and dried blood from razor scratches peppered his face—but for a Cuban man, appearance in front of his family is important, and my father had prepared himself to receive us with dignity and pride. This camp was the new battleground, and he was a soldier to the end: a guajiro, a criollo man with blood in his veins that ran hot and strong like that of a bull. Never would he let us see his pain and defeat.

For Antonio Fernandez, leaving Cuba and freeing himself and his family from the hands of Fidel Castro was his only dream. It was an obsession that gave him strength to fight whatever obstacles stood in the way.

"This is not so bad," Father said as he noticed me looking at his battle wounds. "Last week, we were sent to work in the rice fields. That's the closest to hell I've ever experienced in my life. We were working for days with water up to our waists, digging trenches, bending over, fighting clouds of mosquitoes and other kinds of shit. It's an odd feeling, you know. The men were saying how they could feel their skin shrinking after hours of soaking in the muddy flow. I thought I was losing pieces of my flesh, but taking a breather could cost you your life. Those cabrones milicianos are out there with their guns pointed at you, watching you like fucking guard dogs . . . !"

"Pepe, don't talk like that in front of the children!"

"Well . . . it's the truth! They treat us as if we were criminals. They watch us every minute. They poke into our privacy, not even leaving us alone when we are taking a shower. Look out there . . . See that? See that esbirro walking around, showing off his big machine gun? He is a killer! The other day he kicked one of the men till blood stained the dirt. And why? For no reason! The guy had fainted in the fields from exhaustion and was unable to get up when this hijo de puta screamed at him. I swear I had to swallow my pride and keep my fists inside my pockets."

I was quiet, listening to my father's anger and bitterness. I understood, having experienced myself the abuse of power by those supposedly there to protect me. The night Mrs. Cordoba made me run naked around the camp was still jammed in my soul like a sharp thorn.

What irony! I thought. While my father was treated like a criminal for the simple reason of wanting to leave Cuba, visitors from the United States were being welcomed in Havana by our leader, Fidel Castro. These people, members of the Venceremos Brigade, had no idea of the real conditions in the country. They had no way of knowing that they were taking food from the mouths of our people. Hosted with all the amenities available, they were staying in comfortable air-conditioned rooms and eating in restaurants reserved for the tourists. As they enjoyed tender steaks and savory black bean soup and rice, the rest of us were left to eat food not fit for the pigs.

The Venceremos Brigade arrived in Cuba via Mexico in 1969 to work in the sugar cane harvest, in support of Fidel and his "ten million tons of sugar" goal. To them, this was some sort of adventure. To those of us in the labor camps, it was a slap in the face. We had to put up with their television interviews, where they talked about the wonders of the Revolution and our beautiful island. Of course, their "work schedule" was not like ours. They were given a succulent breakfast in the morning, and by the time they got to the cane fields, it was time to go back for lunch. The same in the afternoon.

I wondered how different their opinion would be if they had a chance to travel across Cuba—if they were allowed to join my father's brigade and eat the food the gusanos had to eat, or deal with the mental and physical tortures these men had to endure. I was sure that if they came to visit my father's camp and saw the agony on the faces of the men, they would immediately return to their country and never come back.

"How is the food here?" I asked Papi, trying to shake off my thoughts.

"Food . . . ? Three tablespoons of rice, a small cup of watery lentil soup, occasionally canned beef from Russia and lots of brown sugar. That's pretty much the menu for lunch and dinner. There are rumors, however, about cats disappearing from the area."

"What's happening to the cats?" asked Jose.

"Let's just say they have passed to a better world in the stomachs of the camp men," said Father, making light of it.

"Pepe . . . that's horrible!" Mother said.

"Horrible . . . horrible! When you're hungry, you eat rocks! The men here are starving, and to survive, we do what we can. Want to know about a delicacy? Try snake meat or bullfrog legs."

According to my father, every night the guards pretended not to notice as a few of the men went down to the pond to catch fat juicy frogs and bijacas, a basslike fish. The price they paid was having to share whatever they were able to catch with the milicianos. The uniformed men waited till the food was cooked and then showed up in the barracks to claim their ration. They constantly threatened to take away the little stove and the handy tarralla, a fishing net my father had brought from home.

"They *love* to see us scared and humiliated!" my father said, and then he looked out the window to make sure nobody was listening. "They *love* to fuck with our minds and terrorize us with threats of canceling our permits to go home or taking away the right to leave the country. They threaten and threaten! They come at all hours of the night to check if we are in our hammocks."

Father stopped and ran his hands over Jose's hair. His hands were covered with yellow callouses and runny sores. Handling a machete for days at a time can eat away the skin and eventually the flesh. Then, slowly, the soft tissue turns hard, like thick tree bark. But my father's hands were still in the raw phase, where the flesh burns. A couple of times I saw his silent "scream" as he tried to handle the coffee can, but of course, he was a man and held it inside.

My gaze followed my father's hands as he poured the coffee into small tin cups. We were all quiet for the first time since our arrival. Mother looked tired and sad. Jose was distracted, watching two kids play outside. I was not too sure of where I was, but I felt nostalgic for the life we once had, the precious and long-gone times when the family was together in our home. Our forced separation was absurd and upsetting, but well justified in the minds of the Communists. Those who wanted freedom were considered traitors and therefore had to be punished. Even more than that, they had to be tortured, and their spirits broken.

155

Yes, freedom! We all dreamed about freedom, and we were willing to pay the price for it. As my Grandmother Patricia would later say
to me: "You must close your eyes, Negrita, and just imagine being free
again. Don't look back . . . don't look back! Don't turn around to say
your final good-byes to this old woman. Keep walking, mi Negrita! You
must not falter. Your steps should be firm."

That's what my father did. And I, too, was quickly learning not
to quiver at thoughts of the unknown. We couldn't afford to think back
to what had happened to our lives, our country . . . all the losses. Our
hearts and eyes were beginning to close. Our anger and pain were becoming the prison that kept us sheltered from any doubt or fear. There
was no room for ambivalence or regret. Once you set out on the path
to leaving Cuba, you were marked as undesirable. Even if you had a
change of heart and decided to stay, you were forever a gusano.

That day in camp, I recognized the jail my father carried within
him: thick brick walls, high towers and electrical fences around the
perimeters of his adventurous spirit. The evidence was there in his light
brown eyes, now turning to somber shadows, haunting him. I knew it
then, but I couldn't afford to peek inside. My mother knew it as well,
and though Jose was too young, in his own way, he understood the loss
of innocence. Even he wasn't able to escape the curse of our existence
in a world that was crumbling and changing faster than we had ever
anticipated.

"Soon as we get to the other side, to the States, this will just feel
like a bad dream," my father said, as he washed the coffee pot.

"I don't believe we'll ever forget these times," Mother said.

"Oh, time heals . . . good food and a different life," Father replied.

"What about the loved ones we'll leave behind?" Mother wasn't
about to give up. She had a need to pour out her own pain about leaving her people behind. "We'll never see them again!"

"I can't afford to think about them, or my own sister . . . or my
mother and father now!" Father turned his face away. "If I do, I won't
be able to do this. Please, Felicia . . . you don't know what it is to be
here in this hell. Every morning, we are marched down to the fields.
We look like a procession of ghosts rather than of men. The milicianos
point their guns at us and laugh aloud.

"'Eh, gusanos,' they say. 'What kind of car are you going to buy when you get to El Norte?' And they laugh and laugh while we push down our rage. I heard one of them say, 'That's if you guys get there, you whole bunch of cabrones.' I wrapped my fingers hard around the handle of my machete, and for the rest of the day, as I was cutting sugar cane, I imagined . . . every single slender cane snapping . . . twisting under my hands as if it were the neck of that militia man."

"You're right . . . I don't know what you're going through," I heard my mother say.

But Father wasn't listening anymore. He was lost in a world of violent images, of unconquerable battles. He was like a little boy with his fantasies of being able to destroy the monsters of his nightmare.

I looked at him. Where was the father I once knew? I searched . . . I tried to get his attention by asking a silly question: "Can we go for a walk, Papi?" There was no answer. He continued talking, now more to himself than to us. Jose had wandered outside. Mother was sitting on the hammock that hung next to the stove. Her face had a flat expression. She was also gone. And I was all alone.

"At night . . . " my father continued, "we go hunting . . . "

"How can you hunt without a gun?" I interrupted.

"We don't need guns. We use traps made out of bamboo shoots."

Oblivious to my desire to connect with him, Father rambled on. His voice sounded as if it were coming from a place far away. I forced myself to listen. He was talking about how they'd go out at night and capture—a rabbit, a wild hen or some other kind of bird, or one of the big rats that overran the camp. My father, I thought to myself, was like a large hawk whose wings had been broken and now fluttered helplessly on the ground.

"Rats!" I said, holding my stomach. The image of Papi eating a roasted rat made me feel like throwing up.

"Yes, Teresa, cats, rats, lizards . . . " Father paused and searched for something inside a small canvas bag hanging from a rusted nail. He pulled out a hand-rolled cigar and held it between his index and middle fingers for a few seconds while he searched for a match in his shirt pocked. Father was known for losing the expensive lighters my mother and his friends gave him.

"You've lost your lighter again!" Mother complained.

"No, you're wrong this time, Felicia. I exchanged it for this leather belt," Father said, showing off the brown leather belt. "Mine got stolen when we first arrived."

"How could that be? All of you are in the same boat."

"It was not one of us. Other men lost stuff, too. We figure it was a young guy who works in the kitchen. He came into the barracks when we were in the fields. A couple of days later, he was seen wearing Benito's watch."

"Did you complain?" I asked.

"Oh yeah, but nothing was done about it. So three of us went and talked to the young gallo. We made it very clear that if anything else was found missing, we were going to come directly to him, but this time not on friendly terms."

"Well, Pepe, what if he tells the guards?"

"He could, but he would be taking the chance of having no teeth left in his mouth."

"Oh, I can't believe what you're saying. I've never heard you talk like that . . ." Mother walked away. She stood by the window with her arms crossed, looking out at the distant blue sky and the green line of the cañaverales merging with the horizon.

"I have never been in a situation like this before. This is survival, Felicia. There is no waiting for justice. Here, there is only one law— the law of the machete."

"Pepe, por Dios. You're beginning to sound like a stranger."

"Sí mujer, like a stranger. I feel that way myself. But you don't know what this kind of place does to a man. You're home, you're protected from this misery!" Father said, lighting his cigar from the blue flame of the stove.

"Wrong . . . wrong! I don't sit around the house all day and do my fingernails. You know better than to say that!"

I didn't recognize my parents. There we were, after weeks of not seeing each other, and all they could do was argue. I could see how my mother's constant fears were irritating my father, but he was not being fair to her. I knew she woke up every morning before sunrise and spent the day standing in food lines at the stores, walking miles and miles to rural areas to bargain with small farmers for food.

I suddenly was furious at both of them for not thinking about Jose and me. I wanted to scream, "Stop your stupid bickering! I'm sick of it! What about me? I'm fourteen years old, but I feel like I'm forty!" But no words came out of my mouth. I knew they loved us, and as my mother told us over and over, "I'm making this sacrifice for you kids. If it weren't for you, I would never leave Mami and Papi and my sister Nelda and . . . " and she'd go on to name all her siblings. I felt responsible for her unhappiness as well as for my father's lost sense of humor and playfulness.

I walked outside. The air was humid. Dark clouds were forming in the sky, and the breeze carried the smell of rain drops mixed with the hot earth. Not far from me, in a clearing before the sugar cane fields began, one of the milicianos was unleashing his fury on a horse. Holding the reins with one hand, with the other he whipped the animal with a leather rod.

I fought the impulse to run to the scene and rescue the poor horse, a futile attempt that would only cost me my freedom. Instead, I stood there with my feet glued to the ground, feeling on my own back the pain of every single stroke of his whip. "Damn milicianos!" I said to myself. Not only have you taken the farm away, but you have stolen my grandparents, my childhood, my family and now my father as well. As you beat him over and over, his heart is hardening and turning bitter, just like the spirit of that horse.

14

THE TELEGRAM

*T*HE AFTERNOON the emigration officer knocked on our door with the telegram—an official notice from the government—I was home on a weekend pass I had earned for harvesting more than a hundred rows of tobacco plants in five days. For four years, our family had waited for that precious piece of paper. It was not just any telegram but *the* telegram, the ticket to our freedom. Our family had been granted permission to fly to the United States.

I was sitting on my favorite rocking chair, a handmade red mahogany and wicker masterpiece that Grandfather José had given my mother on her thirtieth birthday. On the radio a Mexican singer, Roberto Jordan, was singing the Spanish version of "Brown-Eyed Girl," still popular on the island though it was then 1970. With so many dark-eyed women in the country, each felt the verses had been written for her. At least that's how I imagined it every time I listened to Roberto's romantic version.

Another brown-eyed girl, my friend Coki, had been kicked out of school three days before for what the principal called "immoral conduct." Coki had been caught kissing and playing sexual games with another girl in the late hours of the night. We girls were awakened and informed of the situation and of the disciplinary action to be taken, and both girls were sent home the next morning, escorted by one of the teachers.

News spread quickly through town, and Coki was targeted as the tortillera, the lesbian. Parents, including my mother, warned their daughters to stay away from Coki as if she had a contagious disease. The entire community had shunned her. I was sad for my friend, and I was angry with the ignorant people.

I had decided to visit Coki while I was home and was about to leave when I heard a loud knock at the door. When I opened the door, I was face to face with a green-clad military officer. The man didn't smile and simply showed me a piece of paper stamped with a government seal. At first glance, I didn't recognize what it was. I thought he was coming to arrest someone—after all, it was not unusual for people to be thrown in jail for no reason—or that something bad had happened to my father in the labor camp.

"Are your parents home?" His face was hard with a long parrot nose and dark eyes.

"Only my mother. I'll go and get her."

I walked quickly to the kitchen, where my mother was preparing dinner. Carmen had gone out to see if she could buy some salt from one of the neighbors. Mother's eyes opened wide when I told her that some sort of officer was at the door.

"What does he want?" she asked, getting up from the chair where she had been peeling sweet potatoes. She cleaned her hands with an old rag grabbed from the table top and started for the door. "Well, let's go see what he wants."

The officer presented Mother with the telegram and an official order for us to vacate the house immediately and prepare to fly out of the country in three days. Without introducing himself, he read the information to us in a monotone. Then he walked into the living room with intrusive authority.

"I'm Officer Eduardo Galindo, and I'll be doing the final inventory. You know, checking everything that is supposed to be inside the property, as reported in the initial presentation papers." He paused and placed his right hand on the pistol resting on his hip and then looked around with a superior air.

"Let's hope everything is in order." Turning to my mother, he said,

Mrs. Fernandez, start packing the clothes you'll need for the trip. I'll be busy for a while . . . Now remember, the policy is that each member of the family is allowed only forty-five pounds. No more than that. Do you understand? I don't want any games, and by that I mean no hiding of jewelry or any other stuff of value inside the suitcases."

Mother went to her bedroom and opened the dark mahogany dresser where she had been keeping all the clothes for the trip. Inside the drawers, they were carefully folded and organized in such a way that, when the time came, she would just need to place them in the brown leather bags and she'd be ready to go. People in our situation were allowed very little time to pack and leave their residences, sometimes less than a couple of hours. The experience was made to be as humiliating and as difficult as possible, as a way of punishing us.

As I walked across the living room, I saw the officer pull out a pad from his jacket. Then he began opening drawers and throwing their contents on the floor, counting the furniture, checking every corner of every room, with no respect for our precious possessions. For a moment I felt the impulse to yell at him, "You stupid man, get out of my house."

"Hey you, muchacha," he called. "What's your name?"

"Teresa."

"Okay, Teresa, come here and tell me about the two missing chairs in this dining set. There were six in the original inventory."

"There must be some kind of mistake," I said quickly. I knew exactly where the chairs were. My mother had exchanged the six original chairs for four old ones from my aunt's house.

"Well, I'll look around, and if I find anything else missing from this list, you're staying in this country till the missing objects are found," he said, looking me straight in the eye. Then he turned and left the room.

For a brief moment I panicked. I thought of my mother, so invested in protecting her old family furniture from strange hands. She had consistently ignored my father, taking the risk to remove objects of sentimental value one by one from the house. My Aunt Nelda had been her faithful ally, providing inexpensive replacements.

"Hey, Teresa, where is the blender?" the officer yelled from the kitchen.

Oh no, not the blender! I thought to myself, feeling angry at my mother for her stubbornness. "It should be in the right cabinet, sir." I rushed over and searched the cabinets, where I found an old blender, not the original blender, but an old one of the same brand. "Here it is," I said, trying to keep my voice from shaking.

I left Officer Galindo in the kitchen and went to find Jose. It was then that I heard people shouting in front of our house: "Fuera de aquí, gusanos!" I looked outside from the living room window. Standing on the sidewalk was a group of locals, mostly Committee for the Defense of the Revolution members. "Get out of the country, traitors, worms!" It was their way of unleashing their anger and dislike for those of us who had "betrayed" the Revolution. Every family who left the island had to endure this form of last-minute harassment from their own community.

"Okay, Mrs. Fernandez, that's enough," I heard Officer Galindo say.

Mother was not finished yet—she kept trying to pack the suitcases with more and more clothes. Leave it up to her, and she would clean the closets before Galindo had a chance to notice.

"Mrs. Fernandez, I'm finished with the inventory, so let's go."

In a matter of minutes, we'd leave my house forever. I felt the urge just to walk around my home. I wanted to take mental pictures of the entire place. I wanted to feel, taste, touch, smell . . . every single memory of my life was there.

I took a last look at the walls of my bedroom, which I'd decorated myself. When I was around eight, I'd asked my mother for permission to paint the walls with my favorite cartoon characters, Mickey and Minnie Mouse, Donald Duck and Goofy. I carefully drew the figures on the white plaster with a pencil. Then with a combination of fine, thin and wide bristle brushes, I painted them with bright colors. Several friends and relatives had contributed to the masterpiece with donations of leftover paint.

As I looked at my childhood murals, I burst into tears. I turned away, and my glance landed on the old toy box by the foot of my bed. Made of white pine, this treasure chest had been skillfully crafted by the hands of our next-door neighbor Veita, who, having no children of his own, poured his love and attention onto Jose and me.

The smooth varnished surface of the trunk was soothing to the touch. I ran my fingers over the glossy top, thinking of the many times Veita had surprised us with handmade furniture and toys. He had built a wooden truck for Jose that looked just like my father's truck, and on my seventh birthday, he had made me a beautiful playhouse. What a kind man he was! Once he even showed up at my camp before breakfast with a brown bag in his hands. He was working in the area and took the opportunity to bring me some oranges and a tomato and cheese sandwich his wife Nena had prepared for me. I was going to miss Veita and Nena very much.

Slowly I lifted the top of the toy box. Inside were all my favorite childhood toys—rag dolls my mother had made for me, a small guitar, a tea set from Grandmother Patricia, a stuffed white rabbit and a black horse, a game of Monopoly, a few books—*Snow White, Little Red Riding Hood, The Three Little Pigs*. Officer Galindo could be none other then the big bad wolf blowing and blowing, huffing and puffing, running us away from our home.

"Hurry up . . . hurry up!" It was the voice of Officer Galindo in the next room.

I was ready to close the box and walk away when I saw my favorite doll, Tomasito, hidden in a corner among the other toys. No bigger than six inches, dressed in a set of blue pants and white shirt I had made for him with the help of my mother, Tomasito lay there with sleepy eyes, waiting for me to pick him up and play with him one more time. As I took Tomasito in my hands, his soft plastic body felt alive to my touch and his dreamy brown eyes opened. "Hello, my friend," I said, looking at the familiar face as if time had not passed.

"Hello," he said back. "Do you want to play with me?" He smiled.

"No, there is no time. I must go. Officer Galindo wants us out of the house soon," I said, pressing his little figure against my heart. I remembered the day my mother had handed me Tomasito, carefully packed inside a small box. I was five years old and recovering from a severe case of German measles and an allergic reaction to penicillin. Our family physician, Doctor Romero, had given me an injection of the drug, and a few minutes after he left my body had begun to swell.

Uncle Tomás, a doctor as well, had unexpectedly stopped by on his way home and seeing my condition, he administered a shot of epinephrine that saved my life. In gratitude, I named my new doll Tomasito.

"Take me with you," I heard the voice of Tomasito say inside my head.

"No, I can't . . . "

"Have you forgotten all the good times we had together? You used to dress me up every morning and take me to school with you. Remember that mean old first grade teacher, Mrs. Guerra? Once she sent us to the principal's office when we refused to write with our right hand. What a crazy idea! It was easy for us to use our left. That Mrs. Guerra, she had a long ruler to hit the kids with . . . "

"Hey . . . what are you doing? I thought you were helping your mother." It was Officer Galindo right behind me.

"Take me with you," Tomasito cried.

"Leave everything as it is," Officer Galindo said.

"Don't put me back inside that dark box!" Without thinking, I hid the beloved toy under my blouse and started to leave the room. Officer Galindo grabbed me by the arm. "Wait! I said, leave everything as it is!"

"Please, please, Officer Galindo, let me take this doll with me . . . " I was crying. "My mother gave it to me."

Officer Galindo moved his eyes away from me, avoiding my tears, fixing his gaze on the wall. Then he walked around the room, searching my dresser drawers and the toy box. "Is everything that is supposed to be here in here?"

I didn't answer. I was angry.

"Didn't you hear me? Is everything in here?" he asked angrily, making sure I understood he was the authority.

"Yes, sir."

"Well then, leave that doll in there, and let's get going. I don't see any point in your crying for that stupid-looking doll when you're going to get plenty of beautiful dolls in the U.S.A."

Stupid-looking doll? I wanted to kick his big belly.

I could feel all my emotions in the pit of my stomach. I wanted to yell at him, "You're the stupid one," but I didn't say a word. Instead

I followed his directions and put Tomasito back inside the box, next to my guitar, so he wouldn't feel so lonely in my absence. Slowly I closed the toy box. My body felt so heavy and tired that I was afraid I wouldn't be able to walk away from the room.

As I left, I took a few steps backwards to take one last look. I watched Officer Galindo make the final notations on the front page of his report. How easy it was for this man to invade the privacy of my bedroom, scribbling words, inspecting, touching beloved pieces of my existence with his insensitive hands. On top of the night table were three volumes of a book titled *Una Vuelta Alrededor del Mundo, A Trip Around the World*, written by the Spanish writer Vicente Blasco Ibañez. I had devoured each page for information about other countries and cultures. In Cuba, books of this nature were hard to come across. The Communists had removed them from the shelves of every library to keep us ignorant about the rest of the world.

I had borrowed the books from my neighbor Rodolfo, an avid reader himself, who had his own private collection. I panicked. How was I going to get them out of the house? Officer Galindo was now standing out in the hall with his back towards me. The window, I thought. The window was open and the books were right next to it. All I needed to do . . . I hesitated for a second. Then I grabbed the precious volumes and threw them into the garden.

Without even checking if Officer Galindo had seen me or not, I ran out of the room. Carmen, Carmen, where was she? I needed to find Carmen and have her hold me in her strong arms. I found her in the kitchen, making some coffee. She had returned from her afternoon errands to find the house in total chaos.

"Carmen!" I ran to her arms and buried my face in her embrace, crying. She was weeping, too, silently. I felt her tears on my skin as she held me tight.

"Niña, niña de mi corazón, what are we going to do now?"

"I don't know, Carmen, but we have to leave. Would Officer Galindo let you stay in the house?" I asked, hoping at least Carmen could take care of our things till one day we could return.

"No, no, mi niña, I have to leave the house, too."

"Where can you go?" I knew Carmen didn't have any relatives left.

"I have good friends, niña. I'll be okay."

"Carmen, I don't want to leave you or this house," I said.

"Niña, niña. There is no time for that now. You must go. You'll get over this," Carmen said as she stroked my hair.

"Carmen . . . we'll send for you as soon as we get there."

"Yes, mi niña. Don't cry. I'll be waiting for you . . . and someday we'll be together again. Don't you worry about this old negra."

I didn't want to think about what it was going to be like not to have this loving woman in my life. There was no one like mi Carmen when it came to soothing the aches and sores of my soul. She had always been there, a presence I had taken for granted until this moment, never thinking it would be taken away.

"Carmen, come with us, please come with us." Carmen didn't answer, but held me closer and rocked me gently.

Many years later, my mother shared with me that she and my father had tried to convince Carmen to leave the country with them. Over and over, Carmen had refused the invitation.

"This is my home. What's this negra going to do in a big foreign country? My people lived and died here, and I want to be buried next to their bones when my time comes," she had said to my father.

Carmen knew she was not going to see me again, but she didn't want to break my heart or take hope away from me. I held on to her, not knowing but sensing her good-bye. It was best for the moment to believe that, in a few months, my dear nanny would join us in El Norte.

"Come on, Carmen, come on, Teresa, let's go!" Jose came into the kitchen. "Officer Galindo is getting ready to close the house. Mother sent me to get you."

Slowly, Carmen and I let go of each other. Carmen, my dear Carmen, what were we going to do without you? I couldn't imagine a single day without looking at her beautiful, dark chocolate face, or not waking up to her cheerful singing as she prepared breakfast.

Before we left the kitchen, I watched Carmen put away a few pots and pans and wipe off the top of the counters with an old rag. Carefully she washed her hands under the sink faucet, and finally she took off her yellow flowered apron, folded it and placed it in the side pocket of her skirt. It had always been important to Carmen to leave the house in order whenever she went out. This afternoon was no different, even when she knew we were not coming back.

"Now we can go, children, the kitchen is cleaned," she said and grabbed Jose and me by the hand.

"Carmen," I said. "Can we go to your healing room?"

"I don't know if we have time."

"Please, please, let's go just for a second," I begged.

"Okay, okay."

Inside Carmen's sacred space, we stood in front of the familiar altar. The orishas were there by their candles and offerings. In a low voice, Carmen began to pray, "Oh, Elegguá, open the path for these beloved children. Oh, Changó, Ochosí, Oggún, keep your thunder, arrows and machete above their heads. Oh, Yemayá, Oshún, feed and nurture them well. Oh, Oyá, protect them from any strong winds, and keep death away from their doorway." Then Carmen sprinkled Florida water all over our heads and bodies. "This will dispel any evil forces around you two."

Outside, we heard the voice of Officer Galindo calling us to leave the house. Carmen splashed some of the water over herself. "My children," she said, "You go on. I'll be with you shortly." We left Carmen standing by her altar with her eyes closed, still praying.

When we came out, the four suitcases were already sitting outside on the porch waiting for us. There was nothing left to do—all the windows were closed, and the lights were off. For a moment, I felt that maybe this was just a nightmare, that anytime now, I was going to wake up. Then I saw my mother handing the set of house keys to Officer Galindo. At the same time, Carmen was walking out through the gate at the side of the house. My mother called her, "Carmen, Carmen hurry up!" Carmen was moving slowly as if her feet were heavy. I looked at the keys in the hands of the officer, who jingled them in front of my eyes with indifference.

It took Officer Galindo only a few seconds to lock the front door of our house, but it took me decades to come to terms with the unspoken feelings I had that afternoon, when I was thrown out of my own home. Officer Galindo shut the door and placed a seal on it warning

"No Trespassing," a message to others that this was now government property. I remember trying to turn my face away, not wanting to witness the finality of that moment, but I couldn't . . . I couldn't because my gaze was fixed on that door. Behind that door were fourteen years of my life.

"Get out of Cuba, gusanos malagradecidos!" By this time, a crowd of at least fifty people had gathered around the house, but not all of them were against us. A group of neighbors came to our rescue, forming a protective circle around us. They helped with the luggage and walked with us in a silent procession down the street, to my Aunt Nelda's house where we were going to stay for the next two days.

I couldn't resist the desire to look back. Officer Galindo was sitting on his motorcycle, trying to start the stubborn engine, and several CDR members were standing in front of the house, throwing eggs at the walls and windows and screaming, "Out of the country, you dirty worms!" Of course, we knew those eggs were intended for us, but in the presence of Officer Galindo, the anger had to be directed at the physical structure that represented our family. I took a deep breath and for the first time, in spite of all the sadness, I felt relief. I was comforted by the thought that soon no one was going to be able to insult or humiliate us.

The price of freedom was high, considering all we were leaving behind. The precious memories and belongings were sealed away forever. The past was now just a picture hanging on the wall, a toy forgotten in a lonely corner of a room, the family photographs left in the album we were not allowed to take with us. With every step I took away from the house, I tried not to think or feel. Instead I tried to look forward, to how I was going to fill the empty drawers of my life with a new vision.

15

GOOD-BYE, CABAIGÜÁN

*T*HE TWO DAYS that followed the telegram were busy ones. Neighbors and friends paraded through my aunt's house, bringing their best wishes for us and saying their good-byes. There was not a single moment when we were alone. People came in groups and stayed for hours, as I watched the circles under my mother's eyes grow darker and her face become even paler.

Father arrived from the labor camp the day after the telegram came. He looked ill and exhausted. It had taken him more than eight hours to get to town in his friend Alberto's old pickup truck. Halfway through the journey, Alberto had run out of gas and Father and Alberto had been forced to walk to the nearest station, five miles away, only to be told the pumps were empty.

The only reserve of gasoline was in the hands of the army base, another fifteen miles away. Fortunately, the gas station attendant had a brother working at the base, who, for a hundred pesos, the equivalent of a full month's salary, would bring to them fifteen gallons of the scarce fuel. Two hours later, Alberto and my father were on their way again.

As soon as my father recovered from his trip, he asked Uncle Manolo to take us to visit Grandmother Patricia and Grandfather Victor in the

170

neighboring town of Guayos. I sat in the back seat of my uncle's 1957 red Chevrolet Impala, between my mother and Jose. Father sat in the front with Uncle Manolo, and immediately they launched into details of the trip to Varadero Beach Airport, in Matanzas province, a distance of approximately 140 miles. Having enough gasoline was my father's main concern, since it was rationed and, most of the time, the pumps were out of order.

A half hour later, Uncle Manolo parked his "Red Pony," as he called his car, in front of my grandparents' house. The minute I saw Grandmother Patricia waiting for us on the porch in her fine mahogany rocking chair, knots the size of my fist formed in my stomach. As usual, Grandmother looked impeccable in an embroidered cotton dress, her silver hair parted down the center and held back with elegant tortoise shell peinetas. She looked so majestic and wise, sitting there, fanning herself with a palm leaf abanico.

"Victor, they're here!" I heard Grandmother call as I stepped out of the car.

My feet dragged as I walked to the porch. I could tell by the dark expression in her eyes, like deep pools of water, that she was keeping her sadness inside. Grandfather Victor came out and stood right next to Grandmother. His white shirt was starched and finely ironed, his shoes shiny black. They were dressed for the occasion, presenting us as a parting gift, with a final impression of their honorable and humble presence.

We embraced and kissed and then went inside the house and sat in the living room while Grandmother went to the kitchen to prepare coffee. Grandfather Victor sat next to my father on the sofa. He was quiet, and his shoulders drooped. I sensed that Grandfather desperately wanted to put his arm around my father. The distance between them was so small that all he needed to do was reach out. For a moment I thought he would, but Grandfather's arms stayed at his sides frozen. How sad! Not even in this last hour could Grandfather reconcile the many years of silence between them. It wasn't that they didn't love each other. It was just that Grandfather Victor was introverted and very cautious, while my father was totally the opposite. Their personalities had always clashed like fighting bulls.

After coffee was served, Grandmother called me into her healing room. I had known this time would come, yet I dreaded the moment of having to say good-bye. She sat on the cowhide chair by the altar, where all her favorite saints stood watching me, and I sat on the corner of the small bed in the center of the room. Saint Teresa appeared to smile at me. I returned the greeting. With shaky hands, Grandmother lit the two tall white candles and said quiet prayers I couldn't hear very well. Then she turned to me.

"Teresa, mi Negrita, I want you to listen to me carefully." She paused and pulled her chair closer to me. "The day you were born, I was the happiest grandmother in the world. I had dreams . . . many dreams for you and me, but . . . destiny often plays tricks on us. The winding road of life has surprising and painful turns."

She took my hands in her calloused hands. "I never expected for us to be separated."

Silence. I could feel a sob pressing against my chest.

"We'll come back," I said shakily, knowing the futility of my words. Coming back to Cuba would be only possible if the Castro regime were overthrown, but everyone wanted to be hopeful. I wanted to believe that someday I was going to return to my home, because that was the only way to bear the pain of leaving all those I loved behind.

"You will, mi niña, you will. I can see it in your eyes. It is here in the lines of your hand . . . but by the time you return, the color of your hair will be adorned with the silver rays of many moons, and I won't be here to welcome you back." Grandmother's eyes turned darker and smaller. "Remember, Negrita, always remember the gentle rattle of the palm trees swinging with the cool breeze, the rumbling waters of the arroyo rushing through its course, the smell of the sweet guarapo and the taste of fresh raspaduras. That's our Cuba, Negrita . . . and as long as you don't forget, you'll be close to us in your heart and you'll be able to find your way back."

Grandmother's words brought back the memories of my childhood. Soon this moment, too, was going to be a part of the past. I thought about the hot afternoons when Grandmother and I would go to the guarapera, a sort of juice bar, right around the corner from her house, to buy cold sugar-cane juice. We used to walk to the park, a couple of blocks down, and sit on a bench, sipping the refreshing guarapo, while we watched the birds bathe in the water fountain. Once she said to me, "When I was small, every afternoon we went to the arroyo near the farm, to play in the water, just like those birds. It was so much fun!"

How I would miss the special treats Grandmother always saved for Jose and me. Our favorite was raspadura, a hard dark-brown candy made from boiled-down sugar-cane juice, and as much a symbol of Cuba as the royal palm trees and the national anthem. The little pyramid-shaped candies were a special treat to savor after a meal or to sweeten our coffee, and Grandmother always hoarded our favorite, coconut raspadura, for Jose's and my visits.

Those sweet memories were interrupted by Grandmother getting up from her chair and going over to kneel in front of her altar. She asked me to join her. Then she turned to me and raised her arms, the palms of her hands facing down above my head. A current of warmth moved down my body as she began to pray aloud.

"Virgen Maria, San Lazaro, Santa Teresa, Santa Barbara, hear the prayers of this old woman for protection and guidance of my beloved grandchild, Teresa."

Grandmother's prayers slowly turned into a quiet weeping. I closed my eyes and tried to still the emotions that roiled inside me. I was afraid of walking away from Grandmother's healing room, a place where I had been healed and comforted so many times. The smell of incense and herbs, the fresh flowers, the candles burning, the old pictures of the great-grandparents I had heard so much about through Grandmother's stories—it was such a familiar room, so full of Grandmother's spirit and her saints. How could I trust I was going to be safe in a foreign country, so far away from my beloved Grandmother?

"Trust the spirit, Negrita," the old woman said, as if reading my mind.

"Grandmother, I'm scared," I said and began to cry.

"Yes, I know . . . but you must walk out of this room and not turn back. All you need to remember is our tears . . . because that's the price we've paid for your freedom. Any time you begin to forget, these tears

173

will remind you of your people. It is my choice to stay behind; you must not feel bad about leaving. I'm an old woman, my place is here, but you're young and your dreams are like the wings of the eagle, which I must protect."

Grandmother pulled a white cotton handkerchief from her skirt pocket and dried my face. Then, she held my head in her hands and kissed my forehead. I buried my face in her chest and let my pain go in quiet sobs. She held me tight, and every time she hugged me, I could feel each branch and leaf of her being opening and exuding warmth and love.

"Negrita, you must be strong. Come, let me show you something." Grandmother stood up and pulled out a wooden box from underneath her altar. With trembling hands, she opened it and handed me a prayer card of Saint Theresa. "Here, take this with you. It will remind you of your strength. Another name for her is Oyá, the mother of the thunderbolt. She gave Changó the power of thunder and lightning."

I took the weathered picture of the saint and pressed it against my heart. Grandmother put her arm around my shoulders. "That was a gift from my mother. She gave it to me when I was about your age. Now it's yours. Take good care of it, Teresa."

Then, turning back to her altar, she lit another tall white candle and said, "From this moment on, as long as I live, there will always be a candle burning for you in this home."

"Grandmother, I won't forget you."

"Come on, give me a big hug, so it will last me a long time."

An hour later, we all piled inside Uncle Manolo's car and left. As Grandmother asked, I didn't look back. Instead I turned my face the other way, so as not to see the two old people standing on the sidewalk and waving good-bye.

In the car, there was silence. This was only the beginning of our painful trail of good-byes. Our next stop was Villa Petra.

When we arrived at the farmhouse, Grandfather José and Grandmother Petra were sitting in their favorite rocking chairs, side by side, on the front porch that faced the entrance garden. They had been waiting for us, prepared as good warriors. Being immigrants themselves, they knew that when people leave, many times they don't come back.

They had never returned to their homeland in the Canary Islands, and now it was too late. So perhaps they were expecting the cycle to repeat itself, as a part of life.

Almost in a ceremonial way, we sat around the old couple, forming a circle so that we could all join the conversation. Mother was next to Grandmother Petra, crying on and off. For Grandmother, who was not a very affectionate or expressive woman, these moments were probably painful. I could tell how uncomfortable she was with my mother's tears, but in a moment of softness, she reached out with a rough and calloused hand and touched my mother's wet cheeks.

My grandmother's hands were like the earth itself. Almost disfigured by arthritis, her bony fingers were like ancient, twisted canyons, and the backs of her hands were traversed by veins like rivers flooded with silt. These were the same hands that had taught me to find the treasures of yuca roots, potatoes, sweet potatoes and malangas in the moist soil of her vegetable garden. How could I possibly leave her behind, now that her feeble body was no longer able to leap atop a horse and gallop across the valleys, now that her arms were not strong enough to grab the hoe and plough the land.

I looked at Grandfather José. His scalp, shiny and barren as the surface of the moon, was encircled by deep rows of wrinkled flesh just like the rows of the land he had loved so much. Now his tired body was no longer an erect tower, but a crumbling cocoon that housed his unbreakable spirit. I shifted my eyes away. I wanted to invoke the memories of the man I knew as a child, dressed in his beige cotton pants and white guayabera, wearing his Panama hat and his black riding boots; the proud gentleman with a kind heart, who every afternoon would ride his walnut-colored Arabian mare around his farm.

That afternoon, Grandmother Petra and I walked to the garden where flowers of all colors and fragrances bloomed, a place where we had spent so many years working together, planting seeds and caring for the flowers. Wordlessly Grandmother cut a long-stemmed white rose and handed it to me. Then she slowly bent down and began to pull some of the weeds from around a gardenia bush.

"Teresa," she said without lifting her eyes. "When I left the Canary Islands, I didn't know what I was going to find in Cuba. It was all a fantasy, a dream. I was young, and I wanted to see other places, meet other people, but I had no idea that as the years went by I was going to fall in love with this island. Soon, I had no desire to go back home. My home was now here. For a long, long time, I felt guilty about not wanting to return and about not missing my mother and my sisters as much."

Grandmother stopped the weeding. With great effort and pain, she raised her stiff body. I looked at her and thought about what a strong woman she was. Grandmother took a few steps with an unsteady gait. Because of the stroke, her legs were weak, but stubborn as she was, Doña Petra refused to use a cane.

"Look, mi niña." She pointed at the house. "This is my home. Castro took away the land, but not my home. Even without the house, it will still be home. As long as I can see and smell the flowers, the grass, the earth . . . I'm home. Every land has a scent. Cuba smells of rum, sugar cane, wild honey and flowers. Wherever you go, Teresa, the fragrance of your Cuba will follow you. It is like knowing a woman by the perfume she wears. It is in her clothes, her hair, even in her breath. Long after she's gone, you can track her down the road by her scent. It is no different when it comes to finding your home. Your nose, your senses will lead you there."

Without looking at me, Grandmother went back to her digging.

"Go, Teresa, go now," she said finally.

Confused, I stood there watching Grandmother Petra grow even older and more tired. As I took a last look at her, I saw tears running down her face and dropping to earth, mixing with the fertile land. I turned around and ran to the road. Standing there, I read and re-read the big lettered sign in front of the house: Villa Petra . . . Villa Petra. I wanted to engrave the name in my mind forever and take the image of my grandmother's garden with me.

I found Almendro waiting for me in the corral. His nervous pacing and the twitching of his muscles told me he knew I was coming to say good-bye. I patted him on the head and ran my hand over his smooth back and side. There was no time for a last ride, even though we both wanted it. "Almendro," I said with a lump in my throat, "there is no other horse like you. I'm going to miss you. I'll never forget those rides at sunset, galloping across the valleys with the wind on my face and feeling so free and happy."

I knew Almendro had understood my words when he suddenly took off running. I watched the graceful movements of his body as he jumped over the fence. He stopped briefly and shook his head towards me; then he galloped away. That was my last picture of Almendro. Like him, I would soon be leaping over the confining borders of my own existence.

By the time we returned to Aunt's Nelda's house, the sun was beginning to set. Another group of neighbors was there, wanting to say their good-byes. I dreaded going in—I was tired of people. I wanted to go and hide in my bedroom, but I remembered the seal at the door. I didn't have a home anymore. All the familiar objects that had once given me comfort were locked inside an empty house.

I dashed inside the bathroom and shut the door. I sat on the toilet with my face buried in my hands and let loose the sadness I'd held in for so many hours. I cried and cried until I heard a knock. It was my mother wondering if I was okay. "Yes," I lied, not wanting to worry her.

"Come on out, Teresa. The Martinez family has been asking for you."

The idea of more farewells made me dizzy. I waited for my mother to go away and then cracked open the door and looked out to make sure nobody was around. Slipping out of the bathroom, I walked quickly towards my aunt's kitchen, where I jumped out of the large window into the backyard.

The night was warm and heavy with the scents of jasmine and honeysuckle. I thought of my friend, Coki, who lived just a few blocks away. This would be my only chance to see her before I left town in the morning.

I was greeted at the door by Coki's mother, who gave me a warm hug. I could tell she had been affected by the town gossip about her daughter. Her shoulders drooped, and she looked at least ten years older than last time I had seen her two weeks before. I walked down the hall to Coki's bedroom. There, my friend was lying on her bed, her brown eyes fixed on the ceiling. The room was in disarray, with clothes and shoes flung all over the floor and the furniture.

"I knew you would come," Coki said. Under the dim light of a lamp, I noticed her eyes were red and swollen like mine.

"I can tell you've been crying, too." I went and sat on the bed by her side.

"Teresa, I never told you or Mariluz about . . . " Coki broke down in sobs.

"About your love for girls," I said, and I held her hand. "I kind of knew, but I wasn't sure."

"Are you mad at me?" Coki asked, lowering her eyes.

"I'm your friend, your sister, no matter what." I pulled her trembling body close to mine and soothed her.

"You're lucky Teresa. You're getting the hell off this island. I wish I were in your place."

"What are you going to do?" I asked.

"I don't know yet. My parents have been very understanding, but I can feel their shame. This town is too small and the people are too narrow-minded. My mother can't walk to the store without some lady coming up to tell her she won't let her daughter come near me. Can you believe that? They're treating me as if I were a rapist! I can't deal with this. I need to get away from here."

"Maybe I can send for you as soon as I get to El Norte."

"I'm thinking of moving to Havana. I have a cousin there. He's homosexual. Rafael has offered his home to me in the past."

"That's a great idea. You'll be better off in Havana. But you're only fifteen. How are you going to support yourself?"

"My parents will help." Coki became quiet. Then she pulled away from the embrace so that she could look at me. "Hey, Teresa, enough about me. When are you leaving?"

"Tomorrow, early in the morning."

"So . . . this is it." Coki said, a somber expression on her face.

"Yep!" I held back my tears. "I'm going to miss you."

"Me, too."

Just like during the difficult times in camp, we held each other. Soon we were breathing together in a familiar silent rhythm. We both knew there were no words that could express the pain of our separation. I thought about the irony of our destinies. Coki was moving to Havana. Mariluz would continue in the work-study camp, and I was going to the United States. In a matter of days, the three musketeers, who for years had fought together, would be separated forever.

It was close to nine when I returned to Aunt Nelda's house. I found my father and Uncle Manolo talking to some friends about the trip to the Varadero Airport. My uncle was still worried about not having enough gasoline. The local gas stations had been all out for a week. Julio, a neighbor, volunteered to go around the neighborhood and ask for help.

"Chico," he said to my father, "we'll get you to the airport. You can count on your good friends as always." And he left.

An hour later, neighbors began to show up at the door with bottles of gasoline they had been saving in their homes for emergencies.

"Here is all we have, Felicia," said Ernestina, a middle-aged woman who was not even a close friend. She handed my mother a glass bottle filled to the top.

Minutes later, more people arrived with all kinds of small containers. Soon, my aunt's porch was overrun with cans and bottles. Uncle Manolo busied himself pouring the fuel into the tank of his Chevrolet, while my father stayed to thank and shake hands with all those who came.

The next morning before sunrise, we packed the car and started for the Varadero Airport. We didn't expect the neighbors to be up at that early hour, but to our surprise, the street in front of the house was full of friends who wanted to say their farewells. As the car took off, they waved with their hands and handkerchiefs. Uncle Manolo drove slowly till we turned the corner, and then he sped down the street. I sat back in my seat and looked out the window. Everything now seemed like a dream to me.

We drove by my elementary school, Tomás Peres Castro, then by the secondary school, Ernesto Che Guevara. I recalled the faces of my friends and teachers. Would I ever see them again? Probably not. We passed the central park, and soon my small town was just a blur in the distance. I closed my eyes and thought of Carmen. Last night she had promised to be there to say good-bye to me in the morning, but she hadn't been there. It was no surprise to me. Somehow I knew Carmen couldn't bear the pain of witnessing our departure.

Before bedtime, Carmen had asked me to sit with her. We went to the only place where we could find some quiet, the patio. Carmen looked tired, but as usual, she was composed. "Niña," she said, "I have been talking to the orishas about you." Her tone of voice was solemn. "They told me that I must wash your hair before you go." She paused and waited for my response.

"When, tonight?"

"Yes, this night before you go to sleep. It won't take long."

"But Carmen, I'm tired," I protested.

"Niña, I said it won't take long." And with that Carmen took me by the hand. "We're going to do this at Nena's house. Too many people snooping around in here."

In Nena's bathroom I was surprised by all the flowers and lit white candles that filled the room. I could smell rosemary, spearmint, basil, cinnamon and rum. Carmen asked me to sit in the one chair in the room. Next to it was a large white basin filled with a green liquid, the omiero, or sacred water used for the washing of the head ritual. As Carmen explained, she had prepared the water herself by mixing crushed fresh herbs special to each orisha with coconut water, rainwater, sea water and holy water she had obtained from the local priest.

Carmen was dressed all in white. She held in her hand a gourd that had been decorated with cowrie shells. "Niña," she said, "a cool, calm and clear head is the key to keeping confusion, illness and evil away." Then, she reached out and undid my ponytail. Chills ran down my back from the top of my head as Carmen's gentle fingers unraveled my hair. Carmen began to chant the names of the orishas. With her gourd, she scooped up the sacred water and poured it over my head. "Keep your eyes closed," she said.

I relaxed at the soothing touch of Carmen's hands on my head. It was as if she were brushing away all the tiredness of my body. Then she rubbed the mixture of herbs on the top of my head, and she scrubbed and scrubbed. I felt light, as if I were floating in the waters of the ocean.

Once she had poured all the sacred liquid over my head, Carmen combed my hair.

"Niña, it is all done. My job is finished. Your head has been cleared of all unwanted energies; you're now ready to meet a new life, a new world. With a clean head you'll be able to hear the messages from the orishas." With this, Carmen wrapped a white piece of cloth around my head. "You sleep with this tonight. Now you go, niña, I have to clean up this mess."

That was the last time I saw Carmen. She left before dawn while we were all asleep. That morning I recalled what I thought had been a dream. Now I realized that Carmen had come into the room while I was sleeping, knelt by the bed and unwrapped the white cloth from my head. I heard her call Yemayá, Oshún, Changó. She prayed and prayed and asked for my protection. Then she gently kissed my forehead, so careful not to wake me up, and walked away.

16

NIGHT FROM HELL

*I*T WAS NOON on July 3, 1970, when Uncle Manolo drove his red Chevrolet into the gated area of the Varadero Airport. A young military officer, maybe in his early twenties, stood at the entrance of the large iron gate, a machine gun slung over his right shoulder, a cigarette dangling from his lips.

"Passports?" he asked as he walked closer to the car.

"One moment, please," my father said and opened his door. Immediately the officer pointed his weapon at him.

"Don't move!" he said with authority. My father froze.

"Passports," he demanded.

"The passports are in the back in a brown bag," Mother reminded my father.

"Okay . . . okay . . . everybody get out of the car. You, mister, get the passports," the officer said, pointing at my father with his gun.

"I need Manolo to open the trunk," said my father.

"Go ahead." The officer watched every move like a guard dog ready to tear us into pieces.

We stood right next to the car. Jose and I held hands while next to us Mother and Aunt Nelda stuck together like conjoined twins. Uncle Manolo was so nervous he couldn't find the key to the trunk at first. His hands were shaking. He fumbled with the lock a couple of times till finally the door opened and Father was able to get the passports.

The officer examined the passports carefully. He looked at each picture and then matched it to our faces.

"Unload the suitcases and set them next to the gate. You two are not allowed into the airport," he told my aunt and uncle. "So say your good-byes here."

Mother and Aunt Nelda were crying even before the officer finished saying his words. They hugged each other and remained in a tight embrace. Jose and I joined them. We wrapped our thin arms around the two women and squeezed our bodies closer and closer to theirs.

"Come on. It's time to go in. The gate is open." We heard the officer right behind us.

More hugs, more tears. We were getting ready to cross the line that would separate us forever. Only a few more steps. I lifted my head for a few seconds and contemplated the iron bars of the airport gate. A cold sensation filled my stomach. I felt faint.

"Come on, kids . . . let's go." It was the voice of my father. I felt his trembling hand on my shoulder. It was painful to break our bond. Aunt Nelda had been a second mother to Jose and me. She and my uncle had married at sixteen and seventeen, respectively, and decided to wait to have their own family till later in life. For the first six years of my childhood, I was my aunt's favorite niece. We only lived two houses away from each other, which made it easy for Mamina, as I used to call Aunt Nelda, to pour all her maternal instincts onto me.

Mamina and Uncle Manolo had taken great pleasure in taking us places and buying toys and clothes for Jose and me. Even after their son Manolito, and their daughter, Leti, were born, they continued to include us in all their family activities. We became a large extended family.

During the summers, they rented a sprawling house on Varadero Beach, and we vacationed together for two or three weeks. Now we were back to Varadero one more time, except that Manolito and Leti had stayed behind for lack of space in the car, and we were not getting ready to unpack the car and settle in the beach cottage for weeks of fun and relaxation. Instead there was a gated entrance in front of us, and soon, it would divide us into the ones who were to stay behind and those permitted to walk to the other side. It was a cutting of physical ties and the beginning of exile.

Uncle Manolo was the first one to break away from the circle. Putting his arm around Aunt Nelda, he gently pulled her away from us. Mother covered her face with her hands and turned in the opposite direction. I saw her take a deep breath, wipe her tears with the back of her hands, then walk fast towards the entrance. I ran after her, followed by Jose and my father.

Now, standing on the other side of the iron bars, we turned around and waved good-bye. The officer pressed the electric button on the side of a post and the door of the gate began to slide from left to right, till it was totally shut. Uncle Manolo hurried into his "Red Pony" sitting behind the wheel. Aunt Nelda stood by the passenger side.

"Don't forget about us," I heard Mamina say. Then the sound of the engine starting. I turned around and walked with my family into the building. I didn't look back again.

We carried our suitcases down a long hall painted pale blue and decorated with a large picture of José Martí. As we approached the end of the hall, we could hear the rumbling of voices, and then we entered the waiting room where hundreds of other families like our own were crowded together. Thick clouds of smoke from cigarettes and cigars swirled above our heads and the air was sour with the pungent smell of human sweat. Baggage of all sizes was spread across the floor. Several small children were crying while their mothers desperately tried to comfort them. It was suffocatingly hot, and the noise was overwhelming.

Through the double-paned glass windows, I could see three small planes resting on the ground and, far in the distance, the beautiful turquoise waters of the Varadero ocean. All the seats in the waiting room were taken, and some families were sprawled on the granite-tiled floors. I spotted a corner area near the window where a family of five was sitting.

"Let's go," I said and began to walk fast before someone else could get there before us.

Using our luggage for seats, we waited for something to happen, although we knew our flight was not till the next morning. The Emigration Department required everyone leaving the country to check into the airport a day earlier so that the authorities had enough time to check all the legal documents and search belongings. This never made any sense to me, but now that we were there, piled up in a corner of this waiting room from hell, the idea of waiting another twenty-four hours seemed like an unbearable nightmare.

My father didn't sit still for very long. He loosened his tie and unbuttoned the top of his shirt. Hands in his pants pockets he walked around restlessly, engaging in small talk with other men. Twenty minutes later, he returned with sweat running down his face and a big cigar hanging from the side of his mouth.

"Nobody seems to know what's going on," he said, sitting next to my mother.

"Please, Pepe, don't blow the smoke in my face," Mother complained.

"Hey, amigo, how long have you been waiting in here?" Father asked the man from the family next to us.

"Well, we got to the airport this morning around ten."

"Qué mierda!" my father replied.

Time seemed to pass so slowly. We kept waiting and waiting for something to happen, for some officer to show up and tell us what the plan was, but nothing happened. As I glanced around the room, I had the sudden feeling that somewhere from a hidden place, the emigration officers were watching us, laughing and having incredible fun with our misfortune.

By five o'clock we were hungry. Uncle Manolo was right when he'd insisted we stop at a little restaurant owned by his friend Geraldo, twenty miles away from the Varadero Airport. There, the owner and his wife Elisa broke government rules and prepared a delicious lunch of black beans, fried plantains, rice and roasted pork. This was the kind of meal he was only allowed to serve the tourists passing by the area.

Children were now crying for food. Frustrated parents didn't know what to say. The atmosphere was growing more and more tense. Both men and women paced back and forth, chain-smoking till they ran out of cigarettes. Cordial conversations were turning into monosyllables. Mother was taking turns holding the sick infant of the Torres family, next to us. His fragile little body was burning with fever. Pablo, the father, tried several times to get the attention of the emigration officers with no results. Over and over, his request for help was ignored. Emilia, the mother, blamed herself for her selfishness. "I should have taken my child to the doctor this morning instead of coming to the airport."

It was close to seven-thirty at night when a male officer holding a manila folder in his hands made an entrance and proceeded to call a few names: "Marquez, Avellana, Rivera and Garcia. Follow me."

The small group disappeared behind the doors leading into the next room. Whatever took place on the other side was not revealed to anyone. This, of course, increased the level of anxiety and stress in all of us. A few minutes later, a female officer with a similar manila file walked in and called the names of Pablo and Emilia Torres.

"That's us, Emilia! Let's go!" said Pablo, immediately getting up from his place and rushing to the door.

The Torres family was gone for at least a half hour, and when they finally came back, Emilia was tearful and Pablo was having a hard time containing his anger.

"Ay chico, nos jodieron, we are missing some papers! Can you believe that? A fucking piece of paper from my job! We've got to go back home and wait till my supervisor sends in some kind of letter. This is unbelievable. I don't know what to do. Ay madresita, how are we going to get back there without money? I don't have a peseta in my pockets to call my brother, Jesus, for help."

Every single person in the room began to dig into his or her pockets in search of some money. It was like finding a penny in the middle of the desert. We all had been told not to carry any money with us into the airport or else it would be confiscated. Mother found a coin in the bottom of her purse. Another woman happened to be hiding one peso inside her brassiere and gladly handed it to Pablo. In total, the family was able to collect five pesos, equivalent to fifty cents. Not a whole lot, but enough for them to make the phone call to Pablo's brother.

We were saying good-bye to our new friends, when we heard our family name called. Father leaped to his feet. He looked pale.

"Papi, are you okay,?" I asked.

"Yeah, it's just nerves. One never knows—the same thing that happened to the Torres family could happen to us."

Mother appeared calm on the surface, but I could tell by the slight twitch of her upper lip that she was afraid. I knew from listening to town gossip and adult conversations that all sorts of things took place during this final part of the journey. There were rumors of detailed body searches and endless questioning by agents from the Communist Party. Now that we were here, I anticipated the worst.

We were guided into a small lobby surrounded by small offices. Each member of my family was directed into a different room. I was told to sit down and wait for my interviewer. Alone in the cramped office, I felt a wave of terror. Different scenarios ran through my head: What if they put my parents in jail? What if they didn't allow Jose to leave the country because he was a boy and approaching military age? What if . . . what if . . . I jumped up from the chair, took a deep breath and tried to distract myself by looking at the pictures on the pale blue walls around me. One was a photograph of Che Guevara, wearing his military fatigues and a friendly smile on his face. The other was a Cuban landscape of the Havanilla waterfalls.

The image of waterfalls brought memories of the arroyo that ran across my grandparents' farm and the words Grandmother Patricia had said to me as we were exchanging goodbyes: "Remember the river, Negrita . . . "

I was feeling calmer when the door opened and in stepped a woman dressed in the olive-green khaki uniform of the Cuban military and shiny tall black boots, the kind with laces all the way to the top. She shut the door behind her and curtly introduced herself, "I'm Josefa Martinez."

Without sitting down, she opened the manila folder in her hands and took a few minutes to read through my information.

I was sweating, yet my hands felt like two chunks of ice. I wanted to become invisible like the invisible man in that old American movie, *The Invisible Man*, but instead I decided to pray to my grandmother's saints for protection. I looked at Josefa. She was an attractive woman with straight, long black hair, almost down to her midback. She looked up at me, and her dark brown eyes seemed friendly.

"Are you Teresa Fernandez?" She took a step closer to me.

"Yes, ma'am," I replied in an almost inaudible voice.

"Teresa, I'm going to ask you few but very important questions and I want you to respond truthfully. No lies! Understand?"

"Yes . . . yes I do, señora."

"Call me Officer Martinez."

"Yes, Officer Martinez."

"Why are you leaving the country?" She began her interrogation. I thought this was a rather ridiculous inquiry, but then I understood that this was all an unfriendly charade. She knew very well why everyone of us was there.

"My parents are leaving, so I'm going with them," I replied.

"Do you want to go, or are they forcing you to go?"

"I want to go. My parents are not forcing me."

"Why are you going to a strange country?"

"Because my parents are going, and I love my parents." The tapping of her pen on the manila folder was a sign that Josefa was getting impatient with me.

"They are gusanos," she said.

A change in strategy. Her eyes no longer looked so friendly.

"Are you a gusana?" she asked, glaring at me now.

"I . . . I don't know."

"If you are leaving the country, you are!" she screamed. "Listen." Moving closer, until her face was just inches from mine, she repeated, "Listen, you are fourteen years old. You could say no if you don't want to go. Your parents can't force you to leave."

"Yes, Officer Martinez, I know, but I want to go. They are not forcing me. I've always wanted to visit my cousins in California and see the snow on the mountains in the wintertime. I've never seen snow, except in pictures and movies."

"Neither have I, but I don't care to see the white faces of the gringos," she spat out disdainfully. She opened the manila folder again. She flipped through the pages, looking for something. What was she looking for? I tried to control my rising panic.

"I see that you have an excellent school record. You were the best worker in your brigade and a chess player who won several national tournaments. What a shame!" she said as she closed the folder and tossed it on top of a small corner table. "Our country, our Revolution needs young people like you. Think, Teresa, think about the contributions you could make to Cuba if you were to stay. We can send you to the capital, to the University of Havana, where you could train for professional chess tournaments." She paused for a few seconds, then sat on the arm of a small chair next to me.

"I read you want to be a doctor. How would you like to go to Russia? They have the best medical schools, the most advanced research and excellent doctors. Also, it would be a great opportunity for you to learn chess strategies from the Russian masters."

No words came out of my mouth. I knew her game, her bribes. I had witnessed how some of my friends had been successfully brainwashed to abandon their parents and serve the country. I was not going to let in a single one of her lies.

Exasperated with my silence, she got up and opened the door.

"I'll be seeing you again, so think about what I offered you. Go back to the waiting area, and be careful not to say a word about our conversation to anyone, not even your parents."

I rushed out of the small office. My head felt like a balloon about to burst—Officer Martinez's words were rumbling in my mind and my body was shaking with fear. What if this woman decided to send me to Russia anyway? What would I do?

Not being able to tell my parents about what was going on frightened me. Back in the lobby, we were all together again, but for how long? I wondered about the kind of questions the officers asked my parents and Jose.

The atmosphere in the waiting room with the others was tense. We were tired and unable to sleep or rest. Everyone around us looked haggard. Children cuddled next to each other trying to find comfort for their empty stomachs. The crowd was actually getting smaller. At least twenty families had been sent back home through the course of the night. Every time an officer appeared at the door, prayers to all the saints, virgins and God were heard from every corner of the room.

The words of Officer Martinez drifted back to me, this time with memories of the camp and the chess tournaments. My participation in the school chess team had been a key to weekend passes out of the working fields. At least once a month, I and other players were taken to the cities to play against other schools. It was fun! We met students from all over the country, and even some Russians whose parents were technicians sent to Cuba to assist with the Revolution.

These Russian students enjoyed privileges the rest of us didn't have. They were given good homes to stay in, and they went shopping in special stores designated for tourists that were very well supplied with food and clothes, an insult to all of us Cubans starving and wearing patched-up jeans.

I won first place in the championship tournament that took place at the province level, in the city of Sancti Spíritus. I was proud of myself, and I waited for the night of the awards ceremony with excitement. When the moment arrived, I heard my name called out over the microphone. I stood up and walked to the platform, where a glorious trophy awaited me in the hands of a tall woman dressed in the uniform of the Revolutionary army. My friends were clapping and shouting "Viva Teresa!" I reached out to grab the fruit of my victory . . . and I was stopped mid-air by a muscular arm grabbing me from behind. "Hold it!" I froze. *What now?* I asked myself.

A uniformed man snatched away the trophy and stepped between the woman and me. He spoke into the microphone, "We apologize for the interruption. Unfortunately, we were just informed that our first place winner has been disqualified."

"Disqualified?" I asked in disbelief. A moment of silence. Then a bellow of protest erupted from the audience.

"Compañeros, compañeras. Silence, please. The decision was made by the organizing committee after a long debate. The winner of this trophy, Teresa Fernandez, is not a member of the Union of Young Communists. Furthermore, she has been identified as an undesirable elemento who wants to leave this country. Therefore, she is not entitled to receive any awards."

I stepped down from the platform, shaking with shock and rage. Humiliated, I ran out to the street where no one could see me and sank to the ground behind the wide comforting trunk of a flamboyan tree.

The voice of Officer Josefa Martinez calling our names brought me back from that moment. Again, my family was separated and sent into different offices. Once more, I faced Officer Martinez.

"Did you have a chance to think about Russia?" she asked.

"Yes, I did, but . . . I don't want to go to Russia. I want to be with my parents. Please, don't send me to Russia."

"Don't worry. Russia is not for people like you. You're not courageous enough," she said harshly.

"Maybe not," I said, feeling relieved.

"Anyway, I have to do a body search on you," she continued evenly, as if talking about the weather. A wave of nausea rose in my throat. I couldn't feel my legs.

"A body search?" I asked, trembling.

"Yes, we'll do this in parts. First, I need to check your hair. Yours is long and thick, a place to hide a precious stone or a gold ring . . . "

"I'm not hiding anything. See?" I said, taking off the rubber band holding my ponytail. Unconvinced, Officer Martinez ran her long fingers through my hair, checking behind my ears and the back of my neck. I hated the feeling of her hands on my skin. My scalp burned at her touch.

Then, without saying anything or asking for my permission, she moved her hands down to my shoulders, back, waist, buttocks. She searched all the way down to my feet. Not satisfied, Officer Martinez asked me to take my shoes and socks off. What in the hell was she looking for?

"Turn around!" she ordered. "Take your blouse off."

This was no body search. Officer Martinez was taking revenge for my refusal to consider her proposal to stay in the country. She was going to make me pay for it! Rape me! Make me experience her power.

"Now, take your bra off!" She stood back a bit so that she could have a better look at my vulnerable figure. A scream, a loud *No!* almost escaped from my mouth.

"How about your skirt and your panties. I want to make sure your mother didn't try to be smart. You people are so greedy," she said.

I had heard stories about women who hid jewels inside their vaginas and in their bras, but never children. Totally naked under the scrutiny of the hawklike eyes of Officer Martinez, I felt smaller than a grain of rice. Even though she did not touch my body again, I could feel her hands all over me, like the tentacles of an octopus, ripping apart the soft fabric of my adolescent modesty and dignity.

Officer Martinez smiled triumphantly as I lowered my eyes to the floor. I wanted so much at that moment to be able to lift my fist and turn that expression of victory into one of pain. For a few seconds, I enjoyed the fantasy, knowing that was all it could be if I wanted to fly to freedom the next day. Then I heard Carmen's voice from a distance. "Niña, niña, de mi corazón. Call Changó. He's fire, thunder and lightning! He'll protect you."

With silent prayers, I began to invoke Saint Barbara, Changó's Catholic manifestation. I imagined her as the little statue I saw on top of Carmen's altar—a lovely young woman dressed in white robes and a red mantle. On her head she wore a turreted crown and a halo; in one hand she held a golden chalice, and in the other she wielded a sword.

I imagined Saint Barbara's sword in my own hand. I swung it menacingly at Officer Martinez's head and her hateful smile. For a brief moment, I had the sensation of pushing the long pointed blade against her chest. No, I didn't want to kill her. I just wanted her to leave me alone. And she did!

"Get dressed, Teresa, and get out of my sight!"

I pulled on my clothes and rushed out of the room. As I ran across the hall into the waiting room, I saw, through the window facing east, the sun peeking out from behind the gray clouds, surrounded by an aura of red and purple light. In a moment of reverence, I lifted my hand and saluted the golden God. The day was coming. We had made it this far, and a new horizon now awaited us.

17

FLIGHT TO FREEDOM

"FLIGHT ATTENDANTS and passengers, prepare for departure," I heard the pilot say. I turned to look back to where my parents were seated and made eye contact with my mother. For a brief moment, I felt her deep sadness merging with mine, a huge wave of grief for all those we had left behind. I knew my mother was leaving the country for Jose's and my sake, but I also knew she didn't really want to go. And now as the engines of the plane accelerated, my mother's sacrifice was beginning to feel like a burden, a heavy weight on my chest. I looked over at my father. A ray of light coming through the small window revealed the paleness and premature aging of his face, and I could tell by the twitch of his upper lip that he was as nervous and afraid as I was.

The plane began to move, and for a few seconds, I thought the whole world was moving with us. I had never been in a plane before and had no idea what was going to happen next. I reached over and held Jose's hand.

As the plane ran smoothly down the runway leaving behind the Varadero Airport, I leaned back in my seat, feeling dizzy. Even though I was sitting next to the window, I was afraid to look out. Maybe, I thought, it would be easier if I followed the advice of Grandmother Patricia: "Don't look back, Negrita." But this time I didn't want to turn away. Taking a deep breath, I gathered my strength and looked out. We were now facing the horizon of the clear blue Cuban skies and the turquoise waters of the Caribbean Sea.

As we picked up altitude, I could see the coastline of my beloved island, the palms and coconut trees bordering the white sand beaches where I had spent so many summers playing, swimming and fishing from the rocks with friends and family. Not having anything else to compare it with, I had always thought of Cuba as the most beautiful place in the world: an enchanted paradise, with oceans that were treasure bowls of bright pink and black coral, a mulata with flirtatious rumbera hips, swaying with the tides and the strong hurricane winds. Cuba, Cuba, the pearl of the Caribbean.

One more glance down, but now there was only deep blue water topped with whitecaps. Cuba was out of my sight. My island was gone! My people were gone! Except that they existed in a tiny point of the universe for me to remember them but never to touch or see again. How could that possibly be? They had been my life till that moment. I could still smell their scent on my skin, their good-bye kisses on my cheeks, the warmth of their hugs, their smiles and tears, their voices, their loving words. I felt like a plant that had been torn from the earth, its roots left dangling in the air.

I closed my eyes, and scenes from my last three days in Cuba played and replayed in my mind. Grandmother Patricia in her healing room. Grandmother Petra in the garden. Grandfather José in his rocking chair. Almendro jumping over the fence. Carmen's hands washing my hair. Coki staring at the ceiling in her dark, lonely room. All the neighbors coming to say good-bye. The streets of my hometown. The smells of jasmine and gardenias in the warm, moist air of the night. These images were part of a chapter of my life that was now closed.

The moment the pilot informed us we could take our seat belts off, emotions exploded throughout the small plane, like cannons shot from the morros of our hearts. The euphoric screams of release bounced against the cabin's wall. "We are free!" yelled a lady sitting in front of me. Throwing off her seat belt, she stood up in the middle of the aisle and mimicked breaking off the thick chains of Communism. "Let us toast our freedom," she shouted, and we joined in with declarations of independence and our hope to return to a free Cuba in the future.

Amidst all the noise and cries of freedom, I sat quietly, feeling a mixture of disbelief and excitement. For years, my family had waited for this moment when we could fly away from all the nightmares of life in Cuba. There were those times when we thought it was never going to happen, but despite all the obstacles and hardships, we had never lost faith. My father's vision of a better existence in a free country had kept us fighting. I remembered the anguish in the faces of those twenty families sent back to their homes from the airport. They had not made it! I felt at once guilty and lucky. As Grandmother Patricia would say, "A guardian angel was watching over us."

I was deep in my thoughts when the handsome blond flight attendant came around carrying a tray full of plastic glasses of Coca-Cola. It had been years since I had tasted this soda. Jose's eyes popped wide open when he took the first sip, and then he gulped down the rest and asked for more.

"Wooo, qué sabroso!" he said, and the flight attendant handed him a second glass.

Many of the adults behaved no differently from Jose. They had the poor flight attendant running up and down the aisle, bringing them glass after glass of Coke. The same reaction occurred when the small ham and cheese sandwiches were passed out. We were like hungry ants, devouring our portions instantly.

As the distance between Cuba and our plane increased, our fear of expressing our pent-up feelings dissolved. Everyone was talking about the horrible night of waiting at the airport. Soon all the emotions we had carried inside us in silence were spilling out. People were hugging each other and laughing wildly. In the seat right in front of me, a middle-aged man was relating his own tale of how during the body search, the officer on duty had grabbed and pulled his balls. A woman in the rear of the plane broke into hysterical crying and screaming. She had had to leave her oldest son behind because of the military age enforcement. Next to her, the other son, maybe twelve, had his arms around his weeping mother.

"Teresa, Teresa!" It was Jose trying to get my attention.

"I'm here, Jose, what's the matter?"

"I just thought of Conchita and Tofi," Jose said, looking concerned.

Conchita was a river turtle Jose and I brought home after a fishing trip with our father. The creature was tiny then, maybe two inches by three inches, but by the time we left, she had become a mature female, and a very noisy one in her nocturnal wanderings around the back hall of the house. I would miss the *click clack* of her shell in the middle of the night.

Tofi, our three-year-old German shepherd, got along quite well with Conchita. Carmen claimed that once she had even seen them cuddling on the back porch! It was hard to believe, but then again, at the farm I had seen a mother pig nurse a baby goat.

"Don't worry, Jose, Manolito promised he would take care of them."

"Do you think we will ever see them again?"

"I don't know," I said, staring out the window.

Forty minutes after our departure, we could see the contours of a new land. Like Cuba, it had familiar sandy beaches, but as we flew closer, tall buildings and concrete lots became more prominent. A big city surrounded by water and dotted with palm trees, with very wide, long roads snaking in every direction, something I had never seen before. The lines of tiny cars on the highways became more visible as we began to descend. Jose was excited, thinking about all those máquinas, as we Cubans called cars, in all shapes and colors, so unlike the old models we knew in Cuba.

As we landed at the Miami airport, there was a renewed wave of excitement in the plane. "Tierra libre!" people screamed. The pilot welcomed us onto free land and wished us the very best. Then we were given instructions in regard to immigration procedures. We were told that because we were coming to the country as Cuban refugees we would have to go through a series of interviews and medical examinations. None of us seemed to care a whole lot about what was next, we just wanted to be out of the plane.

When we finally walked off the plane, many people knelt and kissed the foreign soil with gratitude. I couldn't bring myself to do anything like that. I decided to save such a moment for a more private occasion, or perhaps for that faraway day when I returned to Cuba.

Once inside the airport, we were guided into a big room painted dull green. Standing in a corner was an aluminum flag pole with the red, white and blue American flag. Right next to it was a picture of President Nixon. His large nose caught my attention. As we waited impatiently, we watched officials come and go, calling people into smaller offices. There were forms to be filled out and more questions to answer about everything in our lives.

It took nearly the whole day to go through the ordeal. Finally, we were taken to a building called El Refugio, the place where all refugees stayed for a few days till all procedures were completed and their destination was decided. For the first time in the endless hours of our journey, we were left alone to rest and shower. El Refugio was not particularly welcoming—the rooms were small, hot, humid and dark, with bunk beds and a simple bathroom—but we felt lucky to be there, with our bellies full after the hot turkey sandwich and mashed potatoes meal we received from the El Refugio workers. We were safe while all our relatives in Cuba were struggling to buy a piece of bread on the lines.

Everything new was a source of joy and pain. "Oh, look at this tiny soap," my mother would say, followed by, "If I could only send one of these to my sister Nelda." My father couldn't say enough about the shaving cream and razor he found in the bathroom cabinet: "Coño! This is the best shave I've had in years. Soon as I get to California, I'm sending some of these inside a letter to Manolo." Our point of reference was Cuba. We couldn't sip a cup of coffee without thinking about our family members across the ocean.

Visitors soon arrived. My Aunt Herlinda, who had flown in from New Jersey, was the first one to knock on the door. She had left Cuba in 1962 and was eager to see us after eight years of exile. My memories of her were vague, as I was very young when she lived in Cuba, but I recognized her from photos she had sent to us with her letters. Although a stranger to me, she was family, and I was happy to see her as well as thankful for her generosity and support. My only aunt in El Norte was there to welcome us! Aunt Herlinda came with a big suitcase filled with presents. Most important of all, she brought us clothes we needed and money to fill our empty pockets.

There were endless hugs and tears and comments about how much Jose and I had grown and how different we looked. My aunt gave me a glance as if measuring me with her eyes. "I think the clothes I brought for you are going to fit perfectly." Then with authority, she opened the fat leather suitcase and handed me a stack of elegantly wrapped boxes. She did the same with Jose. "Here, you kids, try these on." I wasn't quite sure what to do with my gifts. I was nervous and indecisive about which to open first. Then, slowly, I started unwrapping one, trying not to destroy the beautiful printed paper. Inside the box, I found a brand new pair of light brown pants and a dark green blouse.

I stood in the middle of the room holding the gift in my hands. I couldn't remember the last time I had worn a garment that was not used or passed on to me from one of my cousins. I thanked my aunt and ran to the bathroom where I could change, taking my boxes with me. All by myself, I held the fabric against my face and inhaled the mild scent of newness. Then I opened another box. Inside was a pair of short black leather boots. I burst into tears. How much I wished at that moment to have Coki and Mariluz right next to me.

Afraid the new clothes were not going to fit, I stood in front of the mirror and took a last look at the blue cotton skirt and white blouse I was wearing. My mother had made them for me from a couple of dresses from her youth. I hesitated, not quite ready to let go of my Cuban clothes. Trapped in the pores of the cloth were the smells of the soap, the water, the sun, the air of my beloved Cuba, and the sweat from my mother's hands as she struggled to transform her old dresses into fashionable pieces.

With slow and precise movements, I undressed. One by one I folded my old clothes and tucked them carefully inside one of the boxes. Then I slipped into the skin of my "American" bell-bottom pants and blouse. I was shocked by the image I saw in the mirror: a different girl, somewhat taller and even older. I studied myself, not quite happy with the overall picture. Something was missing. "The ponytail. That's it!" I said aloud. And pulling off the rubber band, I let my hair down.

My Aunt Herlinda was the first one to comment on how well both

Jose and I looked in our new clothes. "Now," she said, "we're ready to go out into the world." It was a thrill for us to get out of the El Refugio resort—finally free to explore the new world outside! I was eager to see what it was like to walk on the streets of a free country—to see what people were doing, the clothes they wore, the cars they drove and even the music and dance they were into.

We had been so cut off from the rest of civilization that everything triggered our curiosity: the rental car my aunt was driving, with its automatic windows and seats that adjusted at the press of a button; the stores full of colorful clothing and shiny shoes; the clean streets and brightly painted houses. It was like an adventure in wonderland or waking up from a long, long sleep. Jose poked me to get my attention. "Look at that giant building!" "Hey, kids, look at that red convertible!" my father pointed out. Aunt Herlinda started laughing at our nonstop exclaiming. It was contagious.

My aunt took us to visit Nico, a friend of my parents who had lived in Miami since 1968. Nico had settled in Hialeah, a neighborhood whose residents were mostly Cuban exiles. On the way to Nico's I was surprised to see Spanish names on the signs of restaurants, stores and even buildings. With the windows opened, I could hear Cuban music on every corner. Sidewalk Spanish—"Oye chico, qué pasa?" "Niña ven pa'ca."—mixed with the rumble of car engines. The smells of gasoline, smoke and perfumes in the air made me dizzy. There were so many images, sounds, smells and everything seemed to move too quickly.

My aunt stopped the car right in front of what Cubans called a quiosco, or a small store where cigarettes, cigars, magazines, newspapers, coffee and sometimes pastries are sold. The owner of the place was a heavyset Cuban woman who shouted the orders to her husband just a few feet away from her. My aunt ordered coffee for all of us. "Papi, tirame cinco cafés," the woman yelled. In Cuba husbands and wives often call each other "papi" and "mami." My father fixed his eyes on the large Cuban cigars in a glass box by the counter. My aunt immediately said, "Hey amiga, give him one of those tabacones." She meant big cigars. For a moment, I had the feeling of being back in old Cuba.

The coffee was too sweet for my taste and it reminded me of

Grandmother Patricia's saying, "Coffee without sugar tastes better." Just thinking about my grandmother made my eyes sting with tears. Not wanting to cry, I glanced around the store. It was so amazing just to walk in there and ask for coffee—or anything—and have it right in your hands within seconds!

We finished our cafés and were ready to go back to the car when Jose grabbed my aunt by the arm. "Tía, tía, look! I want some chicles." My aunt turned around and dug out money from her purse to buy one pack of gum for Jose and another for me. Hurriedly Jose unwrapped his and stuffed two pieces in his mouth. I turned my pack over in my hand, thinking about the letters we used to receive in Cuba from our family in El Norte. An uncle or aunt would occasionally send us a piece of gum pasted to the inside of the letter. The thrill from such a small gift would last for weeks. Now, I was holding a whole pack—all to myself, no need to share it with Jose or with my friends.

When we finally arrived at Nico's house, a group of at least fifteen friends was waiting for us. Apparently Nico had telephoned everyone he knew from our hometown who now lived in Miami. The door of the house was open, and people were seated around the porch drinking beer and talking. As soon as we stepped out of the car, we were bombarded with welcoming shouts. I was hugged and squeezed to the point where I couldn't breathe.

Carried inside the house, we were overwhelmed with generosity. The pockets of my father's shirt were ready to burst with the many cigars placed in them. Laughter and cries exploded from every corner as old friends reminisced about the old times in Cuba. Everybody was dressed up for the occasion. Cubans tend to overdo it when it comes to their appearance. The women wear their high heels and elegant dresses even to walk to the store. The men are more subtle but wear thick gold chains around their necks and flash fancy watches as an indication of their wealth or high credit card debts.

Jose and I were mesmerized by the luxurious lifestyle of our new friends. Nico and his wife didn't seem to suffer any scarcities—as we looked around their home, we found a TV in every bedroom, plus another gigantic one in their living room, a total of four sets. Jose and I went from room to room snooping around, trying not to be registrones, that is, invasive; we were simply hungry for information about the world and its modern technology. "These people," whispered Jose, "must make lots of money. They even have a swimming pool in their backyard."

It was a major event when Nico took Jose and me for a ride to the neighborhood grocery, where he needed to pick up a few things for dinner. It was incredible! Jose had never seen many of the fruits on display. As soon as we got there, he began running from place to place, grabbing, touching, smelling and even biting pears, apples, grapes. Finally he hoisted up a big watermelon that he claimed he was going to eat all by himself. The owner caught Jose walking out with the watermelon—he didn't realize he needed to pay for it. The kind man, a Cuban who perhaps saw himself in Jose, gave my brother the watermelon, a gift my poor brother treasured, but which he could barely carry to the car.

The dinner at Nico's was an unforgettable experience. By the time the table was set, we had already eaten lots of plantain and potato chips, but Nico's wife, Olga, outdid herself with the dinner menu. It had been years since I seen such a buffet of Cuban delicacies: congrí or black beans and rice cooked together with cumin, oregano and coriander, a roast leg of pork decorated with slices of papaya, orange and pineapple, steamed yuca with a garlic and cilantro sauce. Also on the table were fried plantains and frituras de malanga, avocado and tomato salad and arroz con pollo, and for dessert, casquitos de guayaba and fresh cheese.

After dinner and coffee, a ride to Miami Beach was suggested. We packed into the cars and a few minutes later were on the road. The city at night was overwhelming with its neon lights and crowds of people walking the streets. I sat in the back with my face glued to the window. My aunt insisted on having the air conditioning on, but this artificial cold air was not pleasant to me—it seemed to dry out my nose and throat and made me cough and sneeze. I preferred the hot and humid breeze we were used to in Cuba.

By the time we arrived, my head was spinning from all the flashing signs and lights on the road. We tumbled out of the car.

"Where is the beach?" asked Jose.

"It's down there," my aunt said. I looked and saw only tall square buildings. Nico and the rest of the clan joined us, and we began our walk down a paved path that took us, finally, to the ocean. The night was clear and the moon was full. Only a few stars were visible in the sky, perhaps because of the reflection of the city lights.

As we walked closer to the ocean, the waves crashed on the shore with a deep, muffled sound. Reflected on the blue-black waters, the silver rays of the moon merged with the multicolored lights of the waterfront buildings. I watched how the surf crashed and receded, leaving behind little shells and algae, as well as plastic bottles and other bits of trash. I heard Nico say, "Some nights when it's clear, the lights of Cuba can be seen from here." I looked across the ocean. I searched for the lights, any light, a sign from my beloved island. But my eyes met only darkness.

We were so close and yet so far away. My Cuba was nowhere to be seen or heard. I kneeled down on the sand and dipped my hands in the cool, salty waters of the ocean. I imagined my fingers stretching, reaching out for the Cuban coastline. I pictured the strong grip of my hands as I held on to the rocks of the Cuban shore, like a crab fighting not to be swept away by the breaking waves.

18

CITY OF ANGELS

LOS ANGELES, city of angels, was not the
land of our dreams. It was a gigantic jungle of concrete that frightened
me with its bustling clamor and crowds. Unlike my hometown, people
kept to themselves. Nobody seemed to be interested in getting to know
their neighbors, and some even seemed afraid of each other. People kept
their doors and windows shut, and on the streets, young blacks and
Mexicans fought deadly battles for turf while the Cubans stuck to their
own territory.

Uncle Manolo helped us find a place to live near the Los Angeles
airport. We moved into the two-bedroom, middle unit of a triplex, between a young couple with an infant, and our eighty-year-old landlord,
Gertrude. The old woman was hunchbacked and half-crippled by arthritis. Her fingers were twisted and swollen, her legs streaked with red
and purple veins.

Gertrude seemed fierce and unfriendly at first. She complained
about the bicycles and roller skates Jose and I kept near the back door.
Every time we wandered outside, she watched us like a hawk. The place
didn't have a backyard, only a narrow sidewalk bordered by a strip of
garden planted with roses, gladiolus and California poppies. At least
twice a day, la Americana, as we called her, would come out of her
house and scream at Jose and me when we played near her roses.

La Americana also took the liberty of disrupting our privacy with unannounced weekly visits. She would simply knock on the door and invite herself into the apartment. Glaring at us, she would inspect every room, saying things in English we couldn't understand and pointing at small stains on the ugly green carpet or at minor scratches on the kitchen tiles. My mother's face would flush with embarrassment.

As shocking as these visits seemed to us, we didn't protest, not realizing that Gertrude didn't have a right to intrude in our lives. We believed that because she was the owner of the property, she could get away with her rude behavior. After a few weeks, the visits stopped. We assumed that somehow she had become convinced we were not a bunch of wild animals from the Cuban jungles.

Gradually, as we learned to speak English in broken sentences and began to communicate with her, la Americana began to soften. I noticed her blue eyes looked kind when she watched Jose and me, though she still yelled at us. Occasionally she and my mother would engage in a dialogue about the roses. Mother spoke Spanish with some words of English mixed in here and there, and Gertrude replied in raspy English as if she understood everything she had heard. Soon they were working together in the garden, pulling weeds and pruning the plants.

One afternoon the old woman came to visit and saw me working on an oil painting, a winter landscape. She watched me in silence for a while and then told me she was impressed with my artistic skills. The next day she was waiting for me when I came home from school. She invited me into her apartment, and I hesitantly agreed. Inside, the place was dark and had a musty smell. In her living room were antique pieces—a heavy brown leather couch and chair, hand-carved wood tables, and two elegant lamps. Several magazines and newspapers were piled on the blue carpet right next to the chair. I was surprised to see on the center table a big box of art supplies—fine bristle brushes of all sizes and dozens of tubes of Grumbacher oil paints in a wide selection of colors.

"Here, these are for you," she said, pointing at the box.

"For me?"

"Yes, they were my brother's. He died ten years ago, and there's no one else in the family who can appreciate their value. I know you can," she said gruffly, as she ran her stiff fingers over some of the brushes.

I couldn't find any words in my limited English vocabulary to express my gratitude to the old woman, so I simply said "Thank you, thank you," and gave her a strong hug. Gertrude was not expecting such an effusive demonstration. I felt her body tense and contract as I wrapped my arms around her, but then she relaxed and returned my embrace.

"Thank you," she said. "I haven't been hugged for years."

After that Gertrude and I became good friends. I visited after school and did her dishes while she sat on her kitchen chair and told me stories of her brother, the painter, and about her childhood in California at a time when there were few houses in the area.

"This was a magical place, Terry," she said, not able to pronounce the shortcut for my name, Tere, as my family called me. "When I was a young girl, we used to ride horses right there"—she pointed at the street, now crowded and noisy with cars. "Except there were no streets, only open fields and a few dirt roads."

My friendship with Gertrude was comforting to me at a time when I was grieving the separation from my grandmothers. Grandma Gertrude, as I began to call her, had a kind heart underneath her stern appearance. Like my Grandmother Petra she loved her garden and her flowers. And like my Grandmother Patricia, she was a great storyteller. The stories Gertrude shared with me about her family and her life gave me some understanding about the people of this country. She was my first and most intimate connection to the new culture.

With both of my parents working outside the home, Grandma Gertrude was the only one waiting for me every afternoon after school. With patience, she listened to my broken English as I shared with her all my frustrations with school. High school in Los Angeles was not anything like my old schools. Kids spent most of their time shouting at the teachers, who had no control over their classes. After the strict military discipline of Cuba, I found the atmosphere chaotic and intimidating.

Mr. Olegno, an old man with big bushy eyebrows and a white wiry mustache that curled up at each end, taught the English as a second language—ESL—class. He was an immigrant himself, from Russia, old and too tired to handle our energetic, highly diverse group, which included students from South America, Greece and Africa. The class met every day for an hour after lunch, a time when our teacher fell prey to his own weakness: the desire for a siesta. While he dozed, we took the opportunity to talk and have fun, sometimes playing the radio and dancing.

Occasionally Mr. Olegno would open his eyes and say in broken Spanish, "No gusta ruido," meaning he didn't like the noise. The whole class was a joke. As we students made friends with each other, we learned to speak Portuguese and Greek, but few words of English.

Then there was my art class with Mr. Bill, a tall, handsome, middle-aged man with shaggy blond hair who interrupted his lesson every day for fifteen minutes to teach me English. He asked every student in the room to stop what they were doing and to sit in a circle around me. He would pull out a book or magazine, and pointing at the picture, ask all of us to repeat, "This is a car, this is a house." Then he would turn to me. "Now, Flora, you try." Besides the fact that he mispronounced my first name, he irritated me with his broken-record style of teaching. The exercise made me feel terribly foolish, especially when my pronunciation was off and the entire group broke into laughter.

All my life I had been called by my middle name, Teresa. In Cuba, it was customary to call people with two names, such as Flor Teresa or Maria Juana, simply Teresa or Juana. In America I was now called by my first name. Hearing my new name, "Flor," was disorienting. It was as if people were talking about somebody else.

I was also not familiar with kids bringing guns and knives to school, but soon I learned from friends certain rules of survival: Never go to the bathroom during the lunch break, don't walk home alone, and if anybody tries to pick a fight with you, ignore him.

I followed the advice of my friends as much as I could, but it wasn't always possible to avoid trouble. One afternoon, while I waited in line to buy my lunch, two tall black girls cut in front of me. "Escuse me," I said in broken accented English, "I here before you." One of the girls laughed and pushed me against the wall. Not knowing what to do, I pretended nothing had happened and went back to my place in line.

"Hey, you, Mexican! What are you doing?" the other girl said and hit me on the shoulder.

"I'm no Mexican."

"Who cares! You're brown." The same girl shoved me again, and then flashed her long, red fingernails at me. "I'll rip your face with these," she threatened, moving closer.

At that point, I knew I didn't have much choice but to defend myself. I looked around in search of a friend, but to my surprise the group of Hispanics had disappeared. How could that be? Five minutes ago, they were sitting at one of the tables, eating lunch. I felt completely alone. These friends were not like my friends in Cuba—they had chickened out. The two girls were circling me. I needed to think fast. Maybe if I ran to the principal's office I would be safe. But it was too late—I saw a fist coming and then felt a hard punch to my nose. I recovered enough to move away. *Kick, kick hard!* I heard a voice inside my head shout.

Fortunately, one of the school guards was nearby, and he stopped the fight before it could escalate, but the girls and I ended up in the principal's office. The girls lied and blamed everything on me, and we all were suspended for two days. From then on, I kept my eyes on those two and avoided them on school grounds. I also signed up for karate lessons.

My parents were having a difficult time adjusting to the new culture. My father became obsessed with the goal of recovering the fortune he had lost in Cuba. Six months after our arrival, he quit his factory job. With the money he had managed to save, he bought an old pickup truck and began to recycle metals, which he sold. Every week, Father took at least a couple of loads of aluminum, tin, copper and bronze to the junkyards and came home with two or three hundred dollars in his pocket. A year later, he enrolled in school to learn about refrigeration. With these new skills, he opened a store where he repaired and sold secondhand refrigerators.

We never saw much of Father. He was always busy with the business and worked during weekends whenever he had the opportunity to make an extra buck. At night, he sat in front of the television and cruised through the channels with a distant look on his face, too tired to talk or to listen to me talk about my day. I began to wonder about my father's promise of going fishing in the green rivers of El Norte. What about the big trout we were supposed to catch together?

Mother worked a forty-hour job in a factory that made fancy boxes for musical instruments. She was having her own difficulties adapting, as she had never worked outside the home. Mother looked tired and sad, but never complained about her job; instead she became more critical of my father. She was constantly on his case about the old shirts he wore to work and the smell of cigars in the house. Like my father, Mother had her own way of escaping reality—her sewing. Every evening after dinner, she sat in front of her sewing machine and lost herself in the quiet world of her creations. For me, it was always a relief when the television was on and the sewing machine was running; finally, there was peace in the house and I could read my books.

Not speaking English was a barrier for both of my parents. At first, they were taken with the idea of going to school in the evenings, but soon they realized they were too tired at night to learn anything. So my brother and I became the designated interpreters. It was a burden for both of us, but especially for me. Being older and female, I was forced by circumstance to go everywhere with my parents—to doctors, the dentist, to stores and any other place where English was required.

My mother's doctor, an elderly Jewish man whose last name I was never able to pronounce, was the worst. In one of our visits to his office, he proceeded to ask my prudish mother questions about her sexual life.

"How often do you have sexual intercourse? Do you experience any pain?" The doctor never lifted his eyes from his notes. He had no idea how difficult my task was, considering sex was a subject my mother had never felt comfortable discussing with me. As soon as I translated the first question, my mother's face turned red. Shyly, she smiled and lowered her face. I waited for an answer.

"Well?" the doctor said, finally looking at me. "Do you understand my question?"

"Not really." I didn't feel good about lying, but the old doctor must have gotten the point because he moved on to another subject.

. . .

I began taking part-time jobs to earn money. I worked four to five hours after school every day, and during the summers I worked full-time. My friends from school and I stuck together and found employment in the same places—mostly factory assembly-line work, such as food packing or assembling electronic parts.

For me, these jobs were just stepping stones—a means to make enough money to buy a car and books and to pay for college. For some of my friends, the factory was it, and only it. Interested only in dating and getting married, they often ended up dropping out of school. The boys bought cool cars for cruising the streets on Saturday nights. The girls spent their money on fingernail polish, sexy dresses and high-heeled shoes to attract a husband.

By the time I became a senior in high school, many of my Latino pals had already married and were on their way to having a family. My best friend, Rosa, a pretty Mexican girl with long black hair and expressive brown eyes, began to miss classes when she got a steady boyfriend. Suddenly, I felt very much alone, as well as angry. There was no Rosa to walk home with after school or to go to the beach with on Sundays. A few months later, during a phone conversation, Rosa told me she was getting married and that she was pregnant. I wasn't surprised by the news, but I felt hurt.

"What happened to our plans to go to UCLA?" I demanded.

"That will have to wait. You understand, don't you?"

No, I didn't understand. I was disappointed. I was going to miss my friend, and I was scared by the prospect of meeting the challenges ahead at the university all alone. Once again in my life, at age eighteen, I had to face another separation from people I knew and loved.

When graduation day came I greeted it with a mixture of feelings. I was happy and proud of my accomplishment. Looking back, it had been hard to go through three years of total frustration, trying to figure out my way in a very chaotic educational system, learn English and deal with the gangs and drugs around me. In many ways, I was amazed by my ability to survive this maze. As I stood in front of my class to receive my diploma, I was also aware that this moment marked a definite separation from my friends. At the end of the summer, only one other friend, Johnny, and I would be going to the university. The rest of the group was staying behind, working their eight-to-five jobs. I was going to miss them.

The University of California at Los Angeles, where I enrolled, was a cauldron of racial and political conflict in the mid 1970s. Chicanos and other Latinos protested against discrimination by boycotting their classes and picketing in front of the administration office with "Chicano Power" signs, and they demanded an increase in the number of brown-skinned students admitted to the schools of medicine and law.

As for myself, I was too new to both the political and educational systems to understand the complexities and struggles of the Latinos and Chicanos. I didn't have the history and trauma of discrimination they had experienced in this country. In contrast to them, I was simply thankful for the opportunity to attend college on a scholarship that covered my tuition and books. Not having to do any type of forced labor in exchange for my education was a gift in itself. Besides, with my background in a very punitive and oppressive school environment, I was truly afraid that any form of protest could get me in trouble.

Gradually, I began to lose myself in the cultural and educational atmosphere of the time. I realized how success, approval and acceptance were linked with a homogeneous identity which required me to tone down the bright colors of my Cuban culture. Soon I learned to fit in by dressing in fashion, by not talking with my hands as Cubans do, by talking more softly and more slowly, not like Cubans who shout and speak rapidly. I stopped listening to salsa music and reading novels in Spanish. In other words, I wanted to be American.

The more I toned down the bright colors of my clothes and Cuban spirit, the bigger the gulf became between me and Cuba and my old friends and family. Cuba and the people there were part of a different reality: everything about them, including their values and beliefs was incongruent with the new ways I was adopting to become more American. In the culture I was now a part of, there was no place for Carmen and her Yoruba tradition, or for Grandmother Patricia and her healing practices, or even for Grandmother Petra and her love for animals and the land. Maintaining two cultures was like being pulled in opposing directions—I just couldn't bear it.

At some point during the second year of my program at UCLA, I stopped lighting candles to the orishas. Even though I kept the altar in my bedroom, it became a dormant spiritual temple. I forgot about Changó, Oshún, Yemayá, and the other deities that had been my allies for so many years. Letters from Cuba were infrequent, and only a few friends and family members continued writing to my family. I tried to write back, but the volume dwindled as I searched for words and experiences they could relate to.

Living at home was frustrating and stressful. I was now a stranger my parents couldn't dare to know, and I was constantly fighting with my mother, who insisted on clinging to Cuban traditions and values. She couldn't understand my not wanting to take her along as a chaperone to the parties I frequented, despite the fact that I was now an adult, and she kept comparing me with Cuban girls who followed the rules.

One Saturday evening, as I helped my mother set the table for dinner, I told her about my plans to go to the movies with my boyfriend, Steve, that night. I knew exactly what her reaction was going to be. First, she would ask if any other friends were going, too. Then, she would lecture me on how inappropriate my behavior was.

"You know how I feel about what you are doing," she said, without looking at me—a sign of disapproval. "A Cuban woman who is decent doesn't go to the movies by herself with a boyfriend." Mother was never direct, but she was good at making hurtful implications.

"So, I'm not a decent woman?" I snapped back, reproaching her.

"Look at your friend Areli. She takes her mother on dates with her boyfriend."

"Of course, Mother. Areli only goes to the Cuban club. Every single girl there is like her. But my friends from school would laugh if they saw me coming to a party with you!"

"Why can't you be more like Areli?" she persisted.

"Because I can't. I live in a different world. Why can't you get that?" I shouted angrily.

"Oh my God, Teresa, if only your grandmother could see you these days."

"She would probably freak out. There's no doubt about that," I replied sarcastically.

Of course, my mother was simply acting out her role as a traditional Cuban mother. She felt responsible for protecting my virginity, or as Grandmother Patricia would say, my honra. She was mistrustful of my ability to take care of myself and never hesitated to tell me so. After many battles, I simply stopped bringing any boyfriends home. I took pains to conceal my outside identity from her and my father, from the rest of the family, even from my Cuban friends.

Eight years after I'd left Cuba, in June 1978, I graduated with a Bachelor of Science degree. I'd successfully completed the rigorous pre-med program, and I was proud of myself, but at the same time I was lonelier than ever. At my graduation, I was overwhelmed with feelings of guilt and sadness. As I stood in front of the faceless crowd to pick up my diploma, I started thinking about everyone I'd left behind and wished with all my heart that my friends from Cabaigüán and the camps could be there to celebrate with me.

Walking in line with the other graduates, I became more and more absorbed in memories of my past and began to envision being back in my beloved home. Someone was whispering, "Negrita, we are proud of you," and I saw my friends and family walking next to me—the spirits of Carmen, Petra, Patricia, José, Victor, Mariluz, Coki. From beyond the crowd, I could hear the distinct sound of drums. Not the drums from the school band but batáa drums. Carmen's drums. Dressed in her blue and white Yemayá cotton dress, she was beside me, dancing and singing. "Carmen," I said "Carmen, Carmen mi negra querida."

The vision continued as I walked across the stage as if in a trance and returned to my seat. And then the batáa heartbeat went silent. Carmen's face turned pale, her dancing slowed and then she dropped to the ground, her robust body coming to rest on the dark soil. Was she asleep? There by her side was Yemayá, rocking Carmen in her arms. Another orisha, Oshún, was offering her fresh river waters for a final cleansing bath. Then, the warriors Elegguá, Oggún and Ochosi came to the scene and danced in a circle around her. Finally thunderbolts, like fireworks, illuminated the sky. It was Changó, coming to welcome

Carmen back home, to pay homage to a great priestess.

There was another sound, rumbling louder and louder. I slowly realized it was not Changó, but the thunder of applause. The vision faded, and I tossed my cap with the other students.

Two days after my graduation, we received a telegram from Aunt Nelda with the news of Carmen's death. She had died of a heart attack two days before, on the evening of my graduation ceremony. The realization that I was not going to see Carmen again filled me with grief. I went into my room and stayed there a long time, thinking of all the years I had fooled myself. I had stripped down my Cuban identity and shut down the voices of my people, their visions and dreams. But Carmen had come to pay me a visit, to remind me of my roots. It was Carmen who let me see the line of spirits who had been walking by my side along the path.

That long afternoon in my room, I cried for all the loved ones left behind, for Carmen and for all the others I would never see again. For years, I had pretended that, someday, we would return to our Cuba. I had lied to myself to avoid the pain of acknowledging that going back was impossible.

My gut twisted. It was the old grief burning inside. I walked over to my window and looked out to the empty street. For a moment I thought I heard the drums calling the spirits to be with me. I thought I saw Carmen once again, chanting the Yemayá songs and reaching out to me with her loving arms. I thought I heard her say: "Let go, niña, let go. It's time for you to let go of all your pain. We chose to stay, and you needed to go."

I sat down on my bed and closed my eyes. I knew the meaning of her words. She was coming to release me from the guilt I'd felt for leaving my people behind in such misery and despair, all those years when I couldn't sit at the dinner table without thinking about my relatives in Cuba who were starving. Guilt for having the privilege to live in a country where I could say and do anything I wanted, while my friends had their tongues and hands tied by Castro's regime. Guilt for not being there when the old roots of our family tree began to die: first Grandfather Victor, then Grandmother Petra followed by Grandfather José.

Every time a family member in Cuba died, the same thing happened. A phone call would come from Cuba. Only four minutes of conversation would be allowed for one of my aunts to tell us the news—"Papi died" "Mami died"— and then, *click*, communication would be cut off by the Cuban operator. No time to talk about the important details of how they died, or the funerals, or their last words. Nothing!—just silence at the other end. After the call, Mother, Father, Jose and I would sit in the kitchen and cry. One more time Mother would say, "We must have courage; we knew this was going to happen. They were getting old, and that's life."

Yes, they were dead, and we were here, so very far away. We would never be able to go back to bury their bodies, to send them on their journey with the proper rituals and prayers, to throw the last handful of earth on their graves. But in my mind I could see their faces as they waved good-bye to me.

That night I cleaned the long-neglected altar in the corner of my bedroom. I dusted the orishas and replaced the old candles. Then I lit them, one by one, and began to call the orishas just as Carmen had taught me.

19

GRANDMOTHER'S VISIT

*I*N 1 9 8 0, ten years after our departure from Cuba, Grandmother Patricia was granted permission to visit us. Fidel Castro, pressured by economic difficulties, needed an easy way to bring dollars into Cuba. His immediate solution was to exploit the emotions of the broken families divided by the ocean and political exile. Castro opened the doors for Cuban elders who wanted to travel to the United States to see their sons and daughters.

The day of Grandmother's arrival, family and friends gathered at the airport. As the airplane bringing Grandmother to us was landing, I could feel the nervous touch of butterfly wings inside my stomach, and my hands were cold and sweaty. I noticed my father pacing near a big metal ashtray. Occasionally he would shake off the gray layer of ash from his burning cigar, and then puff and puff on his puro, blowing thick clouds of brownish smoke into the already saturated air.

"No fumes mas," Mother complained.

"Leave me alone," Father said, blowing more smoke into the room.

The passengers began to come through the gate. Jose moved closer to us and put his arm around Father's back. He was no longer the small, thin boy who'd left Cuba. After a few years of a good diet and exercise, my brother had grown tall and strong. I wondered if Grandmother would recognize us. Both Mother and Father looked better than when they'd left Cuba; they'd had a chance to recover from the hunger and worries they'd suffered. I looked at my dad, noticing the healthy mane of silver hair. At age fifty-five, he was handsome and, like his mother, very charismatic.

The last few travelers walked into the terminal. We were beginning to worry, when out of the long, narrow hall that connected the plane to the gate emerged an old woman. My heart sank. She looked so different from the robust and elegant lady I had known. She was thinner and smaller, her back curved by the weight of her years and the hard times of suffering and inadequate nutrition. I ran towards her.

"Abuela, Abuelita!" I screamed, and I was followed by the rest of the family.

"Negrita, Negrita de mi corazón," she said, embracing me with her long, bony arms. I returned her hug softly. I was afraid that if I put any pressure on her, her ribs would break. Times have changed, I said to myself, remembering, when Grandmother held me, how I'd felt protected by her strength and warmth. Now the roles were reversed. I was the one holding her. I was the solid rock, and she was as fragile as dried clay.

The wrinkles on my grandmother's face reminded me of the deep cracks in the Cuban soil during the dry season. These prints left by time on her pale skin were like pathways into her soul. I looked into her dark eyes, and I was happy to discover that, in spite of all the hardship, there were still bright sparks there, burning like fireworks on a night of fiesta.

"Negrita, mi niña querida, my child. Look at you, so grown-up and pretty. If only your grandfather could see you . . . " She burst into tears.

Gently, I put my arm around her back and helped her walk towards my father. What a moment! As soon as she saw him, she stopped and stood there looking at her beloved son, not uttering a sound, not making a single movement. My father suddenly turned into a little boy reaching out for the maternal hug he had missed for so long.

Grandmother recovered quickly. After two weeks of eating well and resting, she began to look like her old self. She gained weight, and gradually some of the wrinkles disappeared, giving way to a much younger and fuller face. Rather than dragging her feet as we'd seen her do at the airport, she was walking around the house full of energy. The kitchen became her territory. There she spent long hours cooking Cuban meals that required a great deal of time and effort: Cuban tamales and bacalao a la vizcaina, made from salted cod imported from Spain and sold in the local Latino market in town. Another delicacy was her famous tasajo, made from a special dried beef that was boiled till tender and shredded into very fine strips, which she seasoned and slowly cooked in a tomato sauce.

I wanted to spend as much time as possible with Grandmother, and since I was no longer living at home with my parents, I stopped by their house almost every day after work or graduate school. When Grandmother first heard about my having my own place, she became very upset and lectured me for days. Grandmother was truly disappointed with my behavior. She couldn't understand why I had moved away from the family. Over and over I explained my need to be independent, to be more in control of my time and my life. No reason I gave her was good enough. At some point she gave up and never again said a word about the subject. From then on, we sat around the kitchen table just as we had when I visited her as a child. Grandmother's mind was sharp and clear, just as it had been then.

"Eh, Negrita, do you remember that day when I was trying to teach you how to pluck a chicken for soup?"

"Yes, Grandmother, I remember you wouldn't give me any mercy. Even though I knew the chicken was dead, I was crying for the poor creature, somehow thinking I was causing it pain."

"Well . . . " Grandmother paused to look at me with trickster eyes. "When was the last time you had to kill a chicken for a meal?"

"I don't remember," I said. "Let me think. It was probably at the farm with Grandmother Petra, when she asked me to help her kill a couple of chickens for Sunday dinner."

Grandmother got up from her chair and walked to the stove to pour herself some more coffee. She held the tiny porcelain cup in her hands and smiled; then she took a sip of the black liquid, taking time to savor it in her mouth.

"I see you've forgotten what it's like to live in a small farming town with no big stores to buy packaged food, and tasteless frozen chicken and steaks," she said, now back on her chair, right across from me. "It's different when you grow your own chickens and vegetables. Remember my garden? Those big tomatoes and cucumbers we picked together?"

"Yes, those tomatoes were delicious," I said, not knowing where she was going with all this talk.

"Do you remember when you were a little girl and Grandfather gave you a little yellow chick to take care of? You loved that tiny thing so much that when it came time to kill it for dinner, you cried and cried."

"Oh yeah, Grandmother, that day is very clear in my mind. It was terrible to see Rosita's meat in the fricassee you cooked."

It was getting late. I got up from my chair to go.

"Wait, wait, Negrita. We have some work to do."

"What kind of work?" I asked with surprise.

"Your father went fishing last night. I promised him I'd clean the fish he caught, but since you're here . . . maybe you can help."

Clean the fish? I thought. I haven't done that in years, since I was a kid and we went fishing with Father on weekends. The idea of opening up fish and pulling the guts out with my fingers nauseated me. I could almost smell the stinky odor.

"Grandmother, I'll come back tomorrow and help you."

"Sorry, but it needs to be done for tonight's meal. Come on, let's go," she said, sounding like an army captain. She marched in front of me and pulled a bag from the refrigerator. She handed me a short, sharp knife and a plate and, with the same tone of authority, said, "Let's go outside. We don't want all this business to stink up the whole house." We went and sat at the old wooden picnic table under the willow tree.

"Here, this is for you," she said, throwing me a big trout from the bag.

I took the sharp knife in my hand not knowing where to start. Then, as if guided, my hand began to remember how to clean a fish. First, I scraped all the scales from the skin, and then I made an incision on the side from the gills to the tail. It was not as bad as I'd thought.

Two days after the fish-cleaning episode, I went back to visit Grandmother Patricia. She greeted me as usual with a big hug and guided me to her favorite spot, the kitchen, where she could talk to me while tending her cooking. This time she was preparing a big pot of arroz con pollo.

From the moment I walked in the house, I could feel something was bothering her. I sat and waited for her to say something, but she remained quiet while she sliced some onions on the cutting board. A few minutes went by before she washed her hands and was ready to pay attention to me. But instead of sitting on her usual chair across from the window, she walked to the side of the table where I was sitting and grabbed my purse. She took her time examining my old, beat-up leather bag.

"Look at this. You should be ashamed of yourself for carrying something like this to work," she said and dropped the bag on top of the table. "How can you possibly walk around the professional world with this piece of trash?"

I hated it when Grandmother was critical.

"If you're going to be a professional, you better look like one. Otherwise, don't bother. A Cuban woman doesn't go on the streets with a purse that looks like it's been run over by a train," she said, and went to check the pot on top of the stove.

That was one thing about Grandmother, she always dressed impeccably and elegantly. As kids, if we ever arrived at her house with dirty faces, hands or clothes, she would immediately send us to wash up, and she'd complain to my parents about taking us out of the house in such a condition. As a child it didn't bother me much, but now it was beginning to get on my nerves. Every time I came to see her, I could feel her scrutinizing my clothes, shoes, even the way I combed my hair.

"Negrita, don't be upset," Grandmother said as she sat across from me. "I know you don't like me bothering you about your purse, but I really meant what I said. The image you present to the world plays a large part in how people see you and think of you." Her voice was softer and less critical.

"Well, Grandmother, I understand that's a very Cuban way of

looking at things. We are a proud, elegant and colorful people who like to dress up and impress the world."

"That pride is a part of who we are, and you have forgotten much of it by being so far away from us. You don't even talk like a Cuban anymore."

It hurt to hear the old woman talk to me like that.

"You're right, Grandmother, you're right! I have lost my Cuban accent."

I wanted to scream at her. I wanted to tell her that not only had I lost my Cuban ways of talking but my Cubanness as well. That part of me I had buried somewhere in the depths of my being. It had been so well hidden that now I was having problems finding it. Occasionally I glimpsed it when I listened to the Cuban singer Celia Cruz, her songs so full of the passion of the Cuban voice and the vibrant sounds of the rumba drums. Despite my years of numbness, my hips had not forgotten the sensuous undulations I'd learned from dancing in the Carnaval. My heart remembered the toques to call the spirits. Celia, with her music, helped me transcend the dark tones of acculturation.

But I didn't think Grandmother could understand my struggle to be part of a new world and still preserve within myself the fire and the taste of coffee, rum and sugar cane of my forgotten Cuba.

"It's more than that, Negrita. You have changed."

Of course I'd changed. How could I not have changed? And how could I possibly explain to her about the search for my lost spirit, the deep longing to find my place in a melting pot of people? Certainly I didn't belong in the Mexican community surrounding me. Nor could I be a blond Americana. No way! Even if I dyed my black hair as some of my friends did, the dark roots would soon expose the truth. And I was not like the Cubans in Miami. I respected their progress and their efforts to protect a cultural identity away from Cuba, but in their own way, they had forgotten that time had gone by, that we were no longer living in 1959. The dream to go back didn't need to die, but Cuba didn't belong to us any more.

"Have you been in touch with your Cuban friends?" Grandmother asked.

"Yeah." I thought of my last trip to Miami. "You know, Grandmother, appearance is all there is for most of those friends. Remember Victoria, the photographer's daughter who used to live a few blocks from us? Well, I saw her when I was visiting Miami. She stopped by with her boyfriend on the way to a party at the Cabaigüán Club. You wouldn't believe the way those people were dressed. They looked like they were going to a New Year's Eve party." I had to tell Grandmother the rest: "By the way, she was very happy to see me, but she never invited me to dinner at her house, and you know what that means. It was all polite talk. She forgot that when we were all starving in that camp from hell, I shared my tomato and bread sandwich with her."

"People forget," Grandmother said in a soft voice.

"Yes, and they suddenly become the ex-owners of thousands of acres of land and sugar mills. It makes one wonder how big Cuba would be if we were to add up all those acres," I said and laughed.

"Maybe that's what they long and dream for. You know, to own land in Cuba again."

"Maybe, but that's not my dream. I'd love to go back to Cuba and visit someday," I said, feeling somewhat nostalgic.

Grandmother was silent and looking at me as if she'd never seen me before. I wanted to say to her I was sorry, but the words didn't come out. I sat there thinking to myself that what I really wanted was not so much to return to Cuba, but to bring out in me the essence of Cuba, the spirit of the songs, the music and the people. I wanted to free Cuba within me.

Grandmother didn't say a word. And it was at that moment that I realized time and distance had wounded something very sacred between us. I was overcome by grief. All those years of separation had chiseled our visions of the world and of each other in different directions. I could feel the old woman's struggle to find in me the child she had known. I could feel my own despair about disappointing her, but there was nothing I could do. We were strangers to each other.

"Grandmother, I'm sorry."

Grandmother got up from her chair, and facing the avocado tree outside the window, she talked to me in a deep voice, as if her words were coming from the center of the earth. "Negrita, you have not disappointed me. I'm the one who forgot that all the years that have gone by have changed us, just as the wind and the waters of the ocean erode the coastline. I'm sad for all those lost moments when I wasn't here to see you grow and become a woman. I have to catch up with time. You're no longer my little Negrita, the little one who used to sit on my lap wanting to hear my stories. You're now a woman with your own stories to tell." She paused and moved closer to me, and then, putting her hand on my shoulder, said, "Forgive me for that whole thing about your old purse. I was wanting to feel useful."

She walked away from me, looking older and more tired than ever. Her apology moved me. I felt for the old woman who had gathered her strength to come all the way to this country to see us again. Here she was, a foreigner without her status as a medicine woman. No one knew her except for us. No one could see behind her fragile appearance the healing power of her trembling hands and the wisdom of her spirit.

Grandmother never again made any comments about my appearance. One Friday afternoon, I stopped by to see her as usual and found her sitting by the kitchen window, smoking one of her hand-rolled little cigars, and looking out at the avocado tree. Mother was busy with her sewing in another room of the house, and Father was still at work. I noticed that the old woman was distant. I thought that perhaps she was beginning to feel homesick. We talked only briefly about her return to Cuba, a sensitive subject, because we all wanted her to stay.

My father had begged her to reconsider her decision to go back, given the difficult economic and political situation there. On numerous occasions, I overheard him say, "Mami, please stay with us. I will build you a little house next to ours so that you can have your privacy." He tried and tried with no success. Grandmother's response was always the same. "No, hijo, my place is there. That's where my home is."

Every time, my father would walk away, hands in his pockets and a grave look on his face. I tried not to get involved because I understood Grandmother's position, but this day I felt the need to break the rules, and I asked, "Grandmother, why don't you stay with us?"

"Look, Teresa, see this cigar, how it is burning?" She paused and looked deeply into my eyes. "Well, in the same way, my heart is consumed by having to make this decision. I knew when I planned this trip that I was going to be facing this dilemma, so I came prepared for it. You're precious to me, but this vieja is too tired to start all over again in a new land. I came here because all these years I have done nothing but think about all of you, day and night. I wanted to see you again before I die. I promised your grandfather that I would come to see you. There are a few things I need to take care of before I go, but other than that I'm ready to go home, to the land where your grandfather is buried and waiting for me. I want my bones to rest next to his. There, I'm still useful to people. I do my healing work, and I can drink coffee with my friends in the afternoons. Here, I feel lonely. If I stay here, my life will burn out, like this cigar." She got up from her chair and walked to the stove.

Grandmother was looking kind of pale, and her walk was unsteady. I hurried behind her and grabbed her by the arm.

"Grandmother, come sit down. You don't seem well."

The old woman sat on her chair and started telling me one of her stories about life on the farm when she was a child. Suddenly, her words became slurred and then deep sounds like the low roar of a cat or a lion came out of her mouth. I jumped from my chair and went to her side. I held her hands, which were cold like the rest of her body.

I thought of her dying, and I panicked. "Grandmother, Grandmother!"

Grandmother didn't answer. She continued making the guttural sounds, and her eyes rolled up. Then, as if guided by an invisible force, she lifted her arms, the palms of her hands facing out in the direction of the avocado tree outside the window. Unfamiliar sounds continued coming out of her mouth. She looked possessed.

My mother rushed into the kitchen carrying a bottle of rubbing alcohol. Immediately, she began to rub Grandmother's arms, legs and face. "Teresa, call the paramedics! This could be a heart attack or a stroke!" my mother ordered.

I stood there looking at my mother. I had a strange feeling, an intuitive flash that Grandmother was going to be okay. I waited for a few seconds, trying to decide—then noticing the paleness of Grandmother's face, I rushed to the phone.

By the time medical help arrived, Grandmother was recovering from whatever had gotten into her. A young paramedic examined her and asked questions in broken Spanish, "Duele aquí?"

"No, it doesn't hurt anywhere," Grandmother answered with visible impatience.

When the examination was completed, the young man turned to me and my mother: "Well, I don't understand what happened to her. She's doing all right now. Her heart, blood pressure and pulse are better than mine," and he proceeded to put away all his medical instruments. "Where is the phone?" he asked and then put his hand on Grandmother's shoulder and said in a reassuring tone of voice: "We're going to take you to the hospital, just to make sure everything is okay."

As soon as Grandmother heard this, she tried to get up from the chair. She grabbed me by the arm: "No hospitals!"

"But Grandmother," I implored, "you were very sick."

"Por favor, Patricia," my mother begged, "don't be such a hardhead."

"Nonsense!" the old woman said. "Negrita, you need to trust me. I can't explain. You must listen and not let them take me to the hospital."

I was ambivalent at first, but then I remembered the many times I'd witnessed Grandmother's healing power with people who had come from all over the island. Many of them had been given no hope by their doctors and had been sent home to die. Grandmother was as wise if not wiser than any doctor. She had the kind of knowledge medical school didn't teach: a knowing that had been passed on to her by a long bloodline of women healers and their traditions.

"Okay, she is not going," I said to the paramedic.

"Teresa, you must be out of your mind!"

"She doesn't want to go, Mother." For some inexplicable reason, I felt the need to trust her.

"Your grandmother is not a fool, Negrita. Trust me," Grandmother said, smiling at me.

That night, I had many dreams. Several times I woke up with the strange feeling of having traveled to unknown places. One dream in particular stayed with me: I was walking down a long road by myself, when I heard a voice coming from beneath the earth. It was a female voice, but there was also the sound of waves crashing on the rocks near the shore. In the distance, dancing above the water was a dark female figure holding a young infant in her arms. I walked into the ocean and began to swim towards the woman, but no matter how fast I swam, I couldn't reach her.

I woke up agitated, sweating, still struggling. "Yemayá, Yemayá, Carmen," I heard myself say aloud in the darkness of my room. I was surprised by these words and by Carmen's visit in my dreams, accompanied by Yemayá. I took these images as a call from the past. As an invitation to remember.

The next day, I decided not to go to work and, instead, to pay a visit to my grandmother. As soon as I drove into the driveway of my parents' house, I saw Grandmother standing by the avocado tree. To my astonishment, what had been a healthy tree the day before now appeared to be dying, its green leaves drooping lifelessly and turning yellow.

Grandmother ignored my arrival. She stood in front of the tree, her wrinkled hands on the bark of the thick, round trunk. Soft prayers, like the echo of ancient voices springing from the very heart of a forest, were coming out of her mouth.

I stood there witnessing the sacred ritual. Then Grandmother moved closer to the tree and wrapped her arms around the wide trunk. It was a strange but moving scene. It was as if she were one with the avocado tree. Then I heard Grandmother thanking the tree for some kind of sacrifice. I couldn't understand what she was talking about, and as if she could read my mind, she turned and looked at me for the first time.

"I know what you're thinking and I'm not a crazy old woman," she said, inviting me to sit next to her on the nearby bench.

"This tree is a friend. It helped me clear some disturbing spirits that have been dancing with the family for a while."

"I don't understand."

"Let me tell you a story," she said, and she paused to search inside her skirt pocket for one of the thin handmade cigars.

"When I was a child, I suffered from asthma. In those days people didn't go to doctors or hospitals. They took care of things with home remedies or with the help of a local curandero." She took some time to light her cigar with the silver-plated lighter my father had given her a few days before. "My mother did what she could, but when everything failed and I continued having attacks, she asked the healer in town for help. This wise man told my mother to take me to a eucalyptus tree every morning and to have me sit under it for at least an hour. After a month of this daily practice, I got well and never again had any problems with my breathing."

"Amazing," I said.

"This tree," she said, pointing at the avocado, "is going to help you all heal the painful wounds from leaving Cuba. Your souls were shattered by the separation. Yesterday, when you and I were sitting next to the window, I was told by the spirits that it was okay to use the body of this tree to heal that pain."

"What spirits?" I interrupted.

"Spirits. Wise spirits who talk to me all the time."

"Tell me about them."

"There is not a whole lot to say. Spirits are spirits. They come and go in between the worlds. They talk to us. They breathe the same air we breathe, and they live with us. Some people see them with their eyes. Others feel the touch of these beings on their skin. Some simply hear their voices as clearly as you're hearing me."

"Grandmother, I know what you're talking about. I'm not sure, though, that I remember how to connect with them," I said.

"Someday, you'll understand about the spirit world. You will, Negrita. You came to this life with strong protectors. They watch over you and guide you even without your knowing it." She took a long draw from her cigar.

"But . . . you're leaving soon. When would you teach me?"

"When the time is right, Negrita. Don't be so impatient. Even if I'm not around, there will be other teachers you'll meet on your way."

"How can you be so sure?"

Grandmother glanced at her cigar, as if she were searching for just the right words to say to me. Then she spoke in a solemn voice.

"Negrita, you will learn all you need to know. That's your destiny. From the very beginning of your life, there were signs of your sensitivity to the spirit world. Remember? Many years ago, when you were a little girl, maybe six, you became very ill with a severe case of hepatitis. The doctors were not sure whether you were going to make it or not. I'll never forget that day when I walked into the hospital room. You were lying there on the bed with IV needles and tubes in both of your arms. I took your little hand into mine. Your eyes barely opened, and your lips mumbled something like, 'Grandmother, please call the angels.' So I did. I prayed and prayed for your life. Later that day you told me, 'Grandmother, the angels were here. I saw them, but they didn't have wings like angels do in the books. They were like bright lights in the night sky.' I knew then, mi Negrita, that you were going to be well and that you were not alone on your path."

Grandmother placed her hand on top of my head and, looking straight into my eyes, she asked, "Do you believe in destiny, Negrita?"

"I don't know for sure," I said and I thought about the notion of events in one's life being determined by fate. "I just don't like the idea of not having control over my life, that everything that happens to us is part of some master plan."

"Destiny does not mean you're not empowered." Grandmother put out her cigar on the corner of the bench and then turned to me. "Destiny is not passive. It requires you to participate and to take full responsibility for your actions." She paused as if needing to gather her thoughts. Then, she pointed in the direction of a lemon tree in the backyard. "That tree was born to be a lemon tree. Its destiny is to give the best lemons. Like trees, people have different missions in this world. We are born with a purpose to be fulfilled while we're here. Destiny provides us with a sort of road map and pathways. It is up to us to find out who we are and how we want to manifest our potential to the fullest."

With those words, the old woman stood up from the bench and shook off some cigar ashes that had fallen on her dress. Then, without looking at me, she added, "The pain and suffering you've gone through have not been in vain. You, mi Negrita, are exactly where you're supposed to be. This country is the place where you need to set up your own healing room and your altar. You are a curandera. It won't matter what degree or university title you get. Your destiny is to become a curandera."

It was not until many years later that I understood the truth and meaning of my grandmother's words. Behind the appearance of my traditional Western persona was a world of unseen forces, of spirits and of ancient wisdom. Like a subterranean river, it was all there beneath the surface for me to explore and to use, if, and only if, I was to honor the tradition of the women before me.

20

THE CROW

A FEW MONTHS after my college graduation, a vivid dream ended the turmoil I had been feeling about medical school. In the dream, I was in a dark, cold room that smelled of antiseptic and of dead flesh. I was part of a team of students getting ready to practice on a cadaver that rested inside a plastic bag on a large, metal table. We nervously laughed and joked as we tried to decide who was going to "break the ice" and do the first cut on the body. Flipping a coin was suggested, and to my horror I ended up the chosen one.

I moved closer to the table and prepared myself to open the bag. My hands were shaking as I pulled down the long zipper, revealing the wrinkled face of an old woman, so well preserved that she appeared to be in a deep sleep rather than dead. I stood by her side and closely observed her delicate features. I could tell by her peaceful expression that this woman had lived a long and joyful life.

"Come on, Flor. Let's get this thing going." It was one of the members of my team.

"Wait," I said, in a trembling voice.

I took the sharp scalpel in my hand and lifted it above the woman's face. I was ready to make the incision across the forehead, but my fingers wouldn't move. I tried hard to overcome my resistance, but no matter what I said to myself, I couldn't do it. Not even in the name of science. The body in front of me was as sacred as my own. I could not lacerate the skin and flesh of this woman, even if she was dead. I threw the scalpel on the floor and ran towards the exit. Behind me, I could hear the other students laughing and shouting, "You coward. Come back!"

I woke up from my dream in a sweat. That same morning I made a decision that would change the course of my life. Finally I felt certain that Western medicine was not my passion. Instead I wanted to explore healing practices that were not as invasive and that acknowledge the important roles that the human spirit and emotions play in the process of healing.

Like a snake shedding her skin, I felt naked to my own eyes. This new path required me to let go, one by one, of all the layers of accumulated notions and perceptions I had about myself. It meant death to a persona that I had fostered for years to survive the traditional training of the university, an academic persona that had been defined by the boundaries of a scientific and objective understanding of the world. My journey into alternative healing practices would require me to delve instead into the unknown territory of the subjective and the unexplainable.

I found myself at the verge of an identity crisis that was both exciting and terrifying. The structures that had supported me were falling from under my feet. The theories and philosophies that once made sense to me were now useless. Life was no longer a mechanical entity but a fluid and always changing force, a great mystery that science, with its short and limited vision, couldn't see or touch. Once again, I was alone on my path with many questions and no one to turn to. Even my friends thought I was making the wrong decision. "What about all those years of hard work in pre-med?" one friend said. "You're throwing away your future." The same fears that, years before, had propelled me to put away my altar and stop lighting candles to the orishas came back stronger than ever. I was afraid.

Books became my allies. For the next few weeks, I experienced an insatiable hunger for information on folk healing practices. I read every book I was able to get my hands on. Gradually, a clear picture of my vision emerged. The field of psychology began to captivate my heart—not clinical psychology with its emphasis on pathology and dysfunction, but transpersonal psychology with its focus on spirit, mind and body.

Suddenly an entire world of possibilities was opening up to me. I felt guided by the spirits of Carmen and Grandmother Patricia. I was on my way to rediscover a tradition in which women healers were able to cut through the body without surgical knives. Their hands, their intuition and their connection to spirit were their only tools and means.

I knew Grandmother Patricia would never be able to visit us again when, in her letters, she began to make reference to her "final journey." With time, Grandmother's handwriting became less and less legible. The written words reflected the trembling of her hands and the stiffness of her fingers from the painful arthritis. I read every word, sensing her frustration at putting clear thoughts on paper. The soft scribbles were mirrors of her fading spirit.

Not long after visiting us in California, Grandmother Patricia died. She left this world on the same day she was born, August 23, completing the circle of her life. The morning of her death, I woke up with a heaviness in my chest. I took a shower and tried to shake away the feeling, thinking it was probably left over from a disturbing dream I'd had but couldn't remember. The oppressive sensation continued throughout my morning rituals of getting dressed and eating breakfast. It was as if a dark veil were hovering above me, a dense fog permeating my thoughts.

Inside my head danced the fleeting images of my childhood: Carmen and her lullabies, Grandmother Petra walking across the corn fields, Grandfather dressed in his impeccable white guayabera, Grandfather Victor holding my hand as we walked to the park, and then Grandmother Patricia kneeling in front of her altar. With sadness, I realized that of this group of people, Grandmother Patricia was the only one still alive. She was there holding the line as she had promised me before I left Cuba. She was the anchor, the old tree deeply rooted to the heart of the earth.

As I walked by the mirror on the bathroom wall, I was surprised by my own reflection. My hair, short and curly, was graying into the same salt and pepper shades of my Grandmother Patricia. I brushed the curls away from my forehead. I looked so much like the grandmother I had known as a young child: the wide, round face, the deep and penetrating eyes, the broad shoulders and square torso.

I was perplexed by the feelings this mirror image evoked in me. It was as if time had stopped the day of our departure from Cuba. I took a second glance at myself and reflected on how different my life was in the United States. The disparity between the worlds of my childhood and my adulthood was immense. There was no way to compare the two; it felt as if I had lived two lives.

Where were all the people from the past? What had happened to them? My friends from camp, my neighbors, my cousins, my uncles and aunts. Where were they? They were no longer the people I had known then. They were strangers I knew nothing about, except for the few lines we exchanged with less and less frequency. We had been swept in different directions by the whirlwind of our destinies, as well as a revolution.

With all this pondering, I found myself running late for work. I hurriedly left the house and was walking towards my car when the call of a crow caught my attention. The bird was perched on one of the lower branches of an old fir tree near the street. I was puzzled by its insistent, piercing call. Then, as if struck by invisible lightning, the shiny black creature dropped to the ground just a few feet from me.

My first reaction was one of surprise. Searching for a sign, I raised my eyes to the sky, which was blue and clear. I took a few steps so that I could get a closer look at the crow. Then, moved by curiosity, I touched its body with my fingers. It was warm, but there were no signs of life. Death's stiffness was beginning to take over the crow's soft flesh and bones. The eyes, almost covered by the lids, were like opaque marbles.

How strange! I thought to myself. Where had this crow come from? What was her message to me? I had recently learned that the crow was considered a "shape-shifter" by Native Americans, and as a messenger of change, could travel between the physical and spiritual worlds. "Well," I said to the dead bird, "someone is trying to get my attention." And kneeling on the ground, I took the bird in my hands. My fingers tingled with a slight sensation of warmth. Trapped in the feathers were remnants of life, invisible and minute fragments of the bird's spirit left behind as the messenger took her final flight.

With a mixture of fascination and sadness, I watched the bird. My eyes rested on her face, and Crow, the magician, took me into the realms of her most powerful medicine as I witnessed the face of the bird transform into that of Grandmother Patricia. I saw the old woman on her deathbed. She was there, looking at me, reaching out with her hand. The snow-white color of her skin gave her a supernatural appearance. Then, from the center of her chest, I saw a bright light moving away. Slowly, it disappeared and became part of the air.

Mi Abuela Patricia was dead! The crow had been her messenger. She was now free of her pain and could fly like an eagle. But what about me? I heard the voice of denial coming from deep inside me. "Grandmother, please don't leave. Not yet!" I held the dead crow against my chest, a futile gesture of protection from the fierce grasp of death. In my heart, it was no longer the crow, but my grandmother. I was holding my abuelita in a tight and defiant embrace. With my eyes closed, I prayed quietly for a change of fate.

Four hours later, a call from Cuba confirmed Grandmother Patricia's death. She had died of pneumonia, and according to my Aunt Adelfa, our beloved elder had passed away peacefully in her sleep. Cuba was so far from our reach and, as we had so many other times, our family sat around the kitchen table and cried inconsolably for the dead. There was nothing we could do but comfort one another with memories of the last time we'd seen her. The truth of her departure seemed unreal. After all, my memories were all of her alive: standing by her avocado tree, praying in front of her altar, lighting candles to her favorite saints or laying hands on the many children she had healed from mal de ojos.

Later in the afternoon, when I returned home, I went for a long walk to the park. I wanted to feel close to the trees and through their essence connect with the spirit of my grandmother. I wandered around in search of something that spoke to me of Patricia, of her life on this earth and of her existence somewhere in the other world.

"Grandmother!" I cried. "Talk to me. Tell me where you are. Let me know I'm not alone. Can you hear me? Are you all right?"

Only silence. Then I listened even harder. The whisper of the cedar, pine and eucalyptus joined me in my prayers. Up in the blue sky, a red-tailed hawk was circling majestically, dancing a slow waltz with the wind. The narrow trail that I was following forked, and blocking the path on the right was a fallen cedar. I stood there in front of the ancient one, contemplating the exposed roots coming out of the decaying trunk. I was reminded of the many arms that had held me and rocked me as a child, including my grandmother's. I had loved those times when she set me on her lap. Then, she was a strong woman and could make me feel as if the whole universe was on my side. Now, she was gone! She was the last old branch cut away from our family tree.

All the grandparents were dead, and it was up to us—my parents, my brother and me—to carry on the traditions and the stories for the coming generations. My own children, nieces and nephews would someday ask the same questions I once asked. And I thought of those circles within circles of storytelling that somehow had been severed by distance and time—all those years we'd been gone from our native Cuba. We had lost the thread of the dances and the songs, of the people and their passion. We had become foreigners to our own culture.

I moved closer to the cedar and placed my hands on the rough bark. The image of my grandmother's dead body, so cold and stiff, brought tears to my eyes. I thought of her lying on her deathbed, like this tree. She was no longer rooted in this world. Her physical shell was now decomposing in the warm womb of the dark Cuban soil. Her spirit, though, was flying above the green expanse of the park, free as a hawk.

The old cedar, like Grandmother, had a soothing presence. It spoke to me in a very familiar and intimate voice. Not with words but with an eloquent spiral of pictures, intuitive flashes and stories that were unfolded inside my mind. I was reminded of the wisdom within all of us to communicate and to relate to all that exists.

I returned home to the dead crow that I'd left resting on the doorstep. I wondered what I should do with the brave messenger. The idea of a funeral came to mind, along with sadness at not having been able to be present for Grandmother's burial. This was my opportunity not only to mourn and grieve, but to honor the life and death, at least symbolically, of the Great Curandera.

Inspired by the sacredness of the ceremony I was about to perform, I trusted my intuition and childhood memories in gathering what I thought were appropriate ceremonial objects for the ritual. It was a difficult task to figure out Grandmother's predilection. Rather eclectic in her spiritual practices, she prayed to all the Catholic saints, but never went to church. She was not a santera but she had her favorite orishas. Doña Patricia was connected to the healing forces of the planet in whichever channel and frequency she needed to tune in. Sometimes it was Santa Barbara or Changó. For other purposes she called the powers of Santa Teresa or the orisha Oyá.

After I had gone around the house collecting seashells, offerings of corn, and dried herbs, I went out to my garden. There, near a rosebush, I found a place where I could dig a hole big enough for the burial. I placed the bird on the ground and began the process of cleansing and preparing the crow for her final journey. I poured a few drops of Florida water over the feathers and then I burned a mixture of dried sage, lavender and rosemary inside one of the shells and smudged the smoke all over my dead friend.

Once more, I found myself back in Cuba. Grandmother lay naked on the bed, next to her altar, inside the healing room. She looked as if she were asleep. Her silver-gray hair was combed back as usual, but her body was emaciated and bluish. Ripples of wrinkles folded around the sides of her belly and sagging breasts. I imagined how it would feel to be there by Grandmother's side. I thought of the ritual that people in my native culture performed when a beloved died: that final and loving act of bathing the dead.

In my mind, I saw myself lighting the candles on Grandmother's altar. Then, I prepared a warm bath of fresh herbs, flowers and aromatic oils of eucalyptus and lemon blossoms. I lifted Grandmother into the water. With a sponge, I bathed and scrubbed the wrinkles and crevices of her old skin. I remembered Grandmother telling me she had cleaned away the blood and placenta from my body after my birth into this world.

Once finished, I moved Grandmother back to the bed and dressed her in an elegant embroidered white cotton dress. I combed her short hair and placed a purple orchid and a gardenia on her chest. I looked at my grandmother's hands. Resting next to the flowers, her hands were as strong and beautiful as they had been when I was a child and she'd healed me from my illnesses.

Those hands! Grandmother wanted me to remember her hands. Long fingers and perfectly manicured nails, strong and large, those hands had done more than just work in the garden and nurture the family. Those hands were the hands of a healer. The hands of the midwife that had helped pull me from my mother's womb, as lightning illuminated the darkness.

I imagined holding my grandmother's hands in mine. I felt the chill of death somehow melt under the warmth of my flesh. I waited for Grandmother to open her eyes and greet me with, "Negrita, Negrita. You're here!" But her eyelids did not even tremble. Grandmother was dead! I looked at the lifeless vessel, an empty cocoon that no longer housed the colorful butterfly of Grandmother's spirit. She had flown to another place, where she could sip the sweet nectar of a different flower.

The scents of rosemary, sage, peppermint and lavender brought me back to my garden. An occasional breeze carried the aroma of jasmine and honeysuckle blossoms to me from the vines that grew over the fence. As I sat on the moist soil, I began to experience a sense of tranquility and joy, just as I had as a child in my grandmother's garden. I could feel Grandmother Patricia near me, talking to me about the different herbs. Grandmother's voice was becoming clear and vibrant inside my head. The voice I had forgotten was coming back to remind me, to awaken the memories of my own stories.

I was transported again to my homeland. I could feel the summer heat burning my skin, and I could breathe the humid air. The smells of sugar cane and freshly roasted coffee soothed my senses. A soft gust of air blew from the west, from the mountains, the sierras, and I heard my grandmother's voice loud and clear: "Negrita, Negrita," as she used to call me when I was a child, "Negrita, welcome home."

A few minutes later, rain started to fall, and again I was filled with a sense of Grandmother's presence. She was there, somewhere near my heart. She was no longer old, but she was not young either. She was both. She had become part of the air I breathed, of the waters that filled the ocean and ran in the rivers. Grandmother was part of the mountains that surrounded the city, the gentle breeze that caressed my cheeks, the flowers in my garden.

Grandmother was watching me, praying for me, for my return home. The image of my old grandmother sitting in her rocking chair and fanning herself with her Cuban fan made of woven palm leaves came to me from the distance. Once more I heard her soothing voice say, "Negrita, you are not alone, cariño. We are all here with you, forever and ever."

I looked up at the sky, now dark and mysterious. Kneeling on the ground, I reached down and threw a last handful of dirt on the bird's grave. I looked at my own hands and saw the strong hands of my grandmother. These hands were my connection to the many curanderas before me and before mi Abuela Patricia. These hands had the memories of a tradition where women are known to be the carriers of the seeds of life and death. They are the weavers of a fabric called healing, always changing in form, texture and color.

abanico fan

abuela grandmother

abuelita grandma

amigo (a) friend

arado plough

armas weapons

arriba upward, up

arroyo stream

arroz con pollo chicken and rice

Ave Maria Hail Mary

ay carajo oh hell

ay carajo, las cosas que tiene la vida oh hell, the ironies of life

ay chico, nos jodieron hey pal, they screwed us

ay madresita oh little mother

ay, qué cabrón what a shameless bastard

ay, San Lazaro bendito Oh holy Saint Lazarus

banderillas taurs used to taunt the bull during a bullfight

barbudos bearded men; used by Cubans to refer to Fidel Castro's revolutionaries

basta stop

basura garbage, trash

batáa the sacred drums of Santería

bendito blessed, holy

bien well, nice, fine, good

bohío a Cuban peasant's thatched hut

boniato sweet potato

brujo (a) witch

buñuelos fritters

caballeria 33.16 acres

caballo horse

cabrón bastard

café con leche Cuban coffee with steamed milk and sugar

cafesito Cuban coffee, served expresso-style with sugar

calmate calm down

campesino farmer

cañaverales sugar fields

cañones cannons

cariño term of endearment or affection

casquitos Cuban dessert made from guavas

ceiba silk-cotton tree, sacred tree of Santería

cocimiento herbal tea remedy

compañero (a) companion, partner; used by Cuban Communists as a
  mutual address

comparsa Carnival group

congri rice and black beans cooked together

coño all-purpose Cuban curse word; may be used in a variety of ways
  from situations where it simply means "wow" to others where it has
  strong profanity such as "cunt" or "twat"

corazón heart; a term of endearment

criollo Creole, native-born Cuban of European descent

cuentera (o) someone who is gifted in telling jokes, tales and gossip

cuentos tales, short stories

curandera Hispanic woman healer

curanderismo the art of traditional Hispanic healing; consists of a set
  of folk medical beliefs, rituals and practices that is holistic in nature

charro Mexican cowboy

chico pal, young fellow

chirimoya tropical fruit

chistes jokes, funny stories

deja eso mujer leave that alone, woman

descarado a shameless, insolent person

desgraciado someone who brings misfortune to self or others

despojos ritual cleansings

Dios mío, mi Dios my God

Dios te bendiga God bless you

Doña Spanish title used before the first name of a woman who is
  respected

duele aquí? does it hurt, here?

duermete go to sleep

elemento used by Cuban Communists to refer to someone with anticommunist ideas or behavior

empacho   abdominal condition likened to blocked intestines. Most common symptoms are constipation, indigestion and vomiting.

empanada   fried or baked pastry turnover, stuffed with chicken, meat, or fish

esbirro   henchman

espíritu divino   divine spirit

está bien   okay

está pariendo   giving birth

Florida water   aromatic alcohol, an herbal liquid popular in Santería

frituras   fritters

fuera de aquí   get the hell out of here

gallo   a man who is cocky

guagua   bus

guajiro (a)   peasant

guano   palm tree; bird or bat manure

guarapo   sugar cane juice; fermented cane juice

guayabera   a traditional four-pocket cotton shirt, worn not tucked in, that can be either casual or formal

havano   Cuban cigar

hija   daughter

hijita   term of affection for one's young daughter

hijo de buena madre   son of a bitch

hijo de puta   son of a bitch

honra   honor

lomas   low hills, elevations

malagradecida   ungrateful

malcriado (a)   spoiled brat

mambises   nineteenth-century Cuban independence fighters

mamoncillos   fruit which grows in a bunch. The inside of the fruit is fleshy and pink. The mamoncillo trees are found near the riverbeds in Cuba.

mal de ojo   evil eye

malanga   a white root widely used in Cuban cuisine, also known as taro

maldito   evil

malvados   evildoers

matalo kill him

mercenarios mercenaries

mi amor my love

mi querida my dear

mierda shit

milicianos militiamen

mira look (imperative verb)

mojo creole garlic sauce

morros forts

muchacho (a) a child or young person

muchila backpack

mujer woman

mulata mulatto woman

muy bueno very good

navidad Christmas

negro (a) black man or woman; can be used as a term of affection

niña adinerada rich girl

niña de mi corazón my beloved girl; literally means "little girl of my heart"

niña, ven pa'ca girl, come here

no aguanto I can't bear this

no fumes más don't smoke anymore

no puedo más I can't do this anymore

El Norte The North; used by Cubans to refer to the United States

Nuestra Señora Our Lady

ñame a large tuber with thick skin and white, yellow, or red flesh that
is slightly sweet

orisha Yoruba deity, syncretized as a Catholic saint

Padre Nuestro Lord's Prayer

paloma dove

pasteles de guayaba guava pastries

pedazo piece

pelea fight

pequeños de mi corazón children of my heart

pordioseros beggars

peseta twenty-five-cent coin

peso basic unit of Cuban currency

piel morena   brown skin

por Dios   by God

por favor   please

potro   colt

potrero   pasture for horses

puro   cigar

qué bonita   how pretty

qué desgracia   how unfortunate

qué ñoña   what a silly girl

qué pasa?   what's going on?

qué sabroso   how delicious

qué te vas a secar de tanto llorar   you're going to run dry from so
    much crying

querida niña   dear girl

raíces   roots

raspaduras   hard candy made from sugar cane juice

registrones   nosy kids

relajate   relax

ricachones   greedy, rich people

rumbera   female rumba dancer

santa   female saint

santera   a female initiate of Santería

Santería   Afro-Cuban religion in which the orishas, or deities, of the
    Yoruba people are worshipped

sermones   sermons, lectures

sinvergüenza   shameless scoundrel

somos libres   we are free

tachinos   fried green plantains

ten cuidado   be careful

tía   aunt

tierra libre   free land

la tierra es la madre   the earth is your mother

tinaja   large earthen jar

tilo   linden blossom

toque   drum rhythm

tortillera   slang for lesbian; tortilla-makers

tumba Afro-Cuban drum

Unión de Jóvenes Comunistas (UJC) Union of Young Communists

Unidades Militares de Ayuda a la Producción Military Units to Aid
  Production

vea aquí look here

ven come

ven aquí come here

vida life

viejo (a) old man; old woman

viejo estúpido stupid old man

Virgen de color canela virgin of cinnamon-colored skin

Virgen del Cobre another name for Our Lady of la Caridad del Cobre,
  patron saint of Cuba

Virgencita little virgin; used as a term of affection for saints

viva! long live!

yegua mare

yerbera (o) herbalist

yo soy la Virgen de la Caridad I am the Virgin of Charity

yuca cassava root

zafra sugar crop; sugar-making season

ABOUT THE AUTHOR

Flor Fernandez Barrios was born in Cabaigüán, Cuba. She emigrated to the United States in 1970 when she was fourteen years old. Her writing has appeared in several collections, including *Storming Heaven's Gate: An Anthology of Spiritual Writing by Women, Intimate Nature: The Bond Between Women and Animals* and *The Fabric of the Future: Women Visionaries Illuminate the Path to Tomorrow*. This is her first book. She lives in Seattle.

SELECTED TITLES FROM SEAL PRESS

Beyond the Limbo Silence by Elizabeth Nunez. $12.95, 1-58005-013-1. A spellbinding story tracing a young woman's journey from her Caribbean home to the United States during the civil rights struggle.

Nervous Conditions by Tsitsi Dangarembga. $12.00, 1-878067-77-X. Set in colonial Rhodesia in the 1960s, this evocative novel tells the story of a girl's coming of age and the devastating human loss involved in the colonization of one culture by another.

Another America by Barbara Kingsolver. $12.00, 1-58005-004-2. The third edition of this luminous book of poetry by one of America's most beloved writers.

Where the Oceans Meet by Bhargavi C. Mandava. $12.00, 1-58005-000-X. A magical story that captures the lives of Indian and Indian-American women and girls.

Latin Satins by Terri de la Peña. $10.95, 1-878067-52-4. Full of humor, tenderness and salsa, this novel tells the story of the lives and loves of a group of young Chicana singers in Santa Monica, California.

Angel by Merle Collins. $12.95, 1-58005-014-X. A richly textured novel that centers on three generations of women during the Grenadian struggle to achieve political autonomy.

Canyon Solitude: A Woman's Solo River Journey Through Grand Canyon by Patricia C. McCairen. $14.95, 1-58005-007-7. A remarkable solo expedition down one of the world's most spectacular rivers.

Gifts of the Wild: A Woman's Book of Adventure edited by Faith Conlon, Ingrid Emerick and Jennie Goode. $16.95, 1-58005-006-9. A beautifully illustrated and designed collection of outdoor writing by women.

Climbing High: A Woman's Account of Surviving the Everest Tragedy by Lene Gammelgaard. $25.00, 1-58005-023-9. The 1996 Everest disaster, recorded by a woman who made it to the summit and survived.

If you are unable to find a Seal Press book in a bookstore, or would like a free catalog of our books, please order from us directly by calling 800-754-0271. Visit our website at www.sealpress.com.